TO TAMAR,

WITH FOND MEMORIES

OF MANY GREAT YEARS

OF OUR SPECIAL FRIEND=

SHIP.

LOVE,

Alex

12-8-2014

# DISPLACED BY WAR

## A Refugee Remembers

*Alex Bertulis*

# CONTENTS

*Previously published

# Foreword by the Author

This collection of stories and essays is based on my personal experiences and told to the best of my recollection. The passage of time may have led to errors in detail, for which I hope I will be forgiven. Some incidents were too unpleasant or too painful to describe in more detail and I chose to gloss over them. In addition, the brain is known to block out negative or traumatic experiences.

It is no wonder that many veterans with traumatic combat experience are unable to write about those memories. My father refused to write about his close brushes with Russian brutality (he spent time in prison during the time of the last Tsar). My mother, who was a talented writer, came close to writing her memoirs, but kept postponing the project too long (she died at age 58). It's taken me half a century to finally face up to the task of putting some of my experiences and memories down on paper. It had to be done. The saying is, "People who ignore history are condemned to relive it." I don't want that to happen to our future generations. It might, judging by the way global events are developing today. Actually, the vast majority of my writings lean heavily toward the lighter side of life, including this memoir. However, the *whole* story must be told.

To be sure, my life was filled with good fortune and happiness and the occasional "bump in the road." I should have been killed many times, but a guardian angel must have been watching over me. I am sure I've had a more fortunate life than I ever deserved.

I hope I have succeeded in making this memoir readable and entertaining in my attempt to recall the early years of growing up in Europe and adjusting to a new life in America.

A.A.B.

This collection of stories and essays is dedicated to my four children, Eugenia, Ruta, Tomas and Nikolas, who will no longer need to listen to the oral versions of what is recounted herein.

# Introduction

It is my pleasure to introduce my good friend, Alex Bertulis, in his venture to write an auto-biography recounting his early life. On many occasions, whether in camp on a mountain or sitting next to a fireplace at home, he regaled his companions with seemingly endless stories about his life experiences as a child in his native Lithuania, as a refugee in Germany and as an immigrant to the United States. I am glad to see that he is finally putting some of these stories down on paper. He is a remarkable storyteller and I am looking forward to seeing more.

Stimson Bullitt
Seattle

I would rather be ashes than dust!
I would rather that my spark should burn out in a brilliant blaze
than it should be stifled by dryrot.
I would rather be a superb meteor, every atom of me in magnifi-
cent glow, than a sleepy and permanent planet.
The proper function of man is to live, not exist.
I shall not waste my days in trying to prolong them.
I shall use them.


Jack London
1876 - 1916

# Lithuania: A Selection of Notable Times

<u>2000 BC – 800 AD</u>
It has been well established by historians and anthropologists that a people called the Balts populated the southern shores of the Baltic Sea well before 2000 BC. There is ample evidence that various tribes populated this area as far back as 10,000 BC. The issue that is still being debated is whether the Balts arrived from the south (Indian sub-continent) or whether they migrated from the north to the Indian sub-continent. Climate change and continental ice movements played a role in these migrations. One thing that is for sure: the people from these two regions shared languages that were closely related - Sanskrit and Lithuanian. Sanskrit, like Latin, is no longer a spoken language. Lithuanian remains the oldest language spoken in Europe and may be the oldest living language in the world.

One reason that this language has managed to survive so long may be due to the fact that its people were located in an area of no particular importance — commercially nor politically. There was some intermittent trade with Romans (based on archeological findings of old Roman coins). It was well known that Roman ladies were fond of amber from the Baltic Sea.

Warring invaders that did try to conquer the Baltic tribes found it a daunting task. First of all, there were no rich cities to overrun and no big citadels to besiege. When confronted, the local fighters would simply meld into the forest and launch into guerilla tactics. The invaders were often on horseback and wearing heavy armor – no match for the quick and light-footed fighters of the woods, wearing bearskins, and who were deadly at shooting with bows and arrows.

There has been historic documentation that Samogitians (a sub tribe of Lithuania) participated in Hellenic battles in ancient Greece - which would help explain why so many Lithuanian surnames have identical suffixes to Greek ones (e.g., -is, -as, -us, etc.). It has been argued that the Balts were responsible for sacking Rome and not the Goths. Or, were the Balts part of the Goth contingency? There is historic evidence that after the Goth invaders started their retreat back to the Baltic, some of them ventured over to what is now Spain and colonized it. Hence, that would explain why there are many family names in Spain with Lithuanian roots.

800 – 1000
This period saw an increase in foreign activity in the Baltic region. Viking warriors sailed down from the north, raiding coastal areas all the way down to the Mediterranean. Arab merchants arrived looking to buy or trade commodities, such as fine furs, beeswax, amber, etc.

<u>1190 – 1410</u>

The Crusaders of Europe were eventually defeated by Saladin and kicked out of Jerusalem. They returned to Europe in disarray. However, the Germanic brotherhood found a new target for their proselytization: the pagan tribes on the Baltic coast who were the only non-Christians left in Europe! They called themselves, *The Teutonic Knights*. They conquered a Lithuanian subtribe known as *Prussians*. The ethnic name of this tribe was later adopted by one of the noble families of the Teutonic settlers who later became the kings and Kaisers of a united Germany (i.e., Friedrich von Preussen, et al.). The Teutonic knights also conquered the area that is now Estonia and Latvia. For almost two hundred years they tried to conquer all the tribes of Lithuania. However, in 1240 Mindaugas united the remaining Lithuanian tribes, making things more difficult for the Teutonic Knights.

In 1386 Jogaila of Lithuania married a Polish princess and became King of Poland. The Lithuanian population accepted the Christian faith, albeit reluctantly, out of respect for their countryman who was now the King of Poland. The exception was Samogitia: these people preferred to remain faithful to their pagan gods (for a while longer, anyway).

In 1395 the Grand Duke Vytautas led an army that attacked Mongols who had invaded Europe. His forces reached the shores of the Black Sea. Now, the political domain of the Lithuanian – Polish alliance spanned a large part of the European continent. The western countries of Europe became safe from further threats of Mongol incursions. Vytautas brought back a cadre of Tartars (men and women) who became his royal bodyguard. They settled in a village next to the royal castle, Trakai. These raven-haired, dark eyed Moslems remained intact in their adopted home well into the 19th century. It wasn't until the 20th century that they started to assimilate into the predominately blond, blue-eyed population around them.

In 1410 the Teutonic Knights became frustrated by unending skirmishes with Lithuanian tribes which usually resulted in ambiguous outcomes. They decide to enlist the aid of sympathetic member states of the Holy Roman Empire. The Pope gave his blessings. Countries like Hungary, Italy, Spain, France, etc., sent military contingents to what was sure to be a rout. In the meantime, Vytautas the Great enlisted the aid of his cousin Jogaila. Now Lithuania had Poland on its side. The Samogitians had a reputation for being fierce fighters and eager for a showdown with the Germans. It helped that Vytautas' mother was Samogitian.

The battle took place on July 15 on the plains of Tannenberg, near Grünwald. In Lithuanian the name for Grünwald is Zhalgiris. The Lithuanian-Polish forces won the fight decisively. The Teutonic Knights never recovered from this defeat and remained impotent as a military force, henceforth.


1569
A new threat arose from the east as the land of Muscovy gained power. To counter this unfriendly development, Lithuania and Poland formed a Commonwealth. It was successful in preventing Russian territorial incursions. Since some of the Polish kings were ethnically Lithuanians, the royal court in Krakow be-

came home to the Lithuanian nobility, as well. The lingua franca of the court was Polish. Today, the best remembered name of that era is *Radziwill* (as in Princess Lee Radziwill). This name in Lithuanian is Radvila and the family is descended from Lithuanian nobility that moved to Krakow.


## 1795

When her lame brained husband died (prematurely) the German born Tsarina (a.k.a., Catherine The Great) became empress of all Russians. She was reputed to have had series of lovers whom she rewarded wantonly with noble titles and vast estates. But, she was also shrewd politically. Under her rule Russia managed to subjugate Poland and Lithuania into the Russian empire without firing a shot. These two old kingdoms ceased to exist as independent states for the next 123 years.


## 1863

Lithuanians and Poles rebelled against Imperial Russia and were crushed by Cossacks loyal to the Tsar. In the aftermath the Tsarist government became even more repressive. A policy of Russification was enacted. Catholic churches were razed and the teaching of the Lithuanian language was outlawed. The written language remained alive through clandestine schools, mostly in small villages.


## 1918

Russia is defeated during WWI and faced a harsh revolution (de facto, a civil war). Lithuania took advantage of Russia's weakened situation and declared its independence. There were some military skirmishes with the Imperial Army by Lithuanian "Volunteers." Lenin was pleased that the Baltic States were keeping the Russian Army busy in the west and recognized (in official writing) Lithuania as a sovereign country. Twenty-five years later Stalin ignored the recognition of his predecessor.

1940 – 1944

A secret agreement (Molotov-Ribbentrop Pact) between the USSR and Nazi Germany promised a policy of non-aggression between the two countries. It also created "spheres of influence" that allowed the Kremlin to absorb the Baltic States into the Soviet Union. In 1940 the Soviet Army occupied Lithuania without any military resistance. Lithuania was helpless, despite the fact that it officially declared its neutrality in the epic conflict between the great powers of Europe. Lithuania sent diplomatic emissaries to Moscow in order to negotiate a reasonable solution with the Kremlin. Upon arriving in Moscow the delegation was promptly executed. (Stalin does not negotiate.)

However, in 1941 Hitler double-crossed Stalin and invaded the Soviet Union along the whole eastern front. It was the largest military force ever assembled at one time in modern history. The code name for this undertaking was called "Operation Barbarossa." It was a huge setback for the Red Army which was forced to retreat in a hurry. When German troops arrived in Lithuania, hundreds of bodies were discovered — mutilated beyond recognition and apparently tortured to death. Even the battle hardened German soldiers were shocked at the degree of savagery that the Russians perpetrated in their hasty retreat. The Germans took meticulous photographs of the carnage and gave copies to Lithuanians who are identified in a Soviet "black list" — a document left behind by fleeing prison wardens. This list of people now knew what to expect if and when the Russians should ever return.

Hitler's military machine left Lithuanians unharmed, for the most part. However, it is well known what happened to the Jews of Lithuania: they were rounded up and sent to concentration camps. Unfortunately, some Lithuanians were complicit in these crimes.

By 1944 Operation Barbarossa had become a failure. The German army suffered terrible losses and had to retreat. The Red Army occupied the Baltic States again. Hundreds of thousands of men, women and children (the entire intellectual elite) were shipped off to Siberia in cattle cars. Some succeed in fleeing to the West and became "Displaced Persons." This designation is abbreviated ("DP") and the word *"Dypukas"* was coined in Lithuanian. Between the Soviet and German occupations of Lithuania about 40% of the population was either killed or exiled to Siberia (where most of them died). Lithuania became one of the 15 Republics of the USSR

## 1944 – 1953
Resistance to the occupation of Lithuania took on the form of guerilla fighting. These rebels lived in forests for protection. They managed to kill a few thousand Russian military invaders at the cost of 30,000 Lithuanian rebels dead (men and women).

It became a war of attrition. Stalin died[1] in 1953 and Khrushchev took over. He declared amnesty for the rebels in Lithuania and the "war" of resistance ended.

## 1988 - 1990

The Soviet Union was facing economic and political crises. There was an unsuccessful coup attempt in Moscow. Gorbachev introduced new policies (Glasnost and Perestroika) in which the fifteen Republics were given greater freedoms. While visiting Berlin, President Reagan implored: *"Mr. Gorbachev, tear down that wall!"* Eastern Europe was being emancipated. In Lithuania *"Sajudis"* was established which launched a movement for the country's complete independence. It was led by a former musicologist and astute politician named Vytautas Landsbergis. His negotiations with the Kremlin proved to be productive. In March of 1990 Lithuania became the first "Republic" to secede from the USSR and restore its sovereignty. Landsbergis was elected Lithuania's president.

## 2015-2016

Today, Vladimir Putin calls the illegal occupation of Lithuania (1944) *"a liberation."* This is a dangerous harbinger for today's conflagration in Eastern Europe.

---

[1] It is rumored that Stalin was poisoned by members of the Politburo.

# Chapter I: FIRST IMPRESSIONS

*OUR HOME*
We lived in a small resort area called Giruliai, located on the picturesque Baltic coast. Our house was larger than average, three storied, with several guest rooms. The forest around us consisted mostly of pines and an occasional cluster of birch trees. The sand dunes along the coast were within walking distance of our house. The port city of Memel was about fifteen kilometers to the south. It was an idyllic place and my mother looked forward to spending the rest of her life in this bit of paradise that she had created for her family. However, there was a dark cloud on the horizon: World War II was raging not far from the borders of our country, Lithuania.

Hitler had annexed this part of Lithuania into Greater Germany in 1939, the year that I was born. It became known as Memelgebiet (Memel Territory). There was an influx of ethnic Germans, but most local Lithuanians remained and were generally left undisturbed. Lithuanian Jews were not so fortunate: the Nazi government rounded them up and shipped them off to death camps. One of our maids came from a Jewish family. She was eighteen. My father risked his life to hide her on our premises while the rest of her family was sent to a concentration camp. For the most part, I was sheltered from the military and political turmoil of the day and lived in blissful innocence.

I lived here for my first five years. My father, a popular musician, was away in Lithuania most of the time. He did not trust the Germans on the one hand, and he feared the Russians on the other. He had already spent a year in prison under the czar's government.[2]

During the First World War, my father managed to avoid being drafted into the czar's army. Instead, he joined the Lithuanian freedom fighters. He experienced little combat duty since he became the army's chorus master. He had gained early fame as a composer of popular folk songs. These were often patriotic songs and not sympathetic to the Russian occupiers. My parents were educated intellectuals and active figures in Lithuanian society. They knew only too well how they would fare in Soviet hands.

After our home became part of the German Reich, we were incorporated into the Nazi socialist system. The first floor of our house was transformed into a local kindergarten and my mother was appointed as its nominal head. Every day, a dozen or so children, mostly German, would come to our kindergarten to learn and play. I was a natural candidate for this school. However, I refused to participate in any such group activities and my

---

[2]During the first Russian occupation (1795–1918), books written in Lithuanian were outlawed. Clandestine couriers of these books were called *knygnesiai*. My father was caught transporting such contraband and was arrested at age twelve.

mother failed to persuade me otherwise. I preferred to play my games alone or with playmates of my own choosing.

We had a large backyard occupied by a considerable number of exotic chickens, ducks, geese, and a couple of turkeys. Raising domestic birds was my mother's hobby. My father planted blueberries, raspberries, and currants around the perimeter of our property, which was about an acre. He also added a couple of beehives and processed the honey in our barn—located in the far corner of the yard. There was also a large root cellar next to the barn. Refrigeration and electricity were not yet available in this outpost on the Baltic Sea. My father loved farming; it was in his blood.

*MY PARENTS*
My parents built their house before the second world war, never expecting it to be in the path of bloody fighting between two world powers. Lithuania remained officially neutral throughout the war. Unfortunately, that status was largely ignored by the warring parties. My father's name was Juozas Bertulis. He was an old-fashioned Lithuanian—religious, politically conservative, steeped in tradition, and burdened with ancient prejudices. He was also good-hearted and generous. Official documents showed him to be born on January 1, 1893, but the year might have been 1889 or earlier. He once changed the date of his birth to an earlier time, he told me, to avoid being drafted into the czar's army during WWI, and to a much later date when he applied for immigration to the USA. He attended a Catholic seminary for three years and almost became a priest. He had several siblings. His sister, Malvyna, married a Lithuanian air force pilot named Palejus. After the war, they immigrated to Texas and worked in the restaurant business in Dallas. They had no children.

My mother's name was Eugenia Ona Paskievicius. She was about twenty years younger than my father, born in Latvia, and raised in Moscow. Her father (Klement Paskievich) was stationed at the Kremlin as a Lithuanian cavalry officer in the czar's "Guardia." Officially, he was the military attaché representing the territory of Lithuania. He and one of his sons were assassinated during the early days of the Russian Revolution, when my mother was about twelve years old. My mother's other brother (Kasimir) and sister (Sofia) survived the revolution and remained in the USSR for the rest of their lives. Their plight was not dissimilar to the fictional story described in Boris Pasternak's novel *Doctor Zhivago*. Sofia had a son named Felix; he was afflicted with polio. My mother brought him to Lithuania and cared for him until he died at the age of nineteen. My mother said that he was like a son to her and took his death very hard. Felix was a good kid. Often, when my mother was angry with me, she would say, "Why can't you be a nice boy like Felix was?" *Geez, how could I compete against a saint?* I would think.

My mother was happily assimilated while living in Moscow, where she spent eighteen years. She taught Russian literature at one of the colleges and enjoyed the company of many friends. However, she could not endure life under Stalin's reign of terror. Many of her friends would disappear during the night and end up dead or in Siberia. Her brother was being hunted by the NKVD (secret police).[3] He went into hiding and supported himself by playing in chess tournaments. Sofia was jailed but was released a few months later, unharmed. My mother decided to move to Lithuania, where she had family roots. This was a difficult undertaking, since the border was guarded by Russian soldiers. Yet she accomplished this task over a period of many months and at great risk. By then she was in her mid-twenties

[3]The predecessor of the KGB, the notorious secret police agency.

and learned Lithuanian for the first time, though it was the language of her ancestors.

My mother was not overtly religious, but open minded and liberal in her politics. She was cosmopolitan, whereas my father was rather xenophobic—not unusual for a Lithuanian of that era. She was not a pure-blooded Lithuanian—having had a Polish grandparent, for which she was often teased by other Lithuanians. She was proud of the Polish branch of the family at a time when Lithuanians were still smarting from a bitter territorial war with Poland, in which Lithuania lost Vilnius, their beloved capital and the cultural heart of the country. During the middle of the nineteenth century, Poland and Lithuania revolted against the Russian occupation. This revolt was brutally suppressed. Fifteen male members of the Paskievich clan were rounded up and hanged in a public execution. Fortunately, some young males were able to escape the dragnet; otherwise I would not be here today.

My mother was known to be a courageous woman. Once, near the meadow to the north of us, a house caught fire. There was no local fire department, so all the neighbors ran up and formed a bucket brigade, but to no avail. When I arrived at the scene, flames were already spewing out of the second story windows and no more effort was made to save the house. However, everyone was talking about how my mother had run into the burning house as men stood by, raced upstairs, and rescued an infant from his crib. This was a heroic deed that typified her courageous spirit.

Eugenia was a woman of great determination. What she set out to do, she always finished. She had integrity, yet she was not prone to compromise her principles. Her compassion and sensitivity went with nerves of steel. On rare occasions, these traits also made her enemies. For the most part, she was admired and beloved by an inordinate number of people. After her death, I was told that many people owed their lives to her bravery, especially in helping them escape Stalin's purges.

My mother also seemed to have an uncanny sixth sense. One Sunday morning, while she was lounging in bed with her friend Mura Grosch, she announced that her mother had died that night. A telegram later confirmed it. She explained to Mura that her mother, who was living in Moscow (almost a thousand miles away), had visited her in a dream during the night to say goodbye. My mother had many such paranormal experiences.

During the mid-thirties, the frontiers between Lithuania and the USSR were heavily guarded by Soviet troops. Movement across these borders was all but impossible, unless you had official permission from the (paranoid) Soviet regime. Yet this young woman managed to make many trips between Moscow and Lithuania, smuggling much of her family heirlooms—old coins, silverware, works of art, antiques, etc.,—out of Russia. Alas, most of these family heirlooms remained in Lithuania when my mother and I fled the Russian invasion in 1944. My father managed to bury some of it in a secret location. He left me a map in case I ever had a chance to go back and look for these valuables. Most likely, Russian soldiers were on a lookout for such buried treasures and retrieved them for themselves.

Many years later, I asked Mama how she managed to cross the border so often with impunity. She explained to me that one of her close friends at the Kremlin was the minister of finance. I was still young and did not understand this title (or position). So she pulled out a dollar bill from her purse and pointed to the signature inscribed on the face of it. "On the Russian ruble, that's the guy I knew," she said. Now I understood why he was important. Apparently, his signature gave her the safe passage she needed.

It was no surprise that German authorities eventually found out about my mother's frequent travels from Moscow to Lithuania, and later, to the German side of the border. The Gestapo came knocking at our door with a warrant for her arrest. She was an attractive woman, well educated and with a natural sense of social grace. All these attributes made her a good prospect for becoming a spy. Once, when approached about spying for the Russians, she respectfully declined. German security forces found out about her history of smuggling Stalin's victims out, as well as the offer to spy for the NKVD. Now they were eager to know just who she was—a spy or just a homemaker. When they came to take her away, she knew that statistically, once arrested by the Gestapo, you were doomed. Interrogations were conducted the old-fashioned way, i.e., by torture.

Horrified, my mother grasped me in her arms and begged to remain. I had never seen my mother in such a hysterical state and started screaming. The Gestapo was not known for expressions of sympathy. One of them tore me from my mother's grasp and threw me to the ground. The others dragged my mother away and forced her into a waiting car. Crying desperately, I tried to run after the car as it pulled away in a cloud of dust.

A week later, she was delivered back to our house. She was unharmed! Many years later, she spoke of her experience in the Gestapo's custody. The prison cells were shared with many other detainees. She knew some of the incarcerated Lithuanians personally. During interrogations they would be tortured, then dragged back to their cell. My mother watched their physical deterioration day by day. Sometimes, they would return with teeth missing or with fingernails removed. Sometimes, the injuries were more serious. When they did not return, she knew what their final fate had been. My mother was not tortured. She was totally forthcoming with her interrogators. It was a good thing that she was, since the Germans knew her history well. They believed her when she said she had declined to spy for the Russians, and her explanations were corroborated by the information contained in their dossiers.

While in custody, my mother was not molested or humiliated by German soldiers in any way, she said. The Germans were cruel, but disciplined and very businesslike. By contrast, the Russian information gatherers that she experienced were a lot less professional in their approach, she once told me. While she was crossing frontiers, they would often "search" her by ordering her to undress. It was humiliating to be leered at. Obviously, they delighted in seeing a beautiful young woman naked; rules against such abuse were not enforced by Russian authorities.

*THE IDYLLIC LIFE*

My mother enjoyed hosting friends at our home. The house was designed with entertainment in mind. Our neighborhood consisted of about a dozen houses, popularly called "villas." It was strictly a summer resort destination, that is, until my mother became the first resident to stay there through the winter. That was the year before I was born. There were big parties, called "balls," with lots of people attending—the women in elegant long dresses and the men in tuxedos. They would eat, drink, sing, and dance into the night. Lithuanians loved their liquor. However, my parents were exceptions—neither one of them had a tolerance for much drinking. My mother's limit was one drink. If she had more than that, she would fall asleep. I never saw my father have more than two drinks, though he loved sweet liquors.

When I was older, I would help him make home brews concocted from all kinds of berries and grain alcohol. Many years later, my mother said to me that when we were forced to flee, she accepted the reality that she was also leaving her "youth" behind, i.e., she would never again enjoy the freedom that comes with being young. She was thirty-five.

In the spring, we attended Easter egg hunts and other traditional games with family friends and their children. There were numerous birch trees growing around our property, and my father would drill devices into their trunks in order to milk the sap that would drip into hanging buckets. The end product was similar to maple syrup. Winters were cold, but for kids it was all fun. There was a road on a steep grade not far from our house and we used to ride our sleds down it. Once, I exchanged my sled with Mindaugas Pleskys, a neighbor's son. He was a year older and I was not used to his bigger and faster model. I quickly careened off course and smashed squarely into a pine tree. The collision knocked me unconscious. It was dark when I came to as my friends were delivering me to my home. For the next seven years, intestinal bleeding was a reminder of this accident.

I remember the thrill of seeing my first Christmas tree in our living room, decorated with candles and all kinds of old-fashioned ornaments. My favorite was a tiny toy house covered with little licorice diamonds—which I would sneak into my mouth when nobody was watching. On this occasion, I received a flannel nightshirt, which lasted me for the next several years. At first, this nightshirt reached down to my ankles. When I finally wore it out, it barely reached down to my knees. Many years later, I asked my mother which Christmas it was that I was given this nightshirt. She said it was 1940 (when I was seventeen months old). We were both surprised that I remembered so many details of that Christmas without the benefit of photographs.

My father used to spend much of his time across the border in Lithuania and would visit us on weekends. Once, he came home with three big, beautiful oranges. I had never seen one before. They were a delicious treat. He then showed me on the globe he kept in his study where Italy was, the home of this exotic fruit. Foreign lands began to intrigue me. Also in his study was an old-fashioned clock encased in fine walnut veneer, perched high on a bookcase. It chimed every hour and twelve times at midnight. I delighted in winding it up with a big key while sitting on his shoulders. His desk was adorned by an old and elaborate silver ink set, which I greatly admired. It was commissioned by one of my mother's ancestors, two centuries earlier, while he was on a hunt in remote Russia. It was designed to hold quills on a tray with small crystal containers on each side — one for ink and one for powder to dry the ink with. The backdrop was an intricate carving of a bull elk with large antlers. The elk was depicted reaching high up, nibbling on the leaves of an oak tree. Each branch, leaf, and acorn was carved from Russian silver[4] and screwed into the tree trunk. Our walls were covered with paintings that my mother had collected or inherited. A large Turkish kilim adorned the main wall of our living room.

Having a large house in a beautiful resort area means you're going to have lots of friends visiting you. My mother actually enjoyed this aspect of having visitors. Most of our guests were family friends from across the border in Lithuania. My mother was closely involved with the international community, and diplomats from far and wide would come and vacation here. My father enjoyed this lifestyle as well, except when my mother's guests came from Moscow. He did not care for Russians very much, but tolerated them politely. Soviet diplomats that stayed

---

[4]Russian silver is purer than sterling.

with us one summer brought a collection of 78 rpm records with popular Russian music. My father had an aversion to foreign "pop music," especially Russian, and hid the collection in our barn behind a woodpile. My mother discovered the stash one winter as the pile started to diminish. It was an unexpected bonanza and she proceeded to listen to the records when Papa was out of town. I had no prejudices and enjoyed the songs as well. One of the most memorable diplomats that came here was the Japanese consul from Latvia. He was later remembered for helping Jews escape German territories by issuing them Japanese visas. There was a big party in his honor, and we kids were thrilled with the opportunity to play with the little paper flags depicting the rising sun that were handed out to everyone. I always thought that my mother should have married a diplomat of some kind instead of a musician. She had all the attributes required of an ambassador's wife. Actually, she had all the attributes required of an ambassador. She was born too soon.

The house was always full of visitors during summer months. In the winter, it was somewhat underutilized, so my mother would rent rooms out to local students. She loved the connection to young people in college, their hearts filled with political fervor and their minds full of ideas for progressive change. Such social radicalism was anathema to my father, but my mother's ways prevailed. Once, there was an assassination attempt on Lithuania's conservative president. Rumor had it that my mother sheltered the suspected student in our home.

Of the many families that came to stay with us, two had sons who remained my friends after we moved to America. The Grosch family was among my mother's oldest friends. Mura was Russian and Henry was Baltic German. They had a son whose nickname was Schurick. He was a year older and we were great friends. Years later, we ended up as classmates in high school.

The Peteris family had a son named Viktor. He was like a big brother to me and his love for nature became infectious, especially during my teenage years. He was about ten years older than I.

The pristine Baltic coast was the main attraction of this region. During the later occupation of Lithuania, the Soviets considered it their riviera. The coastal sand was fine and the sea was mostly calm during summer months. The water was shallow for a long way out and the sun warmed the water to comfortable temperatures. I would practice swimming in knee-deep water. However, after a storm, the surf would increase substantially with big pounding waves. These stormy seas would cause amber pieces to wash up on shore.[5] Beachcombers would search for new pieces after each storm. After one storm, I found an oval piece of amber the size of a large egg. It was a prize find.

My swimming ability at this time was limited to holding my breath and swimming under water. After one such storm, there were some minor swells that I underestimated. As one of these swells came in, I suddenly found myself in water over my head. I tried to swim but could not keep my head above the water. Desperately, I tried swimming under water and kicking off the bottom. I swallowed water and panicked. Just in time, it seemed, the water receded as suddenly as it appeared, and I found myself standing in shallow water again. The experience terrified me. Living on this coast left me with a lifelong respect for the power

---

[5]Legend has it that Jurate, a mermaid, who was the daughter of Perkunas (Neptune), fell in love with a handsome young fisherman named Kestytis. He succumbed to her enticements and joined her in the amber castle located on the bottom of the sea. When her father found out that his daughter was having an affair with a mortal, he became angry and struck the castle with bolts of lighting—smashing it to bits. Ever since, amber remnants of the castle have been washing up on our shores.

of nature. Yet it did not stop my love for the sea nor protect me from other close encounters later in life.

There was a beautiful meadow just north of our house. Sometime during the war, a Wehrmacht (German infantry) unit established camp there. The young company commander befriended my mother and became a frequent guest at afternoon teas. When I was old enough to understand good manners, I was formally introduced to him. However, I was not invited to participate in the social discourse. These were still the days when children were to be seen and not heard. Instead, I would peek through the open door and observe with fascination the handsome young officer in his military dress uniform. The long saber hanging from his side did not impress me as much as the Luger pistol contained in a holster at his hip. Guns fascinated me and I was tempted to ask him to show it to me. Of course, I never did.

I am sure this cultured young officer was delighted to discover a sophisticated and attractive young lady, albeit married, practically next door to his drab military outpost. His troops were bored and restricted to their encampment. My mother hinted that the soldiers might enjoy some diversion by building a new fence around our property. The lieutenant took the hint. My mother supplied the materials and the soldiers built us an excellent fence!

Not only were the soldiers encamped near our home bored, they got by on limited resources. Not surprisingly, the German army was overextended and strapped for cash during the last years of the war. To replenish their coffers, they would stage fundraisers. This entailed setting up paper targets and allowing local citizens to shoot various military guns for a nominal price. Apparently, they were not short of ammunition. Our young lieutenant invited me to shoot a weapon of my choosing. I picked the most awesome weapon in their arsenal: the MG42 machine gun. I was not big enough to shoot it by myself, so I sat in a soldier's lap and he held me while I pulled the trigger. When I fired, the gun shook me so hard I thought my head would fall off. I'm not sure if I even came close to hitting the target some fifty meters away, but the experience thrilled me.

A small store served our community. It was about a mile away on the coastal highway—an unpaved country road. My mother would send me on errands to purchase various sundry items from time to time. One particular item that I would bring home still sticks in my mind. It was a can of NIVEA hand cream. It was contained in a blue round tin with white lettering, just as it is today. Now, when I purchase such a can for myself, I wonder how a common little consumer item has survived unchanged for so long.

My favorite hangout was our backyard, which also contained a large sandbox. Here I could build sand castles, dig tunnels, or do whatever inspired me. When kindergarten let out, kids would walk past my sandbox on their way home. Some would try to join me, while others showed hostility toward me because they were envious of my independence. In either case, if any kids came too close to my "bodyguard," a gander goose, he would spread his wings, lower his head menacingly, and start hissing and snapping at their bare legs. I was content to be left alone and my bodyguard knew it.

My bodyguard's name was Guzhinas and he was all business. More than once, when the local fox would try to get inside our yard with the intention of grabbing his dinner from the large selection of hens and ducks, Guzhinas would be seen chasing the fox well beyond our property boundary. About once a week, my mother would take the train into the city to buy groceries and other provisions. The local train station was a short walk from our house. Somehow, Guzhinas always knew the day and hour that my mother's train would return, and he would go to meet her. Before the train came to a halt, he sensed exactly which wagon she was on and approached it on the run, wings spread, and honking loudly in an exuberant greeting. People on the concourse were quick to move out of the way of this large and fearless goose.

My mother was the only person Guzhinas respected as his superior. Sometimes, he would go into the woods by himself and return unruffled and unharmed a few days later. It was a mystery what compelled him to wander off like that. In our yard, he was the supreme commander and king of the roost. Chickens are known to have a pecking order. This was true with our chickens, as well. However, Guzhinas would often intervene with that order. When he would see a disadvantaged little chick or scrawny old hen waiting at the rear of the crowd during the feeding frenzy, he would maneuver the poor animal ahead of the bullies so it could eat in front of the lineup. He would patrol the feeding trough like a drill sergeant. Guzhinas would always eat last. This big goose was a local legend and my best friend.

The house and yard gave me ample opportunities for exciting challenges that often got me into trouble. At this early age, I already displayed a natural propensity for climbing. Once, I managed to climb onto the roof of our house. I was unable to climb back down and continued to sit on the edge of the roof with my feet dangling over the eave, much to my mother's consternation. Eventually, neighbors rescued me. Another time, I managed to lower myself to the bottom of our well. Once again, I had to be rescued. Then there was the time I was climbing a tree when the branch I was standing on broke. I fell to the ground and broke my collarbone. While growing up, I never seemed to shirk danger or dangerous activities. If anything, I was drawn to such things. My mother employed a nanny to look after me. She was successful while I was still a toddler. However, once I was old enough to outrun (and outwit) her, she quit in frustration.

If bored with the play options in our backyard, I would cross the dirt road in front of our house and wander off to explore "distant lands," often accompanied by Guzhinas. Exploring the mysteries of the forest where witches, dwarfs, and fairies lived was always a great adventure, but I would not linger long, since I was convinced that these mythic forest dwellers actually existed. Of course, there were real threats, such as wolves and bears, but I did not fear those as much.

(My father once told me the story of how his father had a face-off with a wolf. He lived during the latter part of the nineteenth century and was a talented violinist. For extra cash, he would perform at village festivities and weddings. Late one night, while returning from one of these functions, he was walking through the forest and got off the pathway. In the darkness, he did not notice a hidden wolf pit and fell into it. To his horror, there was already an occupant in the pit: a big Siberian wolf! The wolf growled menacingly. My grandfather had no weapon for defense. Instinctively, he started playing his violin. The wolf started howling. As the night went on, a string on the violin broke, but he kept on playing. Then another one broke. By morning only one string was left on the violin. Fortunately, some passersby heard the sound of the one-string performance emanating from the wolf trap. They promptly dispatched the wolf with a gun and my grandfather became a legend.)

I delighted in traversing the beautiful sand dunes to the open sea. Here I had to be careful, for German soldiers were now patrolling the coast. These soldiers would pace up and down the seashore with big rifles slung over their shoulders. They looked fearsome in their gray uniforms, black boots, and steel helmets. I was convinced that if one spotted me, I would be shot on sight—thanks to Viktor's attempts to scare me. Was he really serious? I was always careful to stay well hidden among the dunes, and my heartbeat would quicken whenever a sentry marched by. It was an exciting life. To be cooped up all day in a kindergarten class with a bunch of snotty kids would not have been a good trade-off for me.

I could not resist staring out over the sea. I tried to imagine what lands lay beyond it and what it would be like to be stranded on a remote island like that fellow Robinson Crusoe. The sea was beautiful, intriguing, and at times, deadly. For hours on end, I would watch merchant ships traversing the far horizon. Usually, these ships would just sail slowly and silently along that line between the sea and sky. On rare but unforgettable occasions, as I lay watching from my position in the sand, a passing ship would suddenly be engulfed in a black cloud. Sometimes, I would hear a dull boom a few minutes later. When the smoke cleared, there would be no more ship on the horizon. It was like a vanishing act. I did not understand it at the time, but U-boats were busy sinking these Allied vessels on their way to Russia.

At times, my father played with the Memel Symphony Orchestra. For performances appealing to children, my mother would take me into town and we would watch staged musicals. I delighted in seeing my father playing the bass in the orchestra pit. The plays were good entertainment. One play sticks in my memory: *Peterchen's Mohnfahrt*.[6] There were scenes of little Peter crossing the sea in a boat and one where he flew over the moon. I knew the scenes were fake and was proud to be able to

---

[6]"Little Peter's Trip To the Moon."

figure out how the props were staged.

If there was a movie theater in town, I had not heard of it. The city was noisy and full of people busy with commercial activities. There was a chocolate factory where we bought candy, and a tailor where I was measured for a custom-made suit. Our dentist was a baldheaded old German with a sense of humor. While I was sitting in the dentist's chair one time, he made a crack about my small stature. Not to be outdone, I responded by saying that he was "Herr *Glatzminister Bombenkopf.*"[7] Both my mother and the red-faced dentist burst into laughter at my quick and witty retort. The city was an exciting place to visit, but I was always happy to return home to my feathered friends and the tranquility of the countryside.

When not attending plays, my mother enjoyed putting them on, using available local talent. One such play was the production of *Snow White and the Seven Dwarfs*. My buddy Schurick and I were cast as dwarfs. It was midsummer and warm. I sweltered in my dwarf outfit and the cotton beard on my face was irritating. During the middle of one of my appearances, I threw up—right there on stage. It was the end of my acting career.

## THE DARK CLOUDS OF WAR
One sunny day, while playing in my sandbox, I heard a new sound in the sky. I looked up and saw a single-engine plane flying by. I had heard of these flying machines, but this was the first time that I actually saw one. Little did I know that soon I would see many more airplanes, and not under such peaceful circumstances.

---

[7]Roughly translated "Mr. Minister Shiny Bullet Head."

Lithuania declared its neutrality during this worldwide conflict, but that did not stop the Russians from occupying our little country. They soon established secret prison camps. Political leaders, intellectuals, and many of my father's friends and colleagues started disappearing during the night. During the summer solstice of 1941, the German army advanced in a surprise attack against the Russians, Operation Barbarossa. German intelligence uncovered a large quantity of records and secret documents that the Russians did not have time to destroy. Some of these documents listed "enemies of the Soviet" who were to be arrested, often brutally tortured, and executed. German security forces made these lists public. One such NKVD blacklist had my father's name on it. When it appeared that the Russian army was about to return, many Lithuanians knew better than to remain. My father went into hiding.

Years later, while living in Los Angeles, I found some black-and-white photographs tucked away in a shoebox located among my parents' belongings. I should have respected their privacy, but curiosity got the better of me. These pictures depicted Lithuanian victims of torture—mutilated bodies in grotesque positions. Each picture had a person's name on it and a date, which coincided with the German solstice invasion of 1941. The Russian occupiers had only hours to make a quick retreat, and they made sure that no one remained alive in their prison camps. The Germans took pictures of the chaos the Russians left behind. These photos were made public so that Lithuanians would be aware of the Soviet menace they could expect if they ever returned.

Some of the people depicted in the pictures were friends and acquaintances of my parents. Some were well-known political leaders. They were people that started disappearing during the first days of the subtle Russian occupation that took place during

1941 (no shots were fired). One of the photographs showed the body of the director of Lithuania's Conservatory of Music. My father had been offered this prestigious position a few months earlier, but my mother urged him not to accept it. If he had, he would have moved higher up the blacklist, and his body would have been in that picture, no doubt.

This rotunda was part of grandfather's estate in Poland. After 1569 most Lithuanian nobility moved to Krakow and spoke primarily in Polish.

Klement Paskevičius (center) with his two sons and two older daughters. Sophia is in the white dress,her brother Kasimir is standing next to her. The son in a cadet's uniform was killed in Moscow at the start of the Russian Revolution, along with his father. Eugenia was still a child when this photo was taken (circa 1916).

Clockwise: Eugenia's communion /
Alex (a.k.a.,"Pupa") and his mother
in Giruliai / Sofia Konn / Felix Konn /
Eugenia with Felix a year before he
died from polio.

Clockwise: Elena Zilinskas (who was suspected of spying for the OSS) & Eugenia (who refused to spy for the NKVD). / Eugenia on the iced up Baltic shore. / Eugenia on the beach near Giruliai. / Pilot Jonas Palejus and his wife Malvina (sister of Alex's father).

Clockwise: A double wedding that took place in Klaipeda. Jonas Palejus seems most interested in the young lady next to him. His future wife,Malvina Bertulite (sitting behind him), does not seem happy. Eugenia Pakevičiute married Juozas Bertulis 1931. Juozas / Eugenia / Kasimiera Murach married Klement Paskevičius in 1891.

45

Lithuanian & German
ID cards and pass-
ports from before,
during and after the
war.

46

# RETURN TO GIRULIAI

When my mother and I fled Lithuania in 1944 I was 5 years old. The next few years were spent in Germany and I kept wondering when we would return to our beloved home in Giruliai—the small enclave on the Baltic coast where our house was located. In 1950 we emigrated to America and the prospect of ever seeing my home again diminished as the "Iron Curtain" fell, separating Eastern Europe from the West forever, it seemed.

Then, in the 1980s surprising events occurred in the communist bastion of the USSR. Cracks in the Iron Curtain started appearing. The leaders in the Kremlin (Yeltsin and Gorbachev) were faced with serious economic problems exacerbated by pressure from strong leaders in the West, primarily, Ronald Reagan and Margaret Thatcher. The handwriting was on the wall: communism could not survive in its current form. It was at this time that I received an unexpected phone call from a Lithuanian Communist official while on a ski holiday with my family. How he tracked me down I never found out. The year was 1987.

The conversation was in Lithuanian:

"Mr. Bertulis, this is professor Grigonis calling. I hope I am not disturbing you."

"Not at all. I'm on a skiing holiday in the mountains. How can I help you?"

"Well, I am visiting the university in San Diego right now and I will be returning to Lithuania soon. However, I would like to meet you in person, if you have the time, to discuss some important matters. Would you be free to meet me in Seattle tomorrow?"

I jumped in my car and drove to Seattle that night. The next day Prof. Grigonis and I met at the Meany Hotel. He explained that he was on an academic tour of the USA and that on his list of objectives was the prospect of extending an invitation for me to lecture next summer at the University of Vilnius, Department of Architecture. Would I be interested?

This offer came as a total surprise to me. Until now, Lithuanian expatriates were not allowed to have any contact with Lithuanians in the USSR, much less visit the country, unless under the auspices of official tour programs. Even then, the people and places one could visit were highly restricted. This was an unexpected opportunity to visit my homeland; I had to give it some thought. Most of all, I wanted to visit my old home in Giruliai, but I also knew that this area was in an "off limits" zone to foreign travelers.[8]

The next day we met again. I agreed to accept the invitation under the following conditions:

---

[8] I later learned that the reason for Giruliai being "off limits" was that there was an ICBM installation nearby, with atomic warheads.

1)  I did not want to have any restrictions put on me as to where I could travel while in Lithuania and whom I could visit.

2)  I did not want to have a guide accompanying me when I was on my own (I knew that such "guides" were KGB agents assigned to spy on the visitor).

3)  My expenses would be paid while in Lithuania.

4)  Lastly, I would be allowed to bring my 16 year old son (Tomas) along with me.

To my surprise, the professor agreed to all my conditions. He added that I would also be given a car and the driver could be someone of my own choosing (one of my friends). His one request was that I should submit to him in advance the architectural topics that I would be prepared to lecture on.

While driving back to the ski chalet to finish my holiday, I wondered why I was invited to lecture at the Lithuanian university by the communist regime? It was well known that not only was my father a vehement anti-communist, but so was I. My father was no longer a threat to the Kremlin because he was no longer alive. I was very much alive, but I had proven my political astuteness by participating in "cultural exchanges" with Soviet alpinists over a number of years without "rocking the boat." (I organized these exchanges as a director of the America Alpine Club.) The Soviet Union was falling apart and communism was on its way out. I speculated that the current communist regime in Lithuania wanted to present a sympathetic face to all Lithuanian patriots by inviting a well-known Lithuanian exile whose credentials were above suspicion. Tomi was delighted to hear that he would be coming to Lithuania with me.

The following summer my son and I flew into Vilnius, the beautiful capital of Lithuania. We were given a comfortable apartment next to the University campus. I was met by Algis, the brother-in-law of a good climbing friend. Algis was willing to be my driver and guide; I trusted him. He was most helpful in showing me the sights and invited me to various cultural events. He also arranged to have me meet with the mountaineering community where I gave slide presentations on my various climbing accomplishments.

I had informed professor Grigonis of the two subjects that I would be lecturing on:

1) *Comparative construction methods between Europe and the USA,* was one. I had worked as an architect in Germany in years past, so I knew the subject well.
2) *The commercial architecture of Frank Lloyd Wright.* I considered myself an expert on Mr. Wright's work since I traveled all over the USA photographing his projects over a period of many years. This lecture proved to be very popular and I was invited to repeat it to groups outside of the university, as well.

High on my list was my desire to visit my childhood home in Giruliai. Algis had heard of this little resort, but he was not sure where it was. So, one weekend Algis, Tomi and I drove to the well-known beach resort of Palanga. From there the directions were simple: 15 km down the old coastal highway, someplace on the left.

"OK, how do we find your house once we arrive in Giruliai?" Algis asked. "You were only 5 years old when you last saw your house. It's in the woods. And how will we recognize it once we find it?"

I responded by asking for a piece of paper and pencil. On the hood of the car I started drawing a map. "Look, here is the old railroad station. It should be easy to find since we were told it is still operational. From the station it is a short walk to my house." I drew a diagonal line from the station indicating a trail through the trees and around some houses ("villas"). I indicated where the trail would connect with a dirt road. On this dirt road will be half a dozen houses. "One of them will be mine," I said, "no problem." Algis shook his head at my misplaced confidence.

When we reached the RR sign on the highway, we turned left and arrived at the station, a short distance in. Here we parked the car. We found the trail that lead to the dirt road just as I had drawn on my map. Sure enough, there were several houses along one side of the road, also as I had shown. Algis was impressed. The problem was, I could not find my house among them. I walked up and down the short stretch of road and studied each house carefully. They were all much smaller than I remembered. Our house was big. Plus, it had a fancy Greek colonnade at the main entry. None of these houses fell into such a category.

Algis was getting impatient and Tomi was getting bored. Finally, I decided to enter one of the houses, and as I did, my heart skipped a beat when I saw the stair in the foyer. This was my house! But it was much smaller than I remembered it. Of course, when I was a lad of 5 years, everything looked big. The Greek colonnade had been removed and the exterior wood siding and color had been changed.

I continued inside and opened the first door on my right. It turned out to be a small bunk-room with a big fat Russian sleeping in one bed. He woke up and grunted: "Stoh ti hotchis?" (What do you want?) I apologized and left the house quickly. I later learned that the house had been converted into a vacation home for retired Russian railroad workers. The original big rooms had been subdivided into small bunk-rooms. The barn in the back was gone. The root cellar was still there, but under lock and key. Everything looked rather neglected and dilapidated.

Driving back to Vilnius I had time to reflect. After almost fifty years I had finally seen my old home again! It was a painful sight. During the communist era properties that belonged to exiles reverted to public ownership — meaning, nobody really owned them and nobody really took care of these properties. Not only the houses but, much of the whole country had gone to pot under this system. I was depressed.

The good news was that Lithuania was one "Republic" in the USSR where much of the land remained under private ownership. Consequently, there were beautiful neighborhoods, well groomed gardens, and the old cities were being rehabilitated with pride. Today, Lithuania is again a proud member of the European community. A few years ago, my daughter Eugenia, visited Giruliai and tried to find my old house, per my description. She could not find it. Instead, she said there was now an upscale townhouse development there.

# HISTORIC REVELATIONS

I have just finished reading *GOTHS AND BALTS*, subtitled, "The Missing Link of European History." It is written by Jurate Rosales (Statkute), who grew up in Venezuela after immigrating there after WWII. Her book is based mainly on two (long over-looked) sources. The first source was by Roman scholars (Jordanes) contemporaneous with the end of the Gothic era (551 AD). The second document was written under the auspices of King Alfonso X of Spain, during the 13th century AD. Rosales found a copy of the latter chronicles in the archives of Caracas University.

Apparently, the Goths were a large and powerful conglomeration of peoples living in northeastern Europe of which the Balts were a major component. I quote: "The thread of ancient history, spinning from eastern Europe all the way to India in the East and Spain in the West, can now be understood..." We are talking of an era starting from about 2,000 BC until about 500 AD. It wasn't the Vandals that conquered Rome. It was the Goths (i.e., Balts)! And they did not "vandalize" Rome, as some historical accounts tend to claim. About 800 years earlier it was the Goths, i.e., the Balts, that were among the army that besieged Troy and lost. There was a long and strong presence of Baltic peoples in Hellenic Greece. This finally explains why we Lithuanians have Greek suffixes in our names (my conclusion).

The military occupation of (future) France lasted less than a century after the Goths defeated Attila the Hun. However, the Goths that occupied Spain never left. The nobility and Spanish Kings were proud to trace their roots going back to the Goths. The Spanish language (and many surnames) are profusely influenced by Baltic (Lithuanian) words. The Lithuanian nobility were proud of their roots going back to Roman times. I always thought the name Bertulis sounded very Italian. Now I know why. By the way, "Bertoli" is a major producer of olive oil in Italy. Is the surname Bertulis related?

After the Goths departed (Roman) Italy they never recovered their pre-eminence. They retreated to their origins on the Baltic coast. Their up and coming neighbors, the Franks, Germans, Slavs and Norsemen, attacked them frequently, causing further demise. Only the ethnic tribes of Lithuania and Latvia survived into the 20th century intact. No, it was not Sanskrit that is the root of "Indo-European" languages. According to this book, the Goths, who spoke various dialects related to Lithuanian, influenced the development of Sanskrit, Latin, Slavic, Spanish and Germanic languages.

This book is worthy of a university level course in historic anthropology.

55

# Chapter II: FLIGHT AND REFUGE

*"Run, the Russians are coming!" This refrain could be heard all over the eastern provinces of Germany after the Soviet troops broke through the Eastern Front. The major part of the population took flight in a wild panic - if not by train, then by foot, by bicycle..., or horse-drawn carts. What followed was an avalanche of human tragedy and catastrophe, by which many thousands of civilians died.[9]*

*ESCAPE*

The war came to our doorstep suddenly, but my mother was forewarned. My father was living and working on the Lithuanian side of the border where he felt safer in the event the German government started conscripting able bodied men into the war (in vain, we later learned). One dark night in May— 1944, the young officer who was our frequent guest for tea awakened us at three in the morning. He was wearing his combat uniform and his Luger was no longer in his holster: it was in his hand with

---

[9] Excerpted from *"Danziger Bucht 1945 - Dokumentation einer Katstrophe,"* by Egbert Kleser, Bechtle Verlag, Munich/Essslingen, 1978.

his finger on the trigger! I was impressed at the sight of the pistol — in full view for the first time. He was wary of Russian soldiers who could appear out of the dark at any moment. I was given fifteen minutes to get dressed and board the truck that was waiting for us outside. Tracer bullets were streaking across the sky above us and artillery bombardment could be heard with ominous frequency in the distance. Flashes of light above the forest line accompanied the sound of explosions. Even though it was practically summer I wore my warmest clothes. All we took with us was what we could carry. We were in the truck ready to depart when my mother asked that the truck driver wait a little longer. I saw her talking to our caretaker, a part-time employee, but I could not hear what she was saying. Years later, I learned that she was giving him instructions to kill all our animals, including Guzhinas, lest they suffer a worse fate while abandoned. I'm glad I did not hear her give this order, for I am sure I would have done something very drastic and foolish to prevent the slaughter. To this day, my heart aches when I think of the fate my feathered friends met that night.

Daybreak found us in front of a big ferryboat docked at the old harbor in Memel. Artillery fire could still be heard in the distance. For all we knew, the Russian army might overrun the city at any moment. People were on the verge of panic. Throngs of desperate civilians were vying for access onto the ferryboat. It was pandemonium. With the intervention of the German lieutenant, we were ushered onto the vessel expeditiously. Then he returned to the truck; we never saw him again. Undoubtedly, he saved our lives, for ethnic Lithuanians were not included in the German evacuation plan. Many of our Lithuanian friends that stayed behind were arrested by the Soviet "liberators" and executed; or, at best, shipped off to Siberia for 15 years or more.

The voyage from Memel to Königsberg[10] was uneventful. The Baltic Sea was calm and no other ships were seen on the horizon. Little did we know that hostile submarines were lurking below the surface. Many years later I learned that only a small percentage of these refugee ships survived the voyage. Allied torpedoes sank most of them and tens of thousands of refugees drowned. This episode has been called "the greatest disaster in the annals of the sea."[11]  Ignorant of this statistic, our vessel's passengers felt safe and relieved to have escaped the impending Russian onslaught.

The ship was packed with people — mostly women and children. I don't recall seeing any adult crew though I'm sure that seamen, somewhere, were operating the ship. My mother and I managed to find a bench to sit on — on the top deck. Adolescent boys of the Hitler Youth maintained order. Like good Boy Scouts, they helped the elderly and mothers with babies find a place to sit and brought them water to drink. The decks were covered with people and baggage. These boys would run around, doing their errands and jumping over obstacles, as if it were a sport. I was impressed with their efficiency and maturity. Many of them were only a few years older than I. During the desperate last days of the war, many of these kids were given rifles and ordered to face advancing Russian soldiers. Very few of them survived.

We arrived in Königsberg safely and began the next leg of our long journey — this time by railway. The train had not arrived yet, but thousands of desperate refugees were already jostling for positions on the concourse. When the train finally ap-

[10] Now, Kaliningrad (Russia), in what was formerly East Prussia.

[11] "*Defeat in the East*," by Juergen Thorwald, published by Random House, Inc.

proached, the pushing and shoving became more intense. My mother managed to position us in front as the train pulled in. Suddenly, I felt a deliberate push from behind and found myself falling onto the railroad tracks. The approaching locomotive was nearly upon me. With so much clothing on, I could not move fast enough to evade it. My mother let out a scream and lunged for me. In an instant, she managed to snatch me out of the path of the train. Undoubtedly, her quick action saved my life. Standing in my previous position was the man who had pushed me. He had a smirk on his face, as if enjoying our brush with death. I recognized him: he was the ex-husband of one of my mother's best friends. He was a notorious sadist (according to my mother) and a former superintendent of a Nazi concentration camp in Lithuania. Reputedly, he was responsible for the torture and execution of many Jews and Lithuanians. Years later, around the mid 1960s, I was browsing through an issue of TIME magazine when I came across his name, Karolis(?) Jakas.[12] The article described his notoriety and how he was finally apprehended in Germany. He was tried, convicted, and sentenced to life in prison. The news warmed my heart. Not all war criminals were German.

When the train left the station, I looked out the window and saw an endless line of cars. I could barely see the lead locomotive. Half way back was a second locomotive tied into the chain of cars for extra pulling power. When the track turned, I could see

---

[12] I remember visiting his home and seeing a large cartoon picture hanging on his living room wall. It was a depiction of him, holding a pistol in one hand and a whip in the other while grimacing prisoners were being trampled under his feet. His wife divorced him (with my mother's encouragement). She and her son Vaidutis eventually immigrated to New York. She and my mother remained close friends. Vaidutis grew up to be a kind and intelligent young man. He joined the US Air Force and came to visit us often while stationed near Los Angeles. Later, he became an architect, but died of leukemia before reaching the age of thirty.

the last car, probably a kilometer to the rear. People were crammed inside the passenger cars and in-between them, as well. I was small and able to lie in the hammock above a window (which was meant for small carry-on articles). I was fortunate to have such a comfortable space all to myself, for I could sleep lying down. And, sleep I did.

The heavily laden train moved slowly. The weather was sunny and the countryside was serene - belying the terrible fighting that was going on not so far off. At night we approached the outskirts of Berlin. The city was in a complete blackout and we could see nothing. The exception was a long line of small, blue lights on the ground that defined the landing strip of the airport. The train stopped briefly at the darkened city station. Except for the wheezing sound of the steam locomotive, all was eerily silent. No one got on or off the train, as far as I could tell. It did not linger for long in that doomed city.

I remember the train ambling along through the German countryside and the occasional small towns. It had been a wet spring and some of the towns were flooded. The sight of streets and houses inundated by water seemed like an awful disaster to me — at the time. I had not yet seen the destruction of war, so the flooding looked like a most horrible tragedy. Occasionally, the train halted for no apparent reason. My mother would point through the window at tiny specs of shiny silver moving in unison, ever so slowly and silently, high up in the blue sky. They were Allied planes on a mission to bomb some German city or factory. Once the planes passed from sight, the train continued on its slow journey south.

A day or two later, while I was napping in my hammock, my

mother woke me, unusually excited: "Pupa!"[13] She said as she shook me, "Look out the window, look up high!" There, for the first time in my life, I saw big mountains — snow capped mountains! We were entering the Alps. I was awestruck. "Could people actually climb over the tops of such peaks," I wondered, "and what would one see on the other side?" The spirit of "Hänshen"[14] was beginning to stir in me. And, for the first time, a feeling of wanderlust struck me.

## RESETTLEMENT

The train disgorged its passengers in the Austrian city of Graz. All "Volksdeutsche"[15] refugees were cared for by social agencies established by Hitler's government. We were Lithuanian foreigners and had to fend for ourselves. I remember holding my mother's hand, going from house to house in the dark, asking for refuge. When my mother's foreign accent was detected, we were angrily rejected with the words, "Verfluchte Ausländer,"[16] and the door slammed in our faces. The first few nights we slept on park benches. Eventually, we found sheltered space in a large basement of a school building with many other refugees. There was a large tin tub and we took turns taking a bath. Outside was a public square where I got a glimpse of an ice cream

---

[13] This was my nickname while I was growing up. I was named Alexander, after the great Russian poet, A. Pushkin, whom my mother admired. My middle name, Arvydas, is of Lithuanian origin and appeased my father's desire for an ethnic name.

[14] A popular German nursery rhyme about a little boy, who leaves home to wander off into the big, wide world. See *Hänschen* story.

[15] Expatriates of German descent.

[16] "Damned foreigners."

stand. Beautiful, big scoops of ice cream were being sold in paper cups. "Mama" could not refuse my pleading look; reluctantly, she gave me a few Pfennig to purchase a serving.

My mother managed to find temporary employment and we were able to pay for a small room in a larger apartment unit. This was in the city of Gratkorn. Before long, the war reached us and Allied planes began dropping bombs on us every few days. We were given rubber gas masks and training on how to use them. I hated putting them on since they smelled bad and made you feel claustrophobic. Sweat caused the rubber to become sticky. During the air raids occupants of our apartment building took refuge in the basement when sirens sounded their dreaded wail. We would listen anxiously for the drone of approaching planes. Then, the sound of exploding bombs could be heard — becoming louder and louder. Terrified, people would hold their breath until the sound of the explosions would start to diminish — signifying that the line of fire was bypassing our building. During these moments, I would sit on my mother's lap, clinging to her desperately. Her calm voice would assure me that nothing could possibly happen to me as long as I was in her arms. It was a terrifying experience that gives me nightmares to this day.

We did not stay long in the Austrian part of "greater" Germany. The job opportunities for my mother were better in a big city. So, after a couple of months we found a house in a farming community called Ismaning - now a suburb of Munich. There was an orchard in the back and meadows extended beyond. A small lake was nearby which was popular for summer picnics. There was a community boat, which was cleverly devised out of a fuel tank from a downed bomber. Across the dirt street was the "Bauernhof" (farmyard), where the owners lived; it included a granary and flour-mill. Once again, I could play outside and enjoy adventures of my own choosing.

There were children around, but being an "Ausländer," I did not fraternize with them. One day I found an abandoned bicycle. It was big, heavy, and meant for an adult male. During those days, a bike had only one gear, and in order to break you simply backpedalled. After many attempts, I learned to ride it by putting my right leg under the top bar and pedaling along, hanging out over the left side. It was awkward to ride around like that but it sure beat walking, I thought. Riding in this contorted position caused the chain sprocket to chafe against my right leg. For years thereafter, I had scars on my right calf where the sprocket scraped against my skin.

### FINAL DAYS
All able bodied men were off at war. Women attended to the daily affairs of the farm. We had a radio in the house and my mother would always listen to any news broadcasts — hoping to hear information of the war and Allied advances. When Hitler spoke on the radio, everyone listened. I listened also, since my mother had explained to me who he was. Of course, I did not have a clue as to what he was talking about, but the awe he evoked in the listeners impressed me. As the fight for the "Vaterland" became more desperate and the bombing of the cities grew more intense, the civilian population steeled itself for "the fight to the finish." Every able-bodied man (including very young boys) was called upon to fight the invaders. I remember a man in his thirties who got around on crutches since he had lost a leg early in the war. He desperately tried to sign up for military service again. When he was refused reentry into the German army, he shot himself! Ironically, the bombing of civilian targets did not demoralize the population, as was intended; rather, it intensified the patriotic fervor.

Air-raid sirens would go off with increasing frequency and we
would rush into the basement of our house for shelter. Most of
the time, the aerial attack by Allied bombers was focused on the
big city of Munich. At such times, we would stand in the doorway of the basement and watch the spectacle taking place over
the city. Allied bombers in large numbers would drop their
deadly load and the sky above Munich would light up with an
orange glow.[17] The anti-aircraft fire from below was fierce.
Every so often, a bomber would get hit and start its fiery descent, trailing a cloud of thick smoke. On some occasions, a
squadron of bombers flying in close formation would be hit with
a flack shell and, as one heavily laden plane burst into a ball of
fire, the adjoining planes would ignite, sequentially — also
bursting into huge balls of fire. The result was a spectacular
conflagration of a dozen or so flaming bombers diving earth-
ward, still in formation. It was a sight I will never forget.

Whenever a few bombers headed our way, the pattern became
familiar. Fear would overtake us as we dropped whatever we
were doing, rushed into our air raid shelter and waited as the
drone of the planes came closer. It was an experience that became repetitious, but one that no one ever got used to. The first
bombs would explode at some distance with dull thuds. Invariably, the intensity of earthshaking explosions would become
greater and louder. The anticipation of being in the line of fire
was unbearable. We were lucky so many times before, we
would think, the odds must now be in favor of the bombs. When
the sound of exploding bombs started to fade, we knew that the
worst was over and breathed easy again. Rosaries would go

---

[17] During the spring of 1937 the bombing of the Spanish city of Guernica by
Hitler's Luftwaffe was considered an atrocity because 1,600 unarmed civilians
died. Eight years later hundreds of thousands of civilians died in German cities
from Allied bombings. There was no international outcry.

back into pockets and the murmuring of prayers would stop. After such bombings, the women would go to the unfortunate houses that had been hit and try to help the survivors. I wanted to go as well, but my mother kept me locked indoors during such occasions. The next day I would see the ruins, often still smoldering.

On less frequent occasions, aerial attacks came during the night. On the ground, all was in a blackout mode. The dark sky would light up with long columns of crisscrossing searchlights. Occasionally, a searchlight would lock onto an unfortunate plane and a barrage of anti-aircraft fire would ensue. Even then, rarely was a plane hit. Conversely, the attacking planes had the same difficulty hitting their intended targets during the night due to a complete blackout below.

Many years after the war I met an Episcopalian minister who was one of the interrogators of suspected German war criminals. His name was Charles Tait. One of these prisoners was a former SS general who was in charge of a small concentration camp (KZ). In the interview the general admitted that his role in running the KZ fell under the definition of "war crimes," he was prepared to accept his fate. Indeed, he was later found guilty at the Nürnberg Trials and hanged. During the interview with Charles Tait, he posed a question in return: "My wife and children lived in a small farming village in southern Germany, away from any strategic war installations, when a squadron of Allied planes flew by and dropped their deadly bombs on them. Most of the villagers were killed, as was my family. Was this a war crime? And if so, who will judge the Allies?" This proposition has haunted Charlie Tait the rest of his life.

In fact, there was an assistant to Winston Churchill by the name of Sir Arthur Harris ("Bomber Harris") who advocated saturation bombing of German civilian cities in order to demoralize the nation. Churchill signed off on the idea and millions of innocent civilians died as a result. This must count as one of the biggest war crimes in modern history.

Squadrons of bombers were not alone in conducting aerial attacks. The British had a little stealth plane, designed to avoid any warning system that German defenses might have had. It was light since it was built out of balsa wood and canvass. It carried only one machine gun and only one pilot sat in its cockpit. This plane could fly deep into German territory and return to England on one filling of petrol. It would fly low and fast, thus avoiding detection until it was too late. These planes never triggered any sirens until they were already gone. The usual targets were civilians caught by surprise. These forays were meant to harass and demoralize the German population; not that it needed any more demoralization, I thought.

One day, while I was playing in the yard behind our house in Ismaning, my mother threw open one of the windows of our veranda and yelled at the top of her voice: "Pupa, quick! Run for the woodpile, right now!" The panic in her voice told me that the situation was serious and I obeyed without hesitation. However, my curiosity got the better of me and as I dove into the woodpile I looked upward to see if I could get a glimpse of what I was running from. Just above the treetops a fast flying plane was banking sharply in my direction. I could see the pilot sitting in the cockpit as clearly as he must have seen me. I fully expected a hail of bullets as he swooped directly over me. The shots did not come. My mother came running out of the house and grabbed me, trembling, in an emotional embrace. She was shaken. It all happened so quickly that I never really had time to get scared.

The pilot could have killed me. He chose not to. Perhaps he recognized that I was just a child, and perhaps, he had a child of his own back home. I still wonder how my mother knew that the plane was coming without being able to see or hear it in advance. Some people are endowed with a strong sense of premonition. I think she was one of them.

During these last days of the war, my mother and I saw a person parachuting into the meadow near our house. She hurried off to search for him and came back with a young man in a soldier's uniform. He was an American pilot, I think his name was Eugene. Had the local farm women gotten to him first, they probably would have killed him with their pitchforks. We hid him in our basement. It was an act for which my mother would have paid for with her life, if discovered. I was allowed to visit our "prisoner" and we enjoyed each other's company. We had no language in common, so the visits were brief. He was always happy to see me and I received my first sticks of chewing gum from him. He indicated that this "candy" was not to be swallowed. The brand name was "DENTINE," I remember, for it came in compact little red rectangles that were different from the gum sticks I would chew after the war.

Our town of Ismaning was trapped on the front lines with advancing American forces on one side and the entrenched German army on the other. With fighting breaking out all around our fate was precarious. Not knowing whether we would live or die during the chaos my mother wrote two letters to a close (Russian) friend who was also a refugee. These letters were never mailed.[18]

---

[18] Translated from Russian.

*Ismaning, April 29, 1945*

*Dear Nina!*

*I don't know if I will ever have a chance to send this letter, but I'm writing it anyway. This is a horrific day and my soul is so heavy that I have to share my feelings with you.*

*Today is Sunday – a wonderful sunny day, but the smoke from all the fires has darkened the clouds.Our apple trees are blooming in the garden. The ground is profuse with dandelions. I am enjoying the scenery and wondering if this will be our last day (alive). Anything can happen. Since Friday the thunder of cannon has prevailed. Saturday was deathly silent since negotiations were underway with the Americans about a possible surrender of Munich. But, the "Waffen SS"[19] destroyed this conspiracy and snuffed out all hope (for a cease fire)... and we were so happy for a while!!!*

*Now we are between two fronts and everything is going through us. What will the night bring?! At the other end of our small village, across the river, a huge fire is blazing. There is gunfire from all directions. At times we climb up into the attic and try to see what is happening and where. The streets look deathly empty. Among the trees in our garden soldiers are hiding with their jeeps and trucks. We have nowhere to run.*

---

[19] An elite German army faction very loyal to Hitler. The Führer's final orders were to never surrender and "fight to the finish."

*Right now our men are sleeping [Eugene and Pupa] because it is very hard to sleep at night. Tonight we will sleep in the cellar, for sure. The sirens stopped wailing and we no longer have any interest in looking at the map (to keep track of the front). My thoughts go back to June 22, 1941.[20] I remember the gunfire — it was also a beautiful Sunday. I'm thinking of the people (caught in the middle) then and what today's end will bring... What horror!!! So much blood and gore.*

*And now, as then, I am beholden with pain and anxiety. I fear not just for myself, but also for many, many other people. Everyone wants to live; life is so beautiful. But here, death is so close we can touch it. Will death fly by or take us with it?!*

*With kisses and hugs, my dearest,*

*Genia*

After two days of intensive and spectacular aerial attacks and carpet bombing, American GI's appeared in numbers. They were all over the place — driving in jeeps, trucks, tanks, and requisitioned motorcycles.[21] For the first time I saw the "Stars and Stripes" waving against the sky. The thrill of that sight has stayed with me to this day. Thanks to my mother's stories, I

---

[20] The day of Germany's surprise attack against the Russian army, "Operation Barbarossa."

[21] The farmers across the street from us had a beautiful BMW motorcycle, which was stored away while the men were at war. I saw it being ridden by two happy GI's.

knew we were being liberated by a democracy of mythic proportions, and this flag symbolized it. Only the Lithuanian tricolors[22] could arouse such emotion in me (during the times that it was outlawed by the Kremlin).

The following letter was written after the dust settled:

*Ismaning, May 3, 1945*

*Dear Nina,*
*Thus, the front is gone and we are alive and in one piece. We were happy to see numerous white flags and (peaceful) silence. Then, again we were soon dashing into the cellar like madmen. But when American tanks were slowly crawling along the streets we could not believe that all the horrors were finally behind us. The following day was the first time that the war was over for us. Much snow fell and the tree branches bent under the burden of fresh snow. There is mud and slush in the streets. Flags are no longer waving (in the breeze) but hanging gray and limp... The streets are empty; people are waiting silently.*

*The following day [when curfew was lifted] foreigners, especially Russians and Poles acted like they were masters of the situation. They dressed up, pinned victory buttons on their lapels and celebrated. Germans that had surrendered were being abused. Stores and warehouses were being looted. There was much drinking in the streets as people would get inebriated, swear, indulge in debauching*

[22] Yellow/green/red in horizontal bands.

*behavior, and throw-up. German civilians were afraid to step outside. American (soldiers) also felt free to debauch at any time (and in some cases) their behavior was no better...*

*This is war! (But) this tiresome and hated war is (now) behind us. We should be happy, but somehow we are not. People's senses are dulled and mistrust is pervasive. I'm in a state of fog. I cannot sleep at night and by morning I feel like I am drunk. My movements are like a robot's. I force myself to eat but my stomach feels painfully empty. The future is very unclear.*

*(P.S.)*

*May 6, 1945*

*Dear Nina! Yesterday we celebrated Eugene's birthday, the end of the front, and the upcoming farewell with him. We celebrated like we used to — with music, dancing and wine. From some of our countrymen he obtained a gramophone [record player] and the wine. He invited one of his friends who brought two female companions along. I was very surprised that these companions were German and made themselves so available, while pretending to be proper ladies; they could not keep their hands off these foreign men.*

## THE WAR IS OVER

A twenty-four hour curfew was enforced until all areas were safely secured. Having sheltered an American pilot from the Germans, we were treated very well. On the other hand, the

Bavarian women living in the farmhouse across the street from us were scared to death of the Allied invaders and feared the worst. They came over to our house and tearfully begged my mother to intercede on their behalf. My mother had no grudge against them and did what she could.

The perception that the majority of Germans were Nazis or Nazi sympathizers is inaccurate. Bavarian farmers and less educated Germans were more likely to side with Nazi policies. Most educated Germans were not fond of Hitler and some tried to overthrow him.

Long after the war, I was visiting friends in Vancouver B.C and became acquainted with the stepson of Willy Messerschmidt, the legendary designer of German airplanes during WWII. His name was Ebohart Strohmayer-Messerschmidt. Ebohart related a fascinating story of how his mother and stepfather enticed Rudolph Hess (an old family friend) to fly to England in order to persuade the British to agree to a negotiated peace settlement early on in the war. Messerschmidt secretly designed a special plane that Hess could fly to England and ditch during the night. Had Messerschmidt been implicated in this plan Hitler would have had him executed, most certainly. Unfortunately, Churchill was not favorably disposed to negotiating with the Germans and demanded nothing short of unilateral surrender. Hess spent the rest of his life in prison. Millions of people on all sides died as a consequence of Churchill's decision.

Almost immediately after the war, my mother was hired as an interpreter by the American forces — she spoke seven languages. Later she got a job with the University of Munich and we rented a room in a large apartment unit in town. Each family was consigned to one bedroom. The kitchen and the only bathroom were communal. Our neighborhood, known as "Bogenhausen," was located not far from the center of Munich. It was a small, two-block street called, "Mühlbauerstrasse." Across the street from us was a boarding school for girls, called Max Joseph Schtift. A ten-foot masonry wall surrounded the premises. The neighborhood boys (myself included) would occasionally climb to the top of this wall to get a glimpse of the uniformed schoolgirls playing ball in the courtyard. Unbeknown to me, my future wife (Gisela) was one of these girls. Destiny would have us meet many years later while attending a university in the United States.[23]

We continued to live among other Germans and refugees of various ethnicities. Most Lithuanian refugees that survived the war were accommodated in "Displaced Persons' Camps," run by Americans. From here, these "DPs," as we became known, awaited the opportunity to emigrate to a country in the "New World." We chose to avoid these camps and were able to manage on our own, for the most part.

---

[23] Chapter IX: "A New Life In the Northwest"

# THE STORY OF HÄNSCHEN

Recently, while sorting through some boxes in my basement, I came across a small, simply framed watercolor painting. Seeing it brought back a rush of memories and mixed emotions. The painting was a caricature of "Hänschen Klein," the little hero of a German nursery rhyme. I will always remember the first stanza:

*Hänschen klein*
*Geht allein*
*In die weite Welt hinein.*
*Stock und Hut*
*Steht ihm gut,*
*Ist gar wohlgemut.*
*Aber Mama weinet sehr,*
*Hat ja nun kein Hänschen*
  *mehr!*
*Wünsch dir Glück!"*
  *Sagt ihr Blick,*
*"Kehr' nur bald zurück!"*

*Little Hänschen*
*Goes off alone*
*Into the big world.*
*Staff and hat*
*Fit him well,*
*And he is quite content.*
*But his Mommy is crying,*
*For she has Hänschen no*
  *more!*
*"I wish you good fortune!"*
*Her last glimpse says,*
*"Just come back soon"!*

In May 1944 the Soviet Army was in the process of overrunning the vicinity where our home was located. My mother and I were forced to flee. My father was caught between the lines of warring factions — the German Wehrmacht on one side and the Red Army on the other. He was trapped. Even though our country was officially neutral during WWII, the big powers ignored this status. If we had stayed, we would have been sent to Siberia, at best, or killed outright. We chose to take our chances with the Germans.

With the help of a sympathetic Wehrmacht officer, whose regiment was encamped near our house, we were able to board a ship crowded with German refugees. It sailed across the Baltic Sea and delivered us to the city of Königsberg (in East Prussia). From there we were able to board a train, which was jam-packed full with "Volksdeutsche" refugees repatriating to Germany. These were mostly old men, women and children.

It was a long and slow ride across the length of Germany, all the way to Austria (then part of "The Reich"). When the train approached the Alps early one morning, my mother woke me up and pointed out a landscape I had never seen before: high mountains encrusted with snowy glaciers. I was transfixed! Lithuania is a coastal country and the terrain is predominantly flat. Here the terrain was mountainous. I could not even imagine what it would have been like to climb over the top of these peaks and behold the other side. Yet, the idea intrigued me. A feeling of wanderlust penetrated deep into my libido which was to remain for the rest of my life.

The train disgorged its passengers in the Austrian city of Graz. We soon moved to the town of Gratkorn, where my mother was able to find work and we were able to rent a small room in an apartment building. At one point I was left to my own devices while my mother remained ill in bed. She gave me some money to buy food with. When I passed a flea market, curiosity got the better of me. What caught my eye was a postcard size watercolor depicting a youngster with a hat, a stick in his hand, and a knapsack on his back. He was surrounded by snowy peaks and about to (blissfully) walk off the edge of a precipice (it was a cartoon). The little fellow was "Hanschen," the hero of a German nursery rhyme, who was in the process of going off "into the big wide world." I decided to buy it as a gift for my mother. Though, it meant I would go hungry that day.

When I handed the picture to her, she was moved to tears, but she forgave me for disobeying her. After we emigrated to America, I noticed that she kept this memento hanging on her bedroom wall for many more years. Of course, her "Hänschen" waited until he grew up and finished school before going off "into the big wide world."

# TRAGIC TIMES IN HISTORY

While reading a book about the bloody Crusades of the 11th and 12th centuries, I was aghast at the carnage and suffering inflicted on the civilian populations who happened to be in the way of armies motivated by greed, politics, or religion. When towns or cities were conquered, the inhabitants — old men, women and children, were often slaughtered. Even Richard the Lionhearted—the "pious King" of England had no compunction in ordering his Christian soldiers to massacre innocent civilians by the thousands when they became an "inconvenience" during his departure from Jerusalem. When I read these accounts, my reaction was always: "boy, am I glad I did not live during those tragic times in history." I then decided to take a closer look at a sampling of such times.

During the era of the Egyptian pharaohs there was frequent mass slaughter of peoples when a city or state was conquered. Life was cheap. If there were survivors, they usually ended up as slaves of the conquerors. What an unpleasant time that must have been to live in, unless of course, you were part of the ruling elite. Even then, life was precarious and few pharaohs lived long enough to die of natural causes.

During Roman times, cities were besieged, conquered, destroyed and multitudes were killed or enslaved. It is surely true that there were more slaves than free citizens in Rome during the apogee of that empire. To diminish the chances of a slave revolt, Romans allowed slaves to dress like free citizens. Romans feared that if their slaves realized what a potent force they could be (if allied together), they would rebel — which they did from time to time, anyway. If you were a young man you might have been inducted into the Roman army. Do you know where the word "decimation" is derived from? Look it up — its etymology is most interesting.

When the Golden Hordes fought their way west during the first millennia AD, they propagated a "scorched earth" policy across much of Asia, even Europe. Nothing and no one was left standing in their way. Thousands upon thousands of innocent people perished. These nomadic conquerors had little use for slaves, so they usually killed everyone. The life span of Mongolian horsemen was not that great either. It was a hard life on both sides of the fence.

In 1258 the Mongol Kahn Hülegü laid siege to the city of Baghdad. When the city's defenders raised the white flag and laid down their arms, the Mongols entered the city and killed every inhabitant (80,000 or so), except for the few Christians that happened to live there (one of his favorite wives was a Christian). The vast collections of books in Baghdad's libraries were thrown into the Tigris River. Arabs still lament that the river flowed red with their blood and black with the ink of their books. Ironically, this tragedy occurred just a few years before these conquerors converted to Islam.

During the middle ages various European nations were constantly at war with each other where the slaughter of civilians was par for the course. On top of that, sanitation was not yet a word in any nation's vocabulary and large percentages of populations succumbed to scourges like the bubonic plague, typhus, cholera, etc.

The Thirty Year war (1618-1648) was the longest conflict in European history. It was fought mainly in the name of religion. It was so bloody and devastating that historians are still trying to figure out who was fighting whom and why.

Before the white man discovered America (1492) the populations living in the Western Hemisphere were constantly warring against each other. Some well established nations would simply vanish (e.g., the Mayans, Toltecs, Anasazi, et al.) and no one knows for sure the causes for such disappearances. Many of these societies lived in constant fear of being killed in war, sacrificed in the name of religion, or enslaved for economic reasons. It was an unforgiving time to live.

The African continent did not fare much better during these times. Wars were fought "savagely." For many centuries Africa was also the harvesting area for the slave exporting business. Even colonial Americans, who were civilized enough to write the Constitution and were pious Christians (in most cases), had no qualms about "owning" innocent men and women from Africa. Is not a basic Christian tenet that we are all "God's children?" Even the Koran states that all people are equal in the eyes of Allah. Ironically, slavery in some Arab countries remained a legal institution until the middle of the 20th century.

During "modern times," when most populations became "civilized" and predominant religions espoused "thou shalt not kill," things got a better. Right? Wrong! It can be argued, that the

20th century must count for enduring the most tragic times in all history.

The "Holy Crusades" in the Middle East are long over, but death and devastation in the name of religion seems to be the norm again in the 20th century (and the 21$^{st}$). Foreign invaders were (and still are) trying to claim land in the name of misplaced religious beliefs, as if *their* "holy book" is as good as a real estate contract for acquiring someone's land. And so it is a tragic time for many indigenous people in the Levant.

40 million (or so) died during the First World War. Millions more died during the Russian revolution. It is estimated that Joseph's Stalin's despotic rule cost around 45 million innocent lives. The whole population of the USSR lived in a virtual state of slavery for most of the 20th century. These were the fortunate ones. Millions more suffered horribly and died as virtual slaves in the Soviet Gulag.

Millions of innocent civilians died in concentrations camps when a self-proclaimed "Führer," named Adolf Hitler, decided to purify the German race. It was not a good time to be there, even if you were a pure blooded German. I lived there during some of that time.

Millions of innocent civilians died when Mao Tse-Tung ruthlessly converted China into a proletariat state. It was supposed to become a "worker's paradise." In reality, it became a "paradise" only for the communist elite.

90 million (or so) died during WWII. Hundreds of thousands of innocent civilians died during the fire bombings of Dresden and carpet-bombing of Berlin, Leipzig, Munich, and numerous other cities and towns across Germany. Thousands of civilians died

during the sieges of Leningrad and Stalingrad.  Thousands of civilians died during the fire bombing of Tokyo.  Hundreds of thousands of old men, women and children, died when atomic bombs were dropped on the cities of Hiroshima and Nagasaki.  This was not a good time to live.  I did live during that time and witnessed the carpet-bombing of one of those cities: Munich.  My mother and I were not citizens of Germany; we were refugees from a *neutral* country.  This officially neutral country, Lithuania, lost more than a quarter of its population in a war it took no sides in!

Comparing the tragic times of the 20th century to the more recent times of the 21st century, things are looking up.  Today, when one or more innocent civilian gets killed in a war zone by a misguided missile, there is an international outcry.  This is good.

Gebeleschule, Munich. This photo was taken in 1920 before it was damaged by bombs during WWII. Note the steep bank in front of the building which Alex used to defend himself against classmate bullies.

After the war a disabled German veteran came to our house and offered to sketch Alex's portrait for a small sack of potatoes.

# Chapter III: LIFE IN BAVARIA

*POSTWAR TRIBULATIONS*
As soon as the war ended, the American command made public the atrocities perpetrated in German concentration camps. The gates to the Dachau KZ were swung open and my mother did not hesitate to take me on a tour of it. I was six years old. The prisoners were gone and the piles of corpses had been removed. But the facilities had not yet been sanitized; piles of prison garb were still lying around. The walls of some areas were covered with black-and-white photographs of what the GIs had found here. It was a horrific sight, especially for a child my age. Mother did not believe in sheltering me from the dark side of mankind, it seemed. I think her intent was to expose me to such evil so that I would always recognize it and oppose it. Yes, it did give me nightmares for years to come, but then, so did the bombing, the fighting, and the abuse I suffered later in various postwar orphanages.

Another example of my mother's intent to educate me by immersion came when we had a heroin addict living in the room next to us. Ivan was a brilliant university student and a descendant of Russian aristocrats. He was tall, handsome, and had just married a beautiful Russian girl. It was a romance I witnessed and admired. Soon they had a baby girl, whom everyone adored. He was also my mentor. Among other things, he introduced me to *Fussball*, a passionate game that I soon excelled at. His happy life changed drastically when he became addicted to heroin. Once, when he was away, my mother took me into his room and let me view the disgusting environment that he was reduced to live in. The room was empty except for an old mattress on the floor and filthy bedsheets. I nearly threw up.

There were several other students living in the same apartment unit at this time. When Ivan would go into withdrawal, they would tie him up to the radiator in his room. He would moan and wail in pain—begging for help. The students would ignore him. During one horrific night, he called out my name for help. Naively, I went to his room and opened the door. It was a pitiful sight, seeing him sitting on the floor with his hands behind his back, tied to the radiator. He was in agony and he begged me to release him. I went to the room where the students were living and opened the door. They were sitting at the table engrossed in their studies. The air was thick with cigarette smoke. I told them about Ivan's plight (as if they did not know it) and relayed his request to be untied. They waved me off nonchalantly and instructed me not to go to his room again.

Ivan never fully recovered from his addiction to heroin. His wife left him and moved to America, where she remarried. Instead of finishing his university education, he went in and out of rehab, and eventually, he became a homeless street bum. This experience, and watching him deteriorate into a tortured human being, turned me against drugs forever.

Munich was a disaster zone—devastated by so much bombing. Many city blocks were reduced to rubble. Renaissance masterpiece art and medieval buildings were either destroyed or badly damaged. On my first visit to the center of town, I was impressed by a huge machine moving around on tank treads, streaming black smoke from its stack and clearing away rubble with a big scoop. It was an ancient bulldozer running on steam fueled by wood. The Frauenkirche, a medieval cathedral with twin steeples topped by onion-shaped cupolas, still dominated the skyline. The symbol of Munich survived despite numerous penetrations from allied bombs. Marienplatz, the central square downtown, was still the principal gathering place for vendors as well as crippled German war veterans reduced to begging.

Demoralized German soldiers were back from the war. Some of them had missing limbs. The most gut-wrenching sight was a former soldier who had lost both arms and legs and was now carted around by his buddy. Some were wearing yellow armbands—indicating that they were blind. For American GIs, however, it was "party time."

On occasion, while waiting for a streetcar, I would watch American soldiers carousing inside a *Biergarten*. Accompanied by willing fräuleins, they would get drunk and indulge in vulgar behavior. These young GIs would often end up in ferocious fistfights among themselves. Their buddies would stand by, and at times cheer the antagonists on. Then, after seemingly beating the bloody hell out of each other, the two fighters would make up, shake hands, and continue drinking beer together as if they were the best of friends. This type of behavior was most bewildering to me.

Along with the occupation force came American culture. Comic books were prized by all us kids. Cowboys such as Red Ryder and Roy Rogers were my favorite. For the benefit of the GIs, some radio stations played country-and-western music. I fell in love with the likes of The Sons of the Pioneers and Hank Williams. I continued listening to country and western while growing up during the rock-and-roll era in America. I considered it a form of folk music. Many of my friends could not understand how a person who liked classical music as much as I did could also listen to "corny" cowboy songs. I have continued to enjoy this type of music to this day.

Movie houses began to reopen. All films were extremely popular with the entertainment-starved public. One evening my mother took me to my first movie. It was a period film about some swashbuckling French musketeers. All the seats were taken and we found ourselves standing in the rear of the small theater. I loved the "staging," for I was still under the impression that this was a live play. However, when a bunch of horses started racing across the "stage," I began to wonder how they accomplished such special effects. Afterwards, Mother explained to me the science behind cinematography and cleared up my confusion.

It was a time for new adventures. There was a huge grass field behind our apartment building and it was pockmarked with craters (from extensive bombing). However, some of the bombs dropped by the Allied bombers had not exploded. They were duds. I was amazed to see so many lying around. They were beautifully made—about a foot long and octagonal in shape. I did not know that they were nasty little incendiary bombs that could still explode. I collected as many as I could carry and brought them home. As I proudly presented them to my mother, she nearly fainted.

I learned not to touch any more unexploded devices, large or small. However, I then explored the craters more closely and was delighted to find numerous deflated "balloons." I enthusiastically collected several dozen with the intention of selling them to all the kids in the neighborhood, thus making lots of money. But first, I had to wash these things, since they were all soggy and dripping slime. When my mother came home and saw me standing at the kitchen sink, busily washing the pile of "balloons," she became upset. She confiscated all of them and told me never to touch another one, ever again! Many years passed before I understood that these were not really balloons but something the GIs used on dates with their fräuleins.

Kids become inventive when conventional (manufactured) toys are not available. A popular toy that we devised was to take a house key and pack it with phosphorus from a match (house keys had hollow cores during those days). Then we would insert a blunt nail up the core. We would run a doubled string through the key so that we could swing it against the pavement or a brick wall. The impact of the nail against the phosphorus would produce a loud crack—much like a firecracker. That was lots of fun.

## GOING TO SCHOOL

The summer of 1945 was a good one for me, but it came to a very sudden and unpleasant end. That year, due to the war, the start of school was delayed until well into November. The thought of school had never entered my mind, until now. I was sure I could avoid it, somehow, like kindergarten back in Giruliai. So you can imagine my shock when mother informed me that school (first grade) was about to start for me. I was in disbelief. Early the next day, she made me wear my tailor-made suit that we brought along from Lithuania. The matching jacket, pants, and cap were made of fine corduroy, gray in color with fine blue pinstripes. I was aghast.

She proceeded to drag me out the door and down the street. I felt I was being led to my execution. No amount of pleading and begging could dissuade my mother from her dire intentions. With a tear-soaked face, I cried, "I promise never to do anything bad again for the rest of my life, but please don't make me go to school!" She ignored my pleadings. Her determination was unwavering and she kept an iron grip on my wrist. This was definitely the worst day of my short life.

We entered a large gray building named Gebeleschule. I soon found myself sitting behind a small, ink-stained desk in a dank classroom, with many of the windows still broken. There were sixty-some Bavarian boys, many of them barefoot and wearing lederhosen, already sitting in class when I arrived. By contrast, being attired in a three-piece suit, I must have looked like someone who just dropped in from another planet. The situation did not look good for me.

On my way home, several classmates going in the same direction followed me. It was a cold day, the skies were overcast and the streets were full of mud puddles. By now the boys knew I was not one of them. To make matters worse, I told them that I was from Prussia. My reasoning was that being a northern German was better than being a Lithuanian Ausländer. Little did I know that admitting to a Bavarian that you are a Prussian was about the worst thing anyone could do. Bavarian kids are raised to despise Prussians (even more so than die-hard American Southerners who learned to hate Yankees). Whereas Lithuanians...who were they? The first casualty was my cap. One of the boys snatched it off my head and threw it into a mud puddle. The others jumped on it with delight. I tried to keep walking but they kept accosting me. Pretty soon, I was shoved into a puddle and thrown to the ground. They proceeded to kick and jump on me. I lost my books and began to run. That was my salvation: I could run fast.

It was dark when I finally arrived at home. My mother was horrified at my appearance. I was covered with mud and my suit was in tatters. Crying, I begged her not to send me to school again. She would have none of it. The next day she dressed me in lederhosen and escorted me to school again. At least I suited more appropriately that day. Matters did not improve. The cat was out of the bag: I was a despicable *Preiss*[24] and that made me fair game.

After school, the boys did not wait to harangue me on the way home. They literally ganged up on me outside the school building and started beating me up. I lost my books again but managed to outrun them. This pattern continued for many days until I learned to defend myself. Outside the main entrance of our school building was a street, and beyond it was an open yard. Actually, the yard lay in a depression that started with a steep bank next to the street. The drop-off was substantial—about six feet. My defense strategy was to stand at the edge of this bank and face the attackers. This way no one could sneak up behind me. I was quick on my feet, and when one or two of the boys would try to accost me, I would maneuver quickly in such a way so as to throw them off balance and push them down the bank.

My tactic worked for a while, but there was only one of me and many of them. In the end, I would get pummeled anyway. However, I was beginning to make the impression that I was no pushover. They were not happy when I got a few licks in.

The turning point came one day when I was standing on the

[24]A Prussian, in Bavarian slang.

edge of the drop-off and desperately fending off my attackers by throwing them over the bank. On the sidelines stood a blond classmate named Fritz. He watched as I defended myself, though it was obvious I could not last long. Then the unexpected happened. Fritz set his books down and calmly walked into the fray —by standing next to me and facing the attackers. Now there were two of us! The odds changed drastically and the bullies were no longer winning. Soon another ally joined us. His name was Augustin. The fight was over. From then on, I was never harassed again and I will always be grateful to Fritz and Augustin. We remained the best of friends for many years.

Another level of acceptance occurred when Fussball season started. As it turned out, I was the best player in the class (thanks to Ivan), and everyone wanted me on their team during scrimmages. Now I was not only being tolerated but sought after. When our class team entered tournament play, I was elected captain two years in a row. My preferred position was center midfield. I would score fewer goals than a striker, but I had more fun using my skill to set up plays that ended up in goals. One important trick that I learned during this time came in handy when I played soccer again in America. Penalty kicks are called *elf meters*. I learned to trick the goalie into thinking that I was going to kick the ball to one side and he would dive that way—when in actuality, I ended up kicking the ball in the opposite direction. This trick was called *Teuscher* (faker).

Before long, I became totally immersed in Bavarian culture. I no longer spoke High German but became fluent in the Bavarian dialect. However, at home, I continued to converse in Lithuanian. We were confident that when Lithuania became free again, we would all go "home." I received a book on Lithuanian folklore and traditions. Some parts of it described ancient pagan rites, of which the Lithuanians are very proud despite being good Catholics.

I soon discovered a new adventure that kept me out of school a lot. It was the exploration of bombed-out buildings and houses. Quite often, the basements of these ruins were still intact and I was able to find ways to crawl inside them. I recruited companions who were happy to join me. Personal belongings did not interest us. The prizes we looked for were guns and ammunition. We found plenty, but by now I had learned not to bring any contraband home. I abandoned these "treasure hunts" when some of my friends got hurt by accidental shootings or explosions.

However, by this time I had skipped too many days of school, and my teacher sent a note to my mother declaring that I would need to take first grade over again. I was flunking first grade! My mother had no clue that I was truant so much. To say that she was upset, disappointed, and very angry with me would have been an understatement. She was furious! The next day she dragged me back to school and we went directly to the principal's office. I sat meekly at her side as she informed Herr Direktor, in no uncertain terms, that her son was not going to flunk first grade. In fact, she assured Herr Direktor that her Alex would excel in all courses while in second grade. The dignified old man did not stand a chance with my mother's powers of persuasion. Reluctantly, he permitted the wayward son to advance to second grade, come fall. Then my mother dragged me back home. I cried all the way, for I knew what was in store for me: I got the trouncing of my life (for my mother believed in "tough love"). I spent the summer practicing the three Rs. The following year I was among those at the top of my class.

My parents grew up in a culture of old-fashioned traditions. One of these was the habit of taking a newborn to a gypsy seer to have his or her future forecast. My mother did this with me. The gypsy told my mother that I had a strong character and that I would have a long and complex life. She also said that I would turn out to be either a very good person or a very bad one—there would be no in between with me. This prediction concerned my mother to no end. It also may explain why she was so ready to use corporal punishment when I transgressed (and I transgressed a lot!). My father was a very gentle person and never laid a hand on me, no matter how angry he may have been. My mother wanted to be certain that I would turn out "good" rather than "bad." She imbued strong moral principles in me. "You did not come into this world for a free ride," she would argue. "I want you to grow up and be productive...and when you die, you should leave this world a better place than when you entered it." This principle stayed in my conscience throughout my life.

She also wanted me to be strong and survive the challenges I was to face in life. To drive the point home, she related the anecdotal story of the lepidopterist observing an exotic butterfly begin to struggle out of its cocoon. Eventually, the scientist began to feel sorry for the little creature and helped it escape. That well-intended gesture condemned the butterfly to a flightless life. The man did not realize that the insect needed to struggle a long time in order to develop the muscles needed for flight. My mother made sure I struggled a lot.

Since I had achieved academic success, my mother permitted me to play in Munich's organized soccer league. I was actually a couple years too young, according to standing rules, but I was an exceptionally good Fussballer. The league officials permitted me to try out and they were impressed. I was accepted on a team called Münchner Kickers. For the first time, I played wearing a real uniform (a jersey with white and green stripes) and wore real soccer shoes with cleats! However, whereas I was the star field player on my school team, here I was relegated to goaltending. I learned to be a smart goalie and eventually enjoyed this unique position on the team.

On this prestigious team, I was a fearless and quick goaltender. I excelled in sweeping the ball from the feet of attacking strikers. This required an aggressive attitude, diving onto the ball just as it was about to be kicked. The danger was that you might get kicked instead of the ball. To avoid such an accident, I learned to tackle the ball in a rolling dive that would place my back at the striker's feet while the ball was tucked against my belly. Getting kicked in the back was preferable to getting kicked in the face or stomach. Actually, I rarely got kicked at all. The older players on my team appreciated my daring approach to goalkeeping.

Playing on both the school team and the city league team was demanding, but I felt as if I could play much more. The intensity of the game caused me to fall on the ground so often that my knees became badly bruised and cut. I proudly carried remnants of these scars for many years.

*HUNGER*
After the war, Germany suffered from economic depression. Inflation was rampant and food shortages were extreme. For a while, money was almost worthless and food essentials could be purchased only with coupons issued by the authorities. Most of the population was living on a starvation diet. I was so thin that I was classified *Unterernehrt*[25] and thereby qualified for extra food coupons. It was still a meager existence for us and I was constantly hungry. I would scavenge through neighborhood garbage cans. Once, I found a dead crow and brought it home. My mother cooked it up and we ate it, pretending it was chicken and savoring every morsel. Bread was readily available, but

[25]A classification given undernourished children.

meat, butter, and sugar were scarce commodities. Once in a while, I was able to treat myself to dessert: a transparent layer of butter spread on a slice of black bread and sparsely sprinkled with sugar. The only candy that I got was a concoction we made ourselves. We would roast oats in a frying pan and let them bond with some melted sugar. These were formed into cookie-sized pieces. I chuckle now when I see people eating granola bars; they are so similar to that oatmeal candy we made. Whole milk was also a scarce commodity because the milk fat was extracted. We drank *Magermilch*, which was nothing more than skimmed milk. Again, I have to smile when I see grocery shelves loaded with such nonfat items as skimmed milk and margarine—made popular by dieters. After the war, we were on a "diet" of major proportions. Ingenious entrepreneurs came up with artificial substitutes for hard-to-get items, such as coffee, sugar, butter, etc. These were called *Ersatz* (literally, substitute).

The dreaded feeling of hunger has stayed with me through most of my life. I still have a compulsive urge to gorge myself once in a while in order to satisfy the craving for a full stomach. The feeling of a stuffed stomach is psychologically reassuring: it's a feeling that one need not worry about being hungry again. Years later, when I had children of my own, my kids often made fun of my policy that everything on our plates had to be eaten. Even worse, I would never throw partially rotten food away. I still tend to shave or cut the rotten or moldy parts off cheese, bread, fruits, etc., away and eat the rest—much to the disgust of my children. They seem to have difficulty understanding their father's eccentric attitude toward food. But then, they never experienced the nagging pain of real hunger.

Eating food found in garbage cans had unpleasant side effects. Worms were prone to invade my intestines. I was constantly on the lookout for them and would visually check my stool after every bowel movement. Sometimes, there were tiny little white worms—lots of them, which could be seen writhing around. On those occasions, I would take appropriate pills, which would kill them (in my intestines). Once, while inspecting my stool, I was shocked to see several huge worms, not unlike the common earthworm, writhing in and out of my feces. I called my mother and showed her the display. At the clinic they gave me some new pills, which I took for a while; the big worms never came back again. Later, I learned that these big worms could be fatal if not treated in time.

Another parasitic problem after the war was the epidemic of lice infestations. All kids had to have their heads shaved every so often and our clothes were powdered with DDT. Behind a framed picture in our room, my mother made an unpleasant discovery: a tight cluster of lice—many thousands of them, infesting the whole backside of the picture. We called the health authorities to have our room fumigated.

Once, while scrounging through garbage cans, I found a gold wedding ring. It was worth a fortune to me. I showed it to my mother and she insisted on posting a notice at the apartment entry describing what I had found. Sure enough, the elderly German couple living in the ground floor apartment claimed to have lost it, and my mother gave them the ring. I was not convinced that these people were the rightful owners. They were never particularly friendly with any of us refugees and they were not poor. They lived by themselves in a five-room apartment while the rest of us were crammed into similar units with one family to a room. My mother also told me that they were former Nazi members. She was particularly impressed that the man had a double-digit Nazi membership number, meaning he was one of the founders of the Nazi Party. It was obvious that they would have preferred Hitler to win the war. They never thanked me for finding the gold ring. To them, I was just another Ausländer.

There was a considerable amount of American relief effort going on. Some of it was totally hokey. Many useless "gifts" were dumped on us, such as yo-yos, crayons, plastic rulers (with measurements in inches, rather than metric), etc. Someone back in the USA must have been making good money by dumping these useless items on refugees in Europe. On the other hand, the most successful relief packages came from an organization called CARE. Their packages contained useful and sought-after products, including canned and dehydrated food. We were always amazed how efficiently packed these boxes were. Americans were ingenious when it came to packaging. These gifts were sought after and usually shared by more than one family. In this manner, I got my first taste of something called peanut butter. The paste stuck to the top of my mouth and the flavor was unlike anything I was used to. It was food for an acquired taste, I thought. Cans of spam would have qualified under the definition of Ersatz, though they were greatly appreciated, as were powdered milk, dark chocolate bars, sugar, sardines, dried fruit, soup mixes, etc. We had heard of soda drinks such as Coca-Cola and 7 Up, but these were out of our reach. Instead, we could buy little packets of a soda-like powder. When the contents were added to a glass of water, it would fizz (much like Alka-Seltzer) and we would delight in the Ersatz soda pop, especially if it was colored to make it look like fruit.

Once, my mother came home with an exotic fruit called a banana. I had heard of this delicacy and eagerly proceeded to eat it. My mother stopped me after the first bite and explained that *it had to be peeled first!*

Hungry street kids soon figured out another source of "relief:" American servicemen. Situated at one end of our neighborhood, just off Prinzregentenplatz, was the US Army headquarters where GIs got their monthly paycheck and bonus rations. Besides a carton of cigarettes, these rations included a box of American candy (chewing gum, Life Savers, chocolate bars, etc.). On these days, a throng of us boys would gather around the entry of the building. As the soldiers came out with the boxes in hand, we would surround them with outstretched hands. Beseechingly, we would say, "give." In fact, "give" was probably the first English word I ever learned. Many GIs would ignore us and walk away. However, some would take pity on us skinny waifs and toss a handful of candy our way, usually over their shoulder and without even looking at us. A free-for-all would ensue among us beggars and, if lucky, I would manage to grab one or two pieces of sweets—a Hershey's bar or a roll of Life Savers. The bigger boys would manage to grab several pieces off the street. I was small in stature but feisty. Still, I felt like a chicken at the bottom of the pecking order. Where was Guzhinas now that I needed him?

*THE BLACK MARKET*
Severe shortages of food and basic necessities begot a flourishing black market. Shady entrepreneurs came from all ethnic groups. Unscrupulous young Jews exploited their privileged position as the heirs of kin who died in Nazi gas chambers. These gangs literally got away with murder sometimes. German law enforcement was reluctant to arrest a Jew for fear of being identified with recent Nazi persecutions. This was unfortunate since the cycle of victim and victimizer was being perpetuated. High in demand were commodities such as cigarettes, ladies nylon stockings, butter, and meat. Men would often knock on our door and beg for cigarettes. Here arose an opportunity for me to make some money. People would drop their cigarette butts before climbing onto a streetcar, where smoking was not allowed. I

would go to these stations and look for discarded butts with a little tobacco left in them. After collecting a bunch, I would roll the salvaged tobacco into thin toilet paper and create new cigarettes. I had no trouble selling these items; it was a lucrative business.

Certain streets of Munich were lined with makeshift sidewalk stands, erected by people selling every imaginable thing, legal and illegal. These were the "black marketers." I would window-shop sometimes, just to see what was hot in this commodities market. Invariably, there were con artists. The most transparent gyp was the proverbial shell game. Why people enduring hard times would be attracted to such foolish gambling always baffled me (this phenomena seems to continue today with the poorest people buying most of the lotto tickets). Once, I had some time to kill before my streetcar arrived, so I decided to watch a shell-game artist do his handiwork. The tactic was obvious: the bean under one of the three shells would be shuffled around slowly enough so that a spectator would always know where the bean was located. Then, when the hapless victim was confident as to the whereabouts of the bean, he would reach for his wallet to pull out a bill to place the bet. The moment that his eyes were diverted to the contents of the wallet, the artist deftly switched the shell one more time. The bettor always lost. Sometimes, when business was slow, a gambler would appear, place bet after bet, and win. It was obvious to me that this "winner" was a partner of the shell-game artist. Once, when business became particularly slow (and there was no partner around), the artist practically begged the audience to place a bet. Failing to persuade anyone, he said, "Please, anybody, pick the shell with the bean beneath it...for free. Show me how easy it is to find the bean." Still, nobody made a move. I knew where the bean was, and after he pleaded for "anybody," I reached out and picked up the shell—exposing the bean. The enraged artist gave me a swift slap in the face and I staggered back a few feet. Thus, I learned that I was not "anybody" yet.

A grim black market appeared for illicit meat. It lasted only briefly before the police succeeded in stopping it. A gang of *Kinderfänger* (kidnappers) started abducting young children, usually on their way home from school. These hapless kids were killed and their flesh was turned into sausages to be sold on the black market as animal products. We school kids were warned not to walk alone anymore, but only in groups. Not far from my home, I witnessed the abduction of a six-year-old who was walking alone some distance in front of us. A car pulled up to the kid on the sidewalk, and two men in black leather jackets jumped out, forced the child into the car, and sped off. We called the police immediately. The abductors were familiar to me. I had seen them around and knew where they lived. I took the police to their apartment. Several of them were sitting around in their living room, still wearing the black leather jackets that must have been the uniform of the "mafia" they belonged to. I was able to identify two of the abductors. I never found out what the outcome of the investigation was. The little boy was never seen again.

*LIFE AS AN ORPHAN*

My mother suffered from a chronic kidney ailment. She had to be hospitalized and ended up staying at a sanatorium for almost two years. My father was still missing someplace in the Soviet sector. Actually, we did not know whether he was alive or dead. During this period I was given over to an orphanage run by Americans associated with the occupation. The orphans were mostly from eastern European countries and had lost their parents during the war. None was German. Technically, I was not a real orphan because my mother was still alive, but I kept that fact to myself. I'm sure I would not have been accepted as one of them if it had been known I had a living parent.

I was first sent to an orphanage that was housed in a large old building. I don't remember its name or exact location; it was someplace in the Bavarian lowlands. The building was plain looking and squarish, three or four stories in height and surrounded by farmland. My stay there was brief. I hated being "imprisoned" with lots of other unruly kids—with strict rules that were more often ignored than followed. Some of the attendants were sexually abusive. I had to get out.

One night, while everyone was asleep, I climbed out of the upper-story window and down the outside wall—to freedom. I was a good climber, even at that early age. Once on the outside, I was able to sustain myself by eating a variety of vegetables growing abundantly on the surrounding farms. Cucumbers with honey were my favorite (I found a jar of honey in a farmer's shed). Fortunately, it was summer and I could sleep out in the open. Unfortunately, the authorities soon found me wandering about. Back at the orphanage, I explained to the administrators why I did not want to return to the place where I was being abused, and they sympathized. I was allowed to transfer to another orphanage, which was housed in a convent—high in the Alps.

I was driven into the mountains in an open army jeep, which was a great thrill. The driver was an American GI and my escort was a very kind and attractive American woman (civilian). She was a wonderful companion, full of good cheer, and I wish I could have stayed with her. Instead, I was soon introduced to grim German nuns in charge of my next residency.

The old convent was beautifully located. Craggy peaks faced us on one side and the town of Mittenwald—famous for producing some of the world's best violins—could be seen far down in the deep valley. The nuns were strict but not mean. There were lots of rules, of course. The only peculiar rule at this orphanage was that we were to sleep in nightshirts and were forbidden to keep our underwear on. The nuns inspected us every evening by looking under our gowns to make sure we conformed to this rule. It was an embarrassing inspection, but we got used to it.

Most of the orphans were older than I. On weekends, these senior boys (teenagers) would rise early and hike up the peaks that punctuated our skyline. I would hear about these daring trips at breakfast the next day. I was about seven or eight years old and much too young to be invited. So I took matters into my own hands. One Sunday morning, I simply tagged along with the "climbing team," keeping behind at a safe distance but not far enough behind to lose sight of them. They hiked at a good clip and I managed to keep up. When the trail ended and they got into scrambling territory on the steep limestone peaks, I followed. I was physically fit (thanks to Fussball) and I was eager to participate in such adventures. Before long, these older boys acknowledged my dedication and enthusiasm and included me in these exhilarating climbing excursions.

I climbed to the top of my first real mountain. It was called Kampenwand. Today you can see it from the autobahn when driving south from Munich toward the town of Prien am Chiemsee. The climbing was not hard by most standards. Nevertheless, I was impressed by a brass plaque mounted on a rock face along the way that commemorated the spot where two climbers fell to their deaths roped together. I realized that we were playing an unforgiving game, but I was hooked by the thrill and beauty of climbing. If our senior orphans took a day off, I simply climbed by myself. During one such outing, I was traversing a ridge that was wooded on one side and had a vertical cliff on the other, facing Austria. A huge bird standing in front of me interrupted my progress. I did not know it at the time, but it was an *Auerhahn*—a bird of near mythical stature related to wild turkeys. For the longest time, we just stood there immobile, staring at each other—no more than twenty feet apart. For a while, I thought it big enough to carry me away and I became scared. The first to "blink" was the Auerhahn. It simply spread its wings, jumped off the precipice, and in a swooping glide disappeared over the Austrian side of the ridge. Encounters with wildlife like this are more likely to happen if you are going solo. On occasions when I could not find a companion to join me, I did not hesitate to travel or climb alone—always relishing the solitude and enjoying unexpected encounters with wild animals.

The summer at this convent was a memorable one. When school started, I was transferred again—this time to an orphanage in the town of Prien. This quaint resort is located at the northern edge of the biggest lake in Germany, called Chiemsee. Here I spent the next winter in an old converted hotel building and in total misery! I was cold most of the time and I found school boring. There was no Fussball activity. To make matters worse, I developed a bladder problem that caused me to wet my bed at night. The supervising attendants considered bedwetting a crime. As punishment, I was made to stand in the hallway displaying my urine-soaked bed sheet for all to see as they passed by on their way to breakfast. Instead of getting breakfast, I was ordered to wash my soiled linen. This humiliating punishment did not stop me from bedwetting. In fact, my condition got worse and the punishments got nastier.

There were also some good times. Americans were expert at staging entertaining events, such as dances and bingo nights. Once, I tied for first place in a bingo game and received half a box of Hershey bars, which I shared with my close friends. Outings often found us up in the mountains where some medieval castles perched, or at one of the islands on the lake (there were two).

During the winter some of us boys discovered a stash of wooden skis in the attic of our building. Departing GIs from the Tenth Mountain Division must have left them behind. The ski bindings were meant for touring rather than downhill skiing. They had leather straps in the front and spring-loaded cables for the heel. Of course, we had no ski boots. We secured our feet to the skis with strands of twine, since the bindings alone were insufficient for street shoes. There was a nice little hill nearby with an open field that we could hike up and then ski down. None of us had any skiing experience. The hill had only one defect: the bottom of the slope was closed off with a barbed-wire fence—there was absolutely no run-out! We learned the technique of stopping on a dime very quickly, usually involving head-over-heels maneuvers. As they say—no pain, no gain. It was great fun.

The town of Prien am Chiemsee is one of the most beautiful resorts in all of Germany. Mad King Ludwig built his extravagant Goldschloss (Gold Castle) on the main island. It was inspired by Louis XIV's Versailles. I made many trips to this tourist attraction, making a little money as a guide (I was about eight years old). Traditionally, the lake was popular with amateur sailors and no motorboats were permitted, that is, until the US military established a base on the south side of the lake. GIs in huge PT boats, started racing up and down the lake. During those days there was constant turbulence and sailing or swimming was no longer safe or pleasant. Eventually, boating returned to normal again when the PT boats were removed. On the southern horizon were the magnificent Bavarian Alps, where I made some of my first real climbs. Overall, my memories of the year in Prien fall more on the positive side than the negative, despite the abuse I suffered at the hands of the people running the orphanage.

After two miserable (mostly) years of life in orphanages, I was finally reunited with my mother when she was discharged from the sanitarium. I was overjoyed to be home again. My mother was the one anchor in my life—the one person that was always there for me, no matter what. Despite her resorting to corporal punishment when disciplining me, I loved her beyond all imagination. I knew without a doubt that she would sacrifice her life for me, if necessary. This time, I was eager to go back to Gebeleschule, where I was in the company of old friends and captained the soccer team.

*BACK IN MUNICH*

A new teacher awaited me in Munich. His name was Herr Pichelmann. He was a veteran of the war, an aging bachelor who lived austerely—like a monk. He was proficient in every academic subject, including math, grammar, history, music, art, and more. He was a no-nonsense disciplinarian. He was also the most influential teacher I ever had in my life. Without a doubt, we were a group of unruly schoolboys; girls were segregated in other classrooms. Most of us were more interested in perpetrating pranks in class and playing soccer after school than enduring math drills or grammar lessons. Herr Pichelmann was serious about teaching and he did it well. He tolerated no foolery in his class and enforced good behavior with corporal punishment. Students who transgressed would be called to the front of the class and required to extend their hands in front of them. Invariably, the hapless fellows would hold out their hands with the palms facing up. Without saying a word, Herr Pichelmann would make a motion with the ruler in his hand, and the boys understood that they had to turn their hands over—exposing tender fingernails. Muted giggles would emanate from the class at those moments. Our teacher would take his wooden ruler and give the fingertips a swift whack. It was not uncommon for some of the fingernails to turn black the next day. This punishment was effective and the class respected their teacher highly, because he was good. I was an occasional recipient of strikes with his ruler, at first. I learned quickly and soon became one of his more obedient students.

As it turned out, my old friend Fritz and I had the best voices in class. The two of us were often picked to sing in duets, with the rest of the class backing us up in chorus. Half your grade in music depended on singing in tune. Each boy would take his turn reciting the different do-re-mis while Herr Pichelmann keyed the piano. When it was my turn, I strode up to the piano confidently as others in the class looked on in envy. Herr Pichelmann played the keys and I intoned the proper scale, or so I thought. I fully expected to get an A. When the grades were read, I was stunned to hear that I merited only a C. As it turned out, I was practically tone-deaf and could not carry a tune, especially when singing alone. Singing alongside Fritz allowed me to stay within range (more or less). My hopes for a singing career were dashed.

At the beginning of one school year, we were asked to identify our religion so that we could attend the appropriate religion class. Out of over sixty kids, only two did not know what religion their family practiced. I was one of them. The two of us were sent to the principal's office, where our records were checked. I turned out to be a Catholic; my companion was a Lutheran (Bavarians are predominantly Catholic). An outside instructor, usually a priest, would teach religion class once a week. Here I learned that just about anything that is fun in life is bound to be a sin. Even thinking about a transgression was a sin. Some sins were so bad that they were considered *Totessinnen* (deadly sins). I concluded that I was destined for hell; the best I could hope for was purgatory. I started going to church twice a week and confession each week. Eventually, I realized that such zealous adherence to this religion was not in my nature. I remained a Catholic, albeit a moderate one.

When summer came again, my mother sent me off to live on a Bavarian farm. In part, it was a tactic to keep me out of trouble during idle times in the big city. Poor city kids become ingenious when they have nothing to do but invent mischief. In part, it was also a way to provide me with a healthy environment while people in the city were still living on marginal food rations. These farmers were hard-working people. To earn my room and board, I had to work hard as well. This entailed doing all kinds of chores and running errands. The one job that I dreaded most was the task of taking the lunch package out to the men working in the field. The wheat had been recently reaped and the ground was left covered with sharp stubble, about an inch high. I had no shoes, and walking across these fields of stubble caused painful cuts to my bare feet. Despite having very tough, calloused soles, my feet became a bloody mess.

The farmers were jovial types and they loved to tease me. I had only one pair of pants, which I would wear to church on Sundays. The rest of the time I wore a homemade pair of shorts that fit poorly around my waist. The men would get a big kick out of sneaking up behind me and jerking my shorts down to my knees (I had no underwear). I did not share their mean sense of humor. The teenage daughter liked me a lot and would come to my rescue, which I greatly appreciated. The matronly farmer's wife worked all day in the kitchen. Her cooking was excellent and she enjoyed watching me gorge myself with the ample food that was placed on the table. For the first time since leaving Lithuania, I was able to eat until I could eat no more.

## REUNITED

For a long time, we had no clue whether my father was dead or alive. As the years passed, the hope of seeing him again diminished. When I was much older, I learned the hell my father endured during the final months of the war and the years following.

When the Russian army had advanced against the Germans, my father was in hiding. He had assumed a new identity and was trying hard to stay out of Russian-controlled areas. During the final stages of the war, the German army became desperate for manpower. Every able-bodied man was recruited to help defend the front lines. If you were German, you were given a rifle and told to shoot Russians. If you were Polish, Lithuanian, Latvian, or any other ethnic minority, you were given a shovel and told to dig trenches for the German soldiers on the front lines. My father was given a shovel. He was digging trenches when the Russian soldiers overran German positions. Most of these defenseless trench diggers became nothing more than cannon fodder and died in the onslaught. My father was one of the few that managed to survive. However, he was now trapped in Russian-held territory.

The NKVD found out that he was alive and began searching for him, but he managed to elude them. Lithuanian friends, relatives, and farmers who sheltered him one night at a time were able to warn him when NKVD agents were hot on his trail. Sometimes, he was only hours ahead of his pursuers. His only hope for survival was to escape to the West. He was fluent in Russian. With the help of the Lithuanian underground, he was able to procure false documents that identified him as a Soviet government official. In East Germany, he purchased passage on a train going to West Berlin. This was a risky venture, since the border police were on constant lookout for anyone trying to escape to the West. As luck would have it, my father got a seat on the train opposite a Russian army officer. He was a friendly guy and engaged my father in conversation. The Russian enjoyed the game of chess. When he learned that my father could play the game, he produced a portable chess set and a game got underway. The communist border police came by to inspect passengers' documents during the heat of the game. My father was sweating hard as the official asked him for his documents, but he pretended to be engrossed in his next move—his opponent had his king in a difficult spot. The Russian major indignantly waved the policeman off. "Don't bother us now," he said, "this game is important." Thus, my father avoided having to produce his fake documents, which may or may not have passed the test. He made it into West Berlin safely, and with the help of the International Red Cross, eventually found his family in Munich.

We were overjoyed to have Papa back, alive and well. Musicians were not in big demand during these depression years, so he managed to get an administrative job with the United Nations Relief and Rehabilitation Administration (UNRRA). He still earned money on the side by giving private music lessons (piano, violin, voice, etc.) and playing the organ at various churches and cathedrals. I would sometimes accompany my father on these trips. I really enjoyed sitting next to him in the organ loft while he played at the keyboard—all the while pumping hard on the big pedals with his feet in order to keep the pipes going. You had to be physically fit to play the organ successfully, I observed. It was cold in the unheated stone churches, and he would rub his big hands together frequently to keep the blood circulating and his fingers nimble. He was a master organist.

The experience of hearing him play the organ was unforgettable.

In one baroque church, the sculpted saints and cherubs seemed to come alive while the powerful sounds of the organ resonated from the ornately decorated walls. I felt the spirituality of music and architecture fuse in perfect harmony. I always thought of organ music as a little austere. Yet, when heard in the spiritual environment of a baroque church or medieval cathedral, the medium reached another dimension.

After such performances, my father would relax in a nearby *Biergarten* and absorb some of that great Bavarian brew. He would allow me to sip the foam off the top of the stein. We both enjoyed going to movies. I'll never forget seeing *The Treasure of the Sierra Madre*, starring Humphrey Bogart and dubbed in German, with him. I admired my father and I loved the idea of becoming a musician, but I could not follow in his footsteps since I was tone-deaf. Besides, I was more interested in sports and worldly adventures. My father could not relate to my preferred interests. Thus, while growing up, I remained closer to my mother, with whom I had more similar interests.

*REVITALIZING ACTIVITIES*

Aside from an occasional movie, we could not afford to spend money on entertainment. Nevertheless, there were times when we did more. The Prinzregenten Theater was not far from our house and I remember seeing some plays there. Cultural events were usually subsidized by the German government and tickets were cheap. Every year, the big circus would come into town with high-wire acts, acrobats, animals, and clowns. I nearly died laughing when a very dumb clown cavorted around while trying to get rid of a roll of flypaper. It kept sticking to his hands, feet, face, and every other part of his body. Comedy was the best medicine for us entertainment-starved kids. During Christmas, many churches and cathedrals gave musical performances commemorating the holy night. Programs were handed out just like at a concert hall. German and Austrian Christmas music is of the highest art form, I always thought. Nonbelievers as well as believers would pack churches for these concerts. And they were free.

Family outings were rare. One night I got practically no sleep because I was so excited about a forthcoming trip into the countryside. Early Sunday morning, we took the train to Berchtesgaden, a beautiful resort area tucked away in the Alps near the Austrian border. We hiked up to Hitler's infamous Eagle's Nest. It appeared to have been recently ransacked. Actually, the Allies had not yet managed to clean up the mess left by withdrawing German forces. I saw many files and Nazi artifacts strewn about in the open. I was particularly impressed by reams of 35 mm film lying around and wondered what they contained. The salt caves were nearby and we visited them as well. The caves were intriguing, but they did not impress me as much as the Eagle's Nest.

I did develop a productive hobby around this time, stamp collecting. I was a good negotiator and shrewd trader. Within a few years, I amassed an extensive collection. My Third Reich–era assembly was nearly complete. Unfortunately, this collection was "borrowed" by a close family friend after I arrived in America and I never saw it again.

Food was scarce and vegetables were expensive. Many residents of our community claimed small plots of ground in the field behind our building and started planting vegetable gardens. Flocks of sheep would pass through this field and I would collect bucketfuls of sheep manure; it made excellent fertilizer. I also started catching and collecting lizards, which I would keep as pets in cages in our "P-patch-like garden". My partner in this endeavor was a neighbor girl named Helga. She was a tomboy and we got along very well. This was when I was about nine years old and she was ten. One thing led to another, as they say, and we had our first kiss. I heard adults did it, so I was willing to try it. I must say, I did not feel the earth move beneath my feet. In fact, I felt nothing. Word of our little secret got out, and our "romance" was the talk of the apartment building for a while.


*THE EXODUS*
In the spring of 1950, Germany was still struggling with a post-war depression. The economic turnaround (*Wirtschaftswunder*) was just around the corner, but nobody foresaw it. My parents, especially my father, always held out the hope of returning to our homeland once the Russians were forced to abandon their illegal occupation. This was not going to happen in his lifetime, my parents concluded, if ever. My parents decided to immigrate to the New World. The countries that opened their doors to refugees displaced by WWII included Canada, USA, Australia, Venezuela, Colombia, Uruguay, Paraguay, and Argentina. The USA was the most desirable destination, but also the most restrictive. Besides having to satisfy all kinds of legal and political requirements, refugees were required to have an American "sponsor" who was financially solvent and willing to support the family, if needed.

We applied to go to Argentina. I took Spanish lessons in my fifth year at Gebeleschule. We tried to prepare ourselves for a new life in an unfamiliar country, but it was hard to plan for the unknown. My father was now fifty-eight years old (officially[26])

---

[26]Once again, my father shifted the year of his birth—this time, to appear younger. There were upper age limits for immigration.

and hardly at an age suited to start a new profession. Nonetheless, he took what little money we had and bought a complete set of carpentry tools. If he could not find work as a musician, he reasoned, he could always find work as a carpenter. My father was good with his hands. My mother took classes that would qualify her to work as cosmetician in the New World. For better or worse, neither occupation ever availed itself.

I had about DM 50 ($12.50) saved up from all my "business ventures," and my mother encouraged me to invest the money in a piece of artwork. Her favorite local artist was a university student by the name of Kurt Moser. She loved his oils and was convinced he would have a great future. I bought one of his big oil paintings to take with us. About thirty years later, Kurt Moser's work became internationally known. His reproductions were displayed at a Sears & Roebuck department store—alongside copies of Monets, van Goghs, Rembrandts, and the works of other famous artists. His originals were displayed in prestigious art galleries in Munich and priced accordingly.

Finally, we packed all we owned and took the train to the port city of Bremerhafen, located on the North Sea. Here we joined thousands of other émigrés waiting to board the ship to Argentina. For two weeks we endured much red tape, medical checkups, and a battery of inoculations. One particular series of shots involved injections with long needles into the upper arm. It was no fun getting poked by these instruments and kids would cry desperately. To demonstrate how tough I was, I would look directly at the injection and refuse to cry. Once, the nurse misdirected the long needle and I could feel it scraping my bone. I began to faint, but I did not cry!

The day before our ship was to depart for Argentina, President Juan Perón decided that he was terminating all further immigration to his country. Apparently, he was concerned that too many left-leaning refugees were infiltrating Argentina and destabilizing the conservative dictatorship. A shipload of Displaced Persons had become stranded. It was a disaster!

My father, having worked with UNRRA, had made some good connections that came in handy now. A ship about to depart for America had an unexpected opening, and we were allowed to fill it. A miracle, it seemed. The sponsor requirement was quickly satisfied from a list of American families kept on file. Later, we learned that it was a farming family named Carter living in Gaston, Indiana. Wow! That was out West, I imagined, as visions of old-fashioned cowboys and Indians danced in my head.[27]

We boarded a decommissioned troop transport named SS *General Greely*. The accommodations were designed for soldiers and were extremely cramped. We slept in bunks at various levels of the ship. For the first time, we were treated to American meals. Once, I saw crew members toss boxes of oranges and grapefruit overboard because they had become somewhat moldy. Many of us were amazed! Any of the refugees on board would have been happy to have that fruit, cut away the rotten part, and eat the rest. It was my first exposure to the casual attitude Americans have toward the overabundance of food available to them. Entertainment was provided in the form of movies, mostly old westerns. The crew even organized an impromptu boxing tournament for the boys on board. I entered in the super flyweight division. I survived a few rounds of punches with ineptness equal to my opponents'.

---

[27]My fantasies of cowboys and Indians were enhanced by Karl May (1842–1912) novels. He was a prolific German author and popular among European kids. He wrote over sixty novels about the American Wild West, yet he never traveled to North America.

The weather was calm and the Atlantic Ocean was as smooth as glass, for a while. Everyone was happy and full of optimism. Then a storm hit. The ship started rolling and pitching. The waves were huge. If on deck, you would see a wall of water in front of the bow and only dark clouds behind the stern. As the ship rode up the wave, the bow was silhouetted against the sky while the stern was in a watery trough. Our little ship behaved like a cork in a turbulent bathtub. People got seasick by the hundreds. The infirmary was packed. One woman became so desperately ill that she staggered to the rail of the upper deck and tried to jump overboard. She was restrained in time. My mother and I seemed to be immune from this affliction and continued to enjoy the voyage without any ill effects. The storm lasted several days.

The ship's first destination was New Orleans. During the night, we passed through the strait between Florida and Cuba. I saw lights on the horizon—we were approaching America. What a thrill!

We docked in New Orleans and remained on board while more than half the passengers disembarked—on the way to their final destinations. The next day, our ship departed for the East Coast. We arrived in the great harbor of New York City a few days later. Lady Liberty seemed to be welcoming us in front of the biggest concentration of tall buildings in the world. Our transatlantic voyage had taken thirty days. We proceeded through immigration control without any problems. In customs, luggage was inspected randomly. Everything we brought with us passed through. While waiting, I observed a wooden crate being opened while its owner, an immigrant in his thirties, stood by—perspiring nervously. Inside the crate, the inspectors found a stash of brand-new Leica cameras, neatly stacked to the brim. There must have been fifty or so. The poor fellow who owned this contraband turned pale and started shaking his head pathetically. This must have been his ticket to a new start in America. The importation of cameras for resale was illegal, and they were confiscated. The man lost a small fortune!

At last, we set foot on American soil—counting our blessings and looking forward to a new life in the land of opportunity. This sentiment was short-lived. For some reason, we were asked to sit in a waiting area. Finally, after the SS *General Greely* had departed, a polite female government official came to speak with us. She had some bad news: the Carter family in Indiana had rescinded their sponsorship.[28] No reason was given. Fortunately, the official waited until our ship had departed for Germany before making it known that we were stranded. This was most considerate of her; otherwise, we may have been ordered to return to Germany on the ship that brought us here. This was a disaster and the lady was truly sympathetic with our plight.

She asked us if we had any relatives in America that could possibly sponsor us. My mother said that she had a distant cousin living in Los Angeles. His name was Nikodemas Jasinevicius.[29] He was contacted and the situation was explained to him. He agreed to sponsor us. The official gave us train tickets to Los Angeles and ten dollars for expenses.

---

[28]My mother did not hold a grudge against the Carter family for declining to sponsor us. On the contrary, she kept up an amicable correspondence with them. In the summer of 1955, when I was sixteen, I was invited to work for Carter Farms in exchange for room and board. See "America's Heartland" in Chapter VI: High School Years.

[29]Nikodemas Jasinevicius had been a port official in Memel. Now, he was employed as a janitor in a Los Angeles factory. I will always remember him as an elegant gentleman, smoking a cigarette held in an ivory holder, like some movie mogul.

The train ride was another adventure for me. We stopped in Chicago for a few hours and I had the opportunity to buy my first hotdog. One stop allowed us to view traditional adobe architecture that was indicative of the true West. I kept my eyes peeled for cowboys, Indians, and buffalo, to no avail. All along this cross-country trip, we saw large billboards advertising all kinds of commercial products and activities. I was fascinated with these expressions of American enterprise and read every one of them as the train passed by.

City kids in post-war Germany. Note that very few children are wearing shoes or sandals. (Photo: Tony Vacero)

Right: Alex after arriving in Munich (1945).

Father and son reunited again (1947), thanks to
UNRRA and the International Red Cross.

# A PATRIOT IN EXILE

At the end of WWII the Soviet army was fully entrenched in the Baltic States (Lithuania, Latvia & Estonia) with clear intentions of remaining there. President Roosevelt and Churchill, at their meeting with Stalin in Yalta, looked the other way. It was a huge betrayal of the three countries that were officially neutral during the war. The Russians wasted no time killing thousands of leading citizens and sending millions more to slave labor camps in Siberia. My parents and I were among the fortunate ones who managed to escape to the West.

However, since the United States did not recognize the Soviet Union's occupation of the Baltic States, the people remaining in those countries, as well as the people that were now in exile, held on to a hope that one day they would be able to return to their country of birth — after the occupation had ended. It took half a century for the occupation to end. Political pressure from within and from abroad contributed to the disintegration of the Soviet empire and freedom for the Baltic States. My activities in exile contributed to that pressure, albeit in modest ways.

During the summer of 1950 my family settled into a new life when we arrived in Los Angeles. All we possessed was what we could carry and $10 in cash. My parents took on menial jobs in order to support the family and to take advantage of "the land of opportunity." We were not alone. By now, thousands of Lithuanian refugees had settled in various parts of the USA—a few hundred of them in the Los Angeles area. The Lithuanian community was tight, for several reasons. First, very few of us spoke any English. Second, we were steeped in Lithuanian culture and traditions; American ways were still foreign to us. Thirdly, we still held out hope that someday we would be repatriated to Lithuania. Hence, most parents tried hard to ensure that the younger generation would grow up speaking Lithuanian and upholding our traditions.

Ironically, many of these traditions were being suppressed in Soviet occupied Lithuania. When freedom finally arrived (1990), I was told by some people in Lithuania that it was we exiles who were primarily responsible for the preservation of many customs and traditions that Lithuanians cherished. They were grateful.

While living in America, I attended American schools and made many American friends. However, Lithuanian culture dominated home life. I spoke Lithuanian with my parents, and when it was my turn to raise children of my own, I spoke Lithuanian to them. Though, by now the prospect of repatriating to Lithuania became less and less realistic — many of the older generation were dying out and most of the new generation was becoming Americanized. None-the-less, Lithuanians in the old country needed support in overthrowing the yoke of Soviet oppressors. To this end many of us never stopped working in every way possible to help our Lithuanian brethren.

Because I had developed some good political connections, I communicated on the subject of Lithuania's freedom with such people as Edgar Eisenhower (the president's bother) — who was a lawyer in Tacoma, with Senator Henry Jackson - who was a stout anti communist, and with Dr. Henry Kissinger - who was dating a friend of mine for a while (Ruta Lee). Through these political contacts I was sometimes able to help Lithuanians who were exiled in Siberia. I agreed to do so on condition that my actions would not get into newspapers. I was not always successful in keeping my efforts out of the press (mainly Lithuanian news reports in the USA).

I always wanted to help Lithuanian alpinists in their endeavor to climb the mountains of the world and in so doing, climb with them as well. There is no lack of challenging mountains to climb in the USSR. However, for financial and political reasons, climbing abroad was not possible for Soviet climbers. As a director of the American Alpine Club I was able to make "official" contact with counterparts of the Soviet Mountaineering Federation. The year was 1973. Thus, we were able to establish a "cultural exchange" with the USSR that allowed Soviet alpinists to climb in the USA and American mountaineers to climb in the Soviet Union. Both countries possess magnificent mountains. The key feature of these exchanges was that we Americans would pay all the expenses for Soviet climbers while in the USA and the Soviet Alpine Federation would pay all the expenses of American climbers while in the USSR. It was a win — win proposition.

My Soviet counterparts knew I was a Lithuanian ex-patriot (I told them so right at the start). They knew that the Kremlin did not look favorably upon any contacts between Soviet Lithuanians and American Lithuanians. Nevertheless, Dainius Mokauskas was secretly included in our climbing exchange when we arrived at base camp in the Pamir Mountains during the summer of 1976. Soviet alpinists were mostly apolitical and willing to help Lithuanians meet whenever they could.

During these years (1957 – 1998) I often came under unfair criticism by fellow Lithuanians (in America) for fraternizing with our "enemy," the Russians. I always felt that the chances of Lithuania regaining her freedom would be better served through friendly relations with Russians rather than through hostility. In the end I was right, I think.

During the Soviet era, I was able to help Lithuanians in many ways. Whenever some of them would visit Seattle, I would help them financially or purchase gifts that they could not obtain at home. Some of these people included two famous basketball players (Modestas Paulauskas and Sarunas Marciulonis), the rector of the University of Vilnius, and various musicians and politicians. In 1988 I initiated the invitation of the Lithuanian rowing team to compete at a regatta in Seattle.

During one of my trips to Vilnius (1988) I had the pleasure of meeting with the Minister of Energy (Dr. L. Ashmantas). I was impressed with his friendly demeanor and willingness to help Lithuania through his contacts in Moscow (where he was educated). His ministry was new and its experience outside of the Soviet sphere was limited. I had contacts with Saudi ministries as well as with World Bank officials. I later learned that Dr. Ashmantas was successful in following up with the contacts I provided him.

Through my friendship with Dainius Makauskas I was connected to the rest of the Lithuanian climbing community. Soon plans were set into motion to climb the highest mountain in the world. But first, I invited a team of six Lithuanians to climb some mountains in the USA (1989). Next, Lithuanians organized an expedition to the Tien Shan Mountains in the USSR (1990). We climbed Kahn Tengri – a challenging 7000 meter peak. Makauskas and I embarked on fundraising efforts in Europe and the USA in order to finance the upcoming Mt. Everest trip. But, our luck ran out: Makauskas died while climbing Daulaghiri (sixth highest mountain in the world). It was a tragic loss for his family, for Lithuania and for our plans to climb Mt. Everest. Now, the burden of raising funds fell on my shoulders alone. I did not feel that I was up to the task and was ready to cancel all plans. Lithuania's postal service jumped the gun and issued a series of postage stamps in honor of our Mt. Everest climb (unbeknown to me). President Vytautas Landsbergis invited me to his office and encouraged me not to abandon plans to climb Mt. Everest. During the fall of 1991 a small group of us made a reconnaissance of the mountain from Tibet. The following year we launched a full-scale expedition. After more than two months on the mountain we were turned back not far from the summit by extremely high winds (the jet-stream).

In the spring of 1993 one of our team members, Vladas Vitkauskas, succeeded in reaching the summit of Mt. Everest and raised the Lithuanian flag at the highest point on earth — for the first time. Upon his return to Lithuania he wrote (in Lithuanian):

*"I am very grateful to you, Alex, that you organized the Lithuanian Expedition to the Himalayas in 1992. Without that expedition my subsequent ascent (of Everest) would not have happened."*

In the spring of 1990, Lithuania was the first of the 15 Soviet Republics to declare its independence from the Soviet Union.

# Chapter IV: ADJUSTING TO LIFE IN AMERICA

*WELCOME TO LA*

We arrived in the city of Los Angeles in July of 1950. The streets appeared to run in endless grids. No other city in the world covered more space, my mother told me. The broad boulevards were lined with tall palm trees. The sun shone all the time, it seemed. We were overwhelmed with the sights of this new paradise. With the help of my uncle Nikodemas, we found temporary lodging in a small rooming house near Sunset Boulevard. It was built in the Spanish style prevalent in Southern California. There was a busy intersection nearby, and the car traffic was controlled by a signal with alternating stop and go flags. These (now-outmoded) devices were noisy when alternating and kept me awake at night.

For the first time since the war, I heard the wailing of sirens again. These sounds would distress me. If asleep, I would wake up in a cold sweat. But they were only ambulances, police cars, or fire trucks. It took years for me to get accustomed to the sound that once signalled incoming allied bombers. The searchlights that lit up the skies above Hollywood during a movie premiere did not bother me—they were silent. However, they continued to remind me of those nighttime air raids. When I hear the drone of a four-engine propeller plane approaching, that old sense of dread still stirs in me (sixty-five years later). Even today, I try to avoid war movies and I'll walk out of a film with gratuitous violence. I still suffer from occasional "persecution dreams," as well as dreams involving aerial invasions—earthly and alien, though they occur less frequently with the passing of time.

My uncle and his wife Helena had arrived in LA a couple of years earlier and had already managed to make a down payment on two small houses in southwest LA (on 106th Street near Normandie Avenue). We soon moved into a bungalow not far away (on 88th Street and Budlong Avenue). It was a working-class neighborhood and the rents were cheap. This part of town was on the edge of an area called Watts. The house had no refrigerator; instead, it had a built-in icebox. Every few days, the iceman would come in his truck and deliver a huge block of ice slung over his back on a leather pad. He was the last of an era.

During the first summer in our host country, most of our contacts were with fellow Lithuanians. There was a small but growing colony of immigrants, and we stuck together socially. The main gathering place was at our church, St. Casimir, the patron saint of Lithuania, located near Griffith Park. Here we would meet for bazaars and other festivities. On Saturday mornings, young children could attend Lithuanian language classes.

In 1951, our community succeeded in establishing a weekly radio program that would broadcast Lithuanian current events, various announcements, music, and poetry. As usual in such situations, there were too many critics and not enough donors to support this community venture. In defense of the program, my mother wrote a public letter[30] that was read on one of the radio broadcasts:

> *...I remember the first radio broadcast in the Lithuanian language: we all gathered around the radio and listened anxiously. Afterward, my son, then a lad of just twelve years, proudly announced: 'Mama, now I'll be able to tell everyone in school that I am a Lithuanian.' Seeing his sparkling eyes, I understood there was a secret yearning for a national identity that seemed to be fading. He now found his rightful place among other nationals...*

My mother was a magnet for numerous other families who decided to move to Los Angeles and be near her. Mrs. Elena Zilinskas was one of these. She was a talented singer, bright, and beautiful.[31] Like most divas, she was temperamentally volatile. She divorced her husband and moved to Los Angeles with her three young sons. They were all close in age and I became good friends with them. Their mother raised them without a man's help; she worked as a laboratory assistant. All the sons finished college. Raymond got a PhD in biochemistry. Gene got his PhD in physics at the age of twenty-two. Viktor became a successful lawyer. Mrs. Zilinskas passed away in her nineties—the last of a

---

[30]Translated from Lithuanian.

[31]While living in exile in Sweden, she was approached by the KGB to spy for the Soviet government. When she refused, threats against her and her boys were made. The US government granted her political asylum and she arrived in America aboard the HMS *Queen Elizabeth*.

unique group of strong and independent women. You might say they were feminists ahead of their time. Since the post-WWII wave of immigrants were mostly political refugees and well educated, their offspring were mostly high achievers and (usually) professionally successful.

Mrs. Zilinskas's brother-in-law, Mikolas Gureckas, was one of my mother's good friends from the early days in Lithuania and was named my godfather. He had two sons, Gintaras and Indris. The latter was technologically savvy and became part of a successful start-up company. When they sold the business, he received just enough money to retire for life. Unfortunately, he became a recluse and spent most of his time reading novels and pulp fiction. His brother became a fighter pilot during the Vietnam War. While on a flight exercise, something went wrong and he crash-landed his plane. His copilot walked away. Gintaras suffered a broken spine. He is now a paraplegic and gets around in a wheelchair. This accident was a hard blow for family and friends. Yet, this handicap has not slowed Gintaras down. He became vice president of the Paralyzed Veterans of America for a while. For many years, he was on the staff of California Congressman Dana Rohrabacher. He's a gourmet cook and a bon vivant. With his positive outlook and cheerful disposition, it is difficult to notice that he is handicapped. The only thing missing in his life, he once told me, is a wife he could share his love of life with.

Older people such as my father had trouble learning English (a baffling tongue for those used to more phonetic languages). Younger adults such as my mother were able to learn English properly and were more prone to make friends among Americans. Kids my age picked up English quickly, and our friends were primarily Americans. However, sometimes such friendships were made the hard way. Fresh off the boat (literally speaking), I met a neighborhood kid my age. I wanted to make friends, but I could hardly speak English. He responded to my overtures by physically accosting me. Little did he know that despite my small stature, I was a survivor of skirmishes at Gebeleschule. I subdued the fellow by wrestling him down with an arm lock around his neck. Then I invoked my favorite English word: "Give?" He understood what I meant and I released him. After that, we played friendlier games together.

## THE FLIGHT KITCHEN

Within days of our arrival in Los Angeles, my mother got a job as a chambermaid at a one-star hotel in Hollywood.[32] For desperate immigrants like my parents, no job was too menial. The other chambermaid at this hotel was a black lady of about the same age. My mother became friends with her and, for the first time, got a glimpse into the mindset of African-Americans. My mother found her to be an appealing woman but could not understand her bitterness at being destined to remain a chambermaid for the rest of her life. She blamed her plight solely on the color of her skin. My mother tried to persuade her to aspire to better jobs by acquiring higher skills. With my mother's encouragement and help, this woman enrolled in a night-school program and eventually earned her high school diploma, thus providing her better work opportunities.

My father got a job as a dishwasher at the United Airlines flight kitchen, located at the airport. If I recall correctly, he was paid sixty-seven cents an hour—the minimum wage. My parents worked hard and saved every penny. Soon we owned our first car, a black 1936 Plymouth Coupe (with a rumble seat!). This convenience allowed my father to drive to work and go on er-

---

[32]It was the old Mission Hotel and no longer exists.

rands around town. I was not used to riding in a car and frequently succumbed to motion sickness. Eventually, I got over this plague.

When I visited my father at the flight kitchen, I was shocked to see how hard the work was. During those days, airline passengers were served meals with real dishes and metal silverware. These were washed in an open dishwashing machine. The dishes would arrive dirty with leftover food. My father would scrape the food from each dish into a garbage can and rinse the dish before placing it on a rack attached to a conveyer belt to be washed. The hot steam emanating from the big machine was stifling. Joe (the name my father chose to go by) had to work fast to keep up with the incoming loads. It was tedious work and tantamount to hard labor in prison, I thought. He stayed at this task for the next eight years until he retired at sixty-five (in reality, he was probably several years older). Since we were still heavily in debt at the time, he took a job as a janitor in an electronics warehouse for three more years.

In addition to his "day job," he taught music students, giving private piano lessons at our house. When he was not giving lessons, he would sit at the piano for hours on end, mainly on weekends, and compose music. These compositions included ballets, operas, symphonies, and anything else that inspired him. I loved the sound of music in our house. I was impressed with his mastery of the piano. My father never offered to teach me to play this instrument, so I talked him into giving me lessons. I did OK when it came to doing practice pieces I could memorize. Learning to read music took effort, but I managed. When it came to my performing more complex pieces, my father realized that I could not play by ear; I could only play mechanically—by reading the score. After more than a year of lessons, my father informed me, "there is no hope for you, my son; you'll never become a good musician." I turned to other endeavors, like drawing and painting.

The crosstown commute to Hollywood by bus became a hardship for my mother. She managed to get hired by the UAL flight kitchen as a salad maker. My father was old and the company was not inclined to train him for a more attractive job than the one he had. Because of my mother's relative youth (forty-one), she was sent to management school and promoted to kitchen steward. This relieved her of menial work but added stressful responsibilities such as keeping the production of meals on time for flights. She also did much of the hiring and firing. Her immediate boss was the kitchen supervisor. This was usually a young college graduate with a degree in business administration. Sometimes, these young men were imbued with too much self-importance and made poor operational decisions. My mother often disagreed with these supervisors over issues of fairness and efficiency in regard to employees and operation methods. At times she would come home and burst into tears. I think it was these battles and the general stress of the job that contributed to her heart problem. Yet she never quit this job because the people who worked under her loved her. She felt needed and that was spiritually uplifting. Over the years, she received many citations and commendations from the president of United Airlines.

For a time, she was also the union representative for the kitchen employees. I remember that on one occasion she opposed voting to strike against the company. The union leaders not only put pressure on her to abide by their dicta but also threatened her physically if she refused to vote their way. She was determined to hold her ground and went to the meeting to vote her conscience. Because union thugs made threats, she asked me to accompany her. I came prepared with my .22caliber target pistol under my jacket. Fortunately, nothing happened.

There were some real benefits associated with working at the airline. All members of the family were allowed to fly for free (standby, of course) to any destination in the USA. We took ample advantage of such opportunities. I remember my first flight in an airplane was to Washington, DC, with my father. When I boarded the plane, I inquired about the location of parachutes. The stewardess laughed and assured me that no such devices were necessary. While in Washington, my father and I spent several days visiting the great institutions, monuments, and museums of that historic city.

Another benefit of working in the flight kitchen was somewhat controversial. The airline served breakfast rolls and other pastries to their passengers. These delicacies were often returned untouched. For a while, it was permissible for employees to take this perfectly good food home. Later, the union decreed that this policy deprived bakers of work, and a rule was adopted that all food returning from planes had to be incinerated. For us immigrants, who had once faced starvation, this was an outrage. Many continued to smuggle such food out of the kitchen. Getting caught meant automatic severance. My parents often brought these pastries home and were never caught. It supplemented our food supply at home and saved us a considerable amount of money over the years.

From the time my mother took over the responsibility of hiring kitchen personnel, the labor force fell into three main ethnic categories: African-Americans, Latin Americans, and Lithuanian refugees. Many of the latter were old friends and acquaintances of my parents. All were well educated, but their former professions were not adaptable to their new country. There were lawyers, teachers, politicians, and one former ambassador (to Switzerland). It was a happy group with a good sense of humor.

Rather than wallow in remorse, these intellectuals were quick to joke about their new professions and daily chores. All were grateful to be alive and thankful to my mother for their employment.

It is an interesting psychological phenomenon that people who have lost everything but the shirt on their back can start a new life, go to work as a janitor, and remain happy—*if they are not alone in their ruin.* I have known gamblers and developers (gamblers, really) who have lost a big portion of their wealth, though not all, and then committed suicide in despair. *They were alone in their bad luck!*

My parents continued their tradition of hosting dinner parties. Christmas Eve celebrations were limited to family and close friends. An assortment of traditional food was served—lots of veggies and fish, but no meat. However, New Year's Eve celebrations involved lots of friends and old-fashioned gaiety. When midnight came, bottles of sparkling wine would pop open and the revelers would burst into song. Not just any song, but the famous "drinking song" from the first act of *La Traviata* (Verdi's classic opera). This aria (for tenor, soprano, and chorus) is an uplifting melody with lyrics of carefree optimism. The following excerpt[33] captures this sentiment:

> *So come, enjoy your happiness*
> *In breathless crowded hours,*
> *For love, like tender flowers,*
> *Is swiftly dead and gone.*
> *My friends, embrace this alluring occasion,*
> *Let's revel and laugh until dawn.*

---

[33] Translated from Italian

I watched and listened in awe, wondering what unquenchable spirit allowed these survivors of a horrible past to be so happy again. *America is great*, I thought.


*SETTLING IN*

During the first year in LA, we could not yet afford to buy an automobile. We commuted mostly by public transportation. The major arterial into downtown was Vermont Avenue. It had a streetcar route and the fare was cheap. My mother and I would take shopping excursions to the farmers' market downtown. There was an amazing array of fruits and vegetables available that we could only dream about in Germany. The prices were remarkably cheap: I remember oranges selling for a penny each.

I was impressed with the big buildings downtown, though they did not compare with those of New York or Chicago. The tallest building was the white-marbled city hall (thirty stories). I was told that zoning codes did not permit any taller buildings. Obviously, this has changed. There was a tram going up Bunker Hill directly from one side of the market, called Angel's Flight. The Hollywood Freeway was under construction. At Pershing Square, men with strange ideas were orating from atop soapboxes. During one of these excursions downtown, I wore my lederhosen that we brought along from Germany. I got teased badly by numerous pedestrians while wearing such a strange outfit. I never wore them again. However, it has to be said, lederhosen must be one of the most practical pieces of clothing ever invented, for you never have to wash them or iron them. The leather gets shiny with age and never wears out; you just outgrow them. I got used to wearing blue jeans.

One day I found an old and inoperable bicycle lying in an empty lot. It was abandoned, like the one that I had found in Ismaning a few years earlier. But this one was a wreck. I brought it home and fixed it to perfect working condition. Then I painted it fire-engine red. It was one of those classic Schwinn bikes. Henceforth, I was able to get around quickly and for free. Unfortunately, I neglected to buy a lock for it. This precaution never occurred to me. One Saturday afternoon, I attended a movie at a local theater[34] and parked the bike outside the entrance. When I returned, the bike was gone. I called the police but they were of little help. They advised me to buy a lock next time. In Germany, especially Hitler's Germany, such thievery was practically unheard of. This was a hard lesson for me. Unfortunately, I learned many lessons in my life the hard way.

Before the end of the summer, we moved one more time in order to be nearer to my future school: appropriately called 95th Street Elementary School. Our new home was a two-bedroom bungalow located on 92nd Street. One of the strange events that would take place while we lived here was the atomic bomb testing in Nevada. Newspaper articles would announce the times and dates of these tests, and the public was encouraged to go up on their roofs and observe the blasts. At just about dawn, the horizon would light up with an orange glow. That was it. We were too far away to see anything more. Fortunately, the prevailing winds would blow from the west, toward Utah. The people who watched from there got a closer view of the bomb blasts and a good dose of radioactive fallout to boot. Many years later, there was an unusually high incidence of cancer among these people. These were the years of the Cold War. At school, we were taught the hazards of nuclear attacks. We practiced "drop" drills, so we would know how to hide under our desks in the event of an atomic bomb attack. Having experienced the threat of Soviet aggression firsthand, I did not mind these drills. I did dread the

---

[34]Saturday matinees cost nine cents in those days.

thought of seeing bomber planes arriving in swarms over this great land.

In the fall, I was introduced to a unique American tradition, that of going trick-or-treating during Halloween. For a candy-starved kid like me, this was too good to be true. All I had to do was to go from door to door and declare the empty threat "trick or treat," and the kind people would give me a handful of candy. During those days, the candy was usually of the hard sugar variety and mostly unwrapped. I was greedy and collected two big bags full. That evening I transferred the candy into a large washbowl and stored the treasure under my bed. It was a warm night and by morning the candy had fused together into one large clump. For the next six months I would use a hammer and chisel to pry off pieces to eat.

Despite the fact that we came to America as destitute immigrants, we never encountered any hostility or prejudice. Here the word "foreigner" did not seem to carry a negative connotation. On the contrary, when people realized that we were newcomers to their country, they usually leaned over backward to help. This was the case with our neighbors on 92nd Street. The McPherson family lived directly next door to us. It was fortuitous that they also had a son and daughter near my age. Their daughter, Barbara, became my classmate from sixth grade through high school.

Our house on Hobart Blvd., near Century & Western.
We got used to the planes flying overhead on their
way to LAX. Note: my mother's '53 Buick parked in
the driveway.

Mr. Jurgis Peteris
posing in the
backyard of our
house, always in
suit and tie and
with a cigarette in
hand.

# The Land of Opportunity

Since the American Revolution no country has equaled the opportunities that this country has offered immigrants arriving on its shores — with only the clothes on their backs and a willingness to work hard. The inscription on the Statue of Liberty says it well:

*"Give me your tired, your poor, your huddled masses yearning to breathe free."*

The miracle that we call the United States of America started with a small group of visionaries known as the "Founding Fathers." What an auspicious time that was, to have men like Washington, Adams, Jefferson, Franklin, et al., come together at the same time and declare independence from suppressive political traditions of Europe. Ever since, many (reborn) countries have tried to emulate the USA by adopting variations of our Constitution. At the very least, it gave them a start in the right direction.

The key to America's success has been due largely to a resistance to institutionalized social barriers and, more recently, opposition to monopolistic business practices. Hard work is at the core of our entrepreneurial spirit. Of course, advancement in one's field of endeavor is facilitated by the acquisition of skilled know-how or through higher levels of education. Lithuanian refugees who came here after WWII knew how to get ahead through education and hard work. It may have taken a generation to get back on one's feet, but economic success was achieved, in most cases, within a few decades. I don't know of any refugees in our circle of friends who remained on welfare for long, if at all.

More recently, there has been an influx of refugees to the Seattle area from Ethiopia. I am impressed by how quickly these people from Africa achieved economic success. Our neighbors south of the border are eager to come to America, one way or another, to take advantage of the opportunities that are far and few between in their native countries. Most of them have shown a willingness to work hard and encourage their offspring to pursue higher education. We should make it easier for them to come here and allow them to join the melting pot that makes America the success that it has become.

Currently, there is a wave of refugees fleeing warfare in the middle-east. This displacement of people is reminiscent of what occurred in Europe during WWII.

# Chapter V: WORK AND SCHOOL

*SCHOOL AGAIN*
In the fall, I entered sixth grade. Being a foreigner gave me special status, it seemed. I would be asked to stand up in front of the class and talk about my life in Germany and Lithuania. The class honored me with applause and asked me many questions. My English was far from perfect, but I was learning quickly. The class was delighted to have a foreigner among them. What a contrast this was to xenophobic Bavaria!

I recently attended our fiftieth high school reunion, where I met many old classmates. Mary Anne LeFlour recalled how she met me in sixth grade, where I was treated like a celebrity because I was "a blond little boy from Europe who needed help with his homework." This was a far cry from the reception I had received at Gebeleschule a few years earlier.

Of course, I had much to learn in this new environment and culture. Children my age are very adaptable. The playground at this school was asphalt (as in most inner cities). I was exposed to such new games as kickball, tetherball, softball, basketball, and touch football. I liked football the most since I could run fast and dodge opponents. But it was my punt that astounded everyone. Because of my soccer experience, I could kick the ball higher and farther than anyone in my age group. Nonetheless, I missed good old European Fussball.

I graduated from grammar school with a respectable B average. Surprisingly, I excelled in spelling, even though I had to spell words whose meanings often eluded me. I attribute this ability to the fact that the Lithuanian and German languages are relatively phonetic. Having learned to read and write phonetically allowed me to visualize English words the same way, and spelling them became much easier.

*SUMMER SCHOOL*

When summer came again, my mother made sure that I would be kept busy by enrolling me in summer school. Unfortunately, the closest junior high school was across town in an area called South Gate. It was a two-hour commute each way. The classes I took included English, beginning typing, and drama. For the first time, I had classmates who were of African-American descent. In drama class, I had my first interaction with black students. There were several black girls of various ages in this class. One fourteen-year-old black girl was rather tall for her age, and I found her most attractive—not in a romantic way, but in the classic sense. I could not keep my eyes off this beauty and my staring began to annoy her. At one point, she turned to me and exclaimed in an irritated voice, "Why don't you take a picture; it will last longer!" I was so embarrassed that I did not dare look at her again.

One of the most useful courses that I have ever taken in school was typing, and by the end of the summer session, I became a proficient typist. For the next ten years or so, I wrote all my school reports on a typewriter. It saved me a lot of time and the teachers were happy because they did not have to struggle with problematic handwriting. By the time I entered college, most of the women knew how to type. However, most male students would have to hire secretaries to have their reports typed up. I was an exception. Now, with the introduction of computers, everyone learns to type at an early age. The only drawback of this high-tech revolution is that the art of good handwriting has all but disappeared. In Germany, we were taught to excel in uniform handwriting at an early age, and I took pride in my calligraphy.

I soon tired of two-hour commutes by bus and learned to hitchhike to my school in South Gate. It probably shaved an hour off the travel time each way. I was blond, fair skinned, and looked a lot younger than my twelve years. People did not hesitate to give me a ride. One time, after school, a man in his forties picked me up. He asked where I was going and indicated that my destination was also in his direction. After a few blocks on the main arterial, he made a quick right turn onto a smaller street and started to accelerate. I realized he was taking me off route, so I quickly opened the door and jumped out. He did not stop for me. I got up, badly bruised, clothes torn, and took the next bus back home. When my mother saw me, she made me promise not to hitchhike again. I kept the promise, for a while.

*ARRIVAL OF THE GROSCH FAMILY*

My mother continued to correspond with her dear friends Mura and Henry Grosch,[35] who were stuck in Austria. She offered to sponsor them. Consequently, they arrived in Los Angeles during the summer of 1952, along with their son Schurick. I was delighted to have my old friend from those wonderful days in Lithuania with me again. When we met, I tried to talk to him and realized that I had lost the ability to speak German (Schurick spoke German with his father and Russian with his mother). In just two years, I had forgotten the language, or so it seemed! Actually, I had just blocked this language out. Within a week or two, I was fluent again. In the fall, he joined me at Bret Harte Junior High in the eighth grade.

Henry Grosch must have been in his seventies by then, but he was in good physical shape and looked years younger. Like my father, he had falsified his real age in order to qualify for immigration to the USA. He got a job as a janitor at the University of Southern California. There he worked for many years in this humble capacity. One night he was cleaning out the metallurgy laboratory and got distracted by his love for and familiarity with his old profession. While he was examining various specimens of metal, a professor walked in unexpectedly. The professor noticed that Mr. Grosch's curiosity was inconsistent with a janitor's and inquired what his interest was. Mr. Grosch explained that his background and education was in metallurgy. The professor asked him to identify various samples of metal ore and compositions of alloys. Mr. Grosch answered flawlessly. The professor

---

[35]Henry Grosch was of Baltic German origin—a region that has been passed back and forth between the Germans and Russians for centuries. As a young man, he came to America to study and graduated from Columbia University (1908) with a degree in metallurgy. During WWI, he served the czar as an artillery officer. During WWII, he served as the director of steel production in the northern sector of Hitler's Germany.

was so impressed that the next day he arranged for an interview with a major industrial company that employed scientists in metallurgy. They hired him at a salary commensurate with his professional experience. We were all elated! However, it was a short-lived miracle. The company was also a defense contractor and Mr. Grosch failed to pass security requirements. It was at the height of the Cold War, and Henry Grosch's past with Hitler and the Russians made him a security risk. He went back to sweeping out classrooms and cleaning toilets.

*JUNIOR HIGH SCHOOL*
In the fall of 1951, most of our sixth grade class at 95th Street Elementary School matriculated to Bret Harte Junior High. This major urban school was located in a part of Los Angeles (Hoover and 92nd Street) now called Watts. I was definitely in the ethnic minority again. The experience that I gained in "public relations" during the early school years in Bavaria came in handy here. Compared to Germany, school in America was a lot more fun. The academic classes were good, but one could get by with doing very little homework. There were a lot of shop classes for the boys: wood shop, electrical shop, ceramics, metal shop, etc. These courses were fun because most boys like to build things with their hands. Also, there was ample opportunity to goof off. A course in mechanical drawing prepared me for future architectural drafting classes in high school. My mother made sure that I took classes in Spanish as well. "Forget French," she would say. "With Mexico for a neighbor, it is important to speak their language and know their culture." She was so right.

Again, the large playgrounds surrounding the school buildings were all paved in asphalt. The exception was a large sandy area in one corner of the grounds. This sandpit contained steel apparatus for gymnastics (high bar, parallel bars, climbing rope, jungle gym). There was no formal class or teacher who would show us how to do tricks on the high bar or parallel bars, so the more daring kids would experiment. I was one of the kids who was attracted to such acrobatics. The most daring trick was a backflip swinging off the high bar. I think some kids probably learned this maneuver from older brothers in high school. Most of us learned by derring-do. More than once, I would swing into a backward somersault and land flat on my back—knocking the wind out of me. At first, I would struggle for air and get none. Then I would pass out; this was not pleasant. A few minutes later, I would regain consciousness, staring up at the sky, with a crowd of kids looking down at me as if they had placed bets on my odds for survival. When I began to realize where I was and what had happened, embarrassment would take over; I would get up and try to regain my composure. After a few such attempts, I soon learned how to complete the somersault and land on my feet.

Race relations at this school were amicable for the most part. There were occasional skirmishes between various troublemakers. Schurick and I would hang out together, and we made friends with many of the boys, black and white. We let everyone know that we were cousins (an exaggeration—although I did call Schurick's parents my aunt and uncle). When together, we spoke in German. This may have annoyed some. One such troublemaker, I think his name was Billy, had it in for me and informed a black kid (Trevor) with a bad reputation that Schurick and I referred to him as "negro." In those days, the proper term for this racial minority was "colored." The words "negro" or "black" were considered offensive (as "nigger" still is today). In German, there is no other word for this race other than *Neger*, which is the generic name for Africans.

Trevor confronted Schurick and me with this concocted insult and let it be known that he and his buddies would be looking for us after school. We did not relish the idea of getting beaten up by a gang of toughs. Fortunately, I was friends with a big black kid, Leroy, who had the reputation of being the toughest fighter of them all; he had the physique of a young Mike Tyson. Even though he was a feared fighter, he had a mellow personality and was not a troublemaker. I explained our dilemma to him. He listened carefully and my story made sense to him. Leroy sided with us. The conflict was defused. Later, I settled the score with Billy privately.

One racial incident did not get defused as easily. Two of the fourteen-year-olds in our class got into a fight. The following day, each kid brought in fighters from his racial side and a larger brawl was in the making. Though there were lots of taunts and insults, actual fighting did not break out at this stage. What happened next electrified this part of Los Angeles. These troublemakers (white and black) had older friends and brothers and recruited them to join in for a showdown. Over a hundred kids (and young men) showed up at our junior high school ready to fight. The LAPD was forewarned and showed up as well. Arrests were made (mostly older boys with guns) and the fight never materialized. This was a racial conflagration that did not ignite. A few years later, a similar conflagration started by two fourteen-year-olds did explode. It became known as the Watts Riots; it lasted for weeks. While I was away at college I had to pass through a police barrier each time I visited my mother at our home.


*FILMS, STORIES, AND POLITICS*
During my adolescent years, I developed a passion for reading and listening to stories. With money that I had saved, I mail-or-

dered a set of fifteen volumes of the Western world's great literature. These books included novels such as *A Tale of Two Cities*,
*Les Misérables, The Count of Monte Cristo, David Copperfield*,
and *Gone with the Wind*, and two volumes of poetry. Since I
liked history, especially American history, I also bought a set of
books depicting great figures of early America. These biogra-
phies were simplistic, since they were written with school-
children in mind, but I loved them. They included romanticized
heroes such as Daniel Boone, Davy Crockett, Kit Carson, Buffalo Bill, et al. My mother introduced me to the writings of Mark
Twain, and we both shared his wonderful stories.

Television was just becoming popular when we arrived in America. I first glimpsed this technological marvel in storefront windows. We did not actually buy one until I was almost through
with high school. Looking back, I don't ever remember anyone
in our family turning it on and watching it. I think its main purpose was to serve as a flower bouquet pedestal. I did develop an
appreciation for certain radio programs. These included American classics such as *The Jack Benny Program, Amos 'n' Andy,
The Lone Ranger, Boston Blackie,* and a fifteen-minute program
that would come on at ten o'clock on Sunday nights; it was
called *I Love a Mystery.* It was a most unusual series that would
transport me to the unexplored jungles of South America and tell
tales of high adventure and intrigue. I would lie in bed with the
lights out and imagine the sights more vividly than any television display ever could have portrayed. Visions of man-eating
flowers, rain forests, impenetrable jungles, prehistoric animals,
and undiscovered civilizations would  appear in my mind. The
program would begin and end with the sounds of an old-fashioned locomotive passing through and fading out in the distance.

My mother was a great storyteller. Having taught Russian literature in Moscow, she was well read. Sometimes, she would sim-

ply make up stories as she went along. Her tales always enthralled me and the two of us would sometimes stay up until two or three in the morning (on weekends). Many of her stories described women performing great deeds, especially mothers sacrificing their lives for the well-being of their sons. During this period, I was convinced that women were a superior race. My mother also enjoyed a good card game (e.g., Hearts), and we often played Chinese Checkers. Humor was always a part of these activities.

She would also impart words of wisdom. We came from a European society that was extremely class conscious. She did not believe in archaic social traditions. She viewed everyone as an equal, unless they proved themselves otherwise. One Lithuanian saying she often repeated was "don't look for someone dumber than you" (meaning, don't assume you can put one over on someone). When it came to class distinction, she loved to tell the story (or anecdote) about an aristocratic old general who attended a fancy ball in the court of St. Petersburg. Upon meeting a young lieutenant whom he considered an upstart, the stuffy old man looked down his nose and asked, "And to which great family do you belong?" The lieutenant replied, "Sir, I am aware that you come from a noble family and you are the last of a long line. I, sir, do not come from such a family, but I shall be the first of my line." Touché!

My mother was a feminist of the old-fashioned kind. She was romantic, feminine, and did not flaunt her superiority. At the same time, she expected her son to grow up independent and self-sufficient and not become dependent on the "weaker sex." So she taught me domestic skills such as cooking, ironing, sewing buttons on my shirts, darning socks (a lost art), etc. "Too many men end up marrying for the convenience of domesticity. I don't want that to happen to you," she counseled. Actually, these skills were really helpful for living on a tight budget during my college years.

One of the best pieces of advice that she ever gave me was "Beware of people who speak badly of others. Someday they may speak of you the same way." Probably the most contagious social disease transmitted by word of mouth is that of character assassination. Ironically, the more accomplished a person is, the more likely it is that people, i.e., "old friends," will badmouth his or her accomplishments. The Old Testament identified envy as one of the seven deadly sins for good reason.

I frequented movies, but not always the kind that were popular with teenagers my age. I enjoyed epics like *Quo Vadis*, *20,000 Leagues Under the Sea*, and *Gone with the Wind*. I also discovered a genre of film that was just beginning to gain attention in America: the foreign film. There was a small movie house near Western and Wilshire that showed imported German B movies. I liked to see them for nostalgic reasons. Then they introduced films by a Swedish director named Ingmar Bergman. Wow! I was smitten by his work. A Danish film called *One Summer Of Happiness* was about first love, which moved me deeply. When I saw Francois Truffaut's film *The 400 Blows*, I was disappointed. I thought my own experience of being abandoned in orphanages to be more compelling. Though the film struck close to home. When I was about thirteen years old, a sensational science-fiction film appeared at our neighborhood theater. I remember it as simply, *The Thing*. A bunch of us kids went to see it. Most of the kids seemed to like it, and it became a big hit. I was horrified and scared to death while watching the film. In fact, I would have walked out of the theater early, but that would have made me look like a weakling. I endured it to the end, and then I endured nightmares of extraterrestrial monsters for the next few years. I never saw another horror film ever again.

My mother was fond of dance and we would go to ballet performances together (mostly films). When the Bolshoi Ballet came to town, we attended a performance. Outside the Shriner's Auditorium, where the Soviet dancers were performing, a crowd of people gathered. They were holding up signs protesting Soviet occupation of several countries, including Lithuania. My mother took the position that artists are not to blame for the actions of their governments. My father would take me to opera performances (on film), which I found boring at that time; I was not yet ready for this art form.

It was the presidential election year of 1952. Two former generals, Eisenhower and MacArthur, were vying for the Republican nomination. My mother was not fond of Ike because of what he did after the war in Germany. During World War II, one of the Russian army divisions turned against the Kremlin and joined forces with the German army. The leader of this revolt was a highly respected general by the name of Andrei Vlasov. His hope was to defeat Stalin's brutal regime and build a new and democratic Russia. He was not a fan of Hitler, by any means. When the war ended, Vlasov's army surrendered to the Americans. They were promised good treatment as prisoners of war and eventual release, along with their German comrades in arms. Above all, they were promised that they would not be delivered into the hands of Stalin. This promise was broken by General Eisenhower, the commander of the Allied forces. Over three thousand of Vlasov's soldiers were rounded up and shipped back to the USSR in cattle cars. When the decision was made to repatriate these soldiers, many committed suicide rather than face Stalin's wrath. Many who did return were tortured and killed; the more fortunate ones were sent to slave labor camps for the rest of their lives.

My mother argued that Eisenhower was willing to appease Stalin. "He is a weak leader," she said. "You cannot be weak in the face of a brutal dictator like Stalin! We need someone strong, like General MacArthur. Look what he did in Japan: he stood up to the Russians and kicked them out of the country. The Russians will never give us Lithuania back if Eisenhower is elected. They know he is weak."

She was right. The Cold War lasted for almost fifty years. The Baltic states regained their freedom when a strong president was at the helm in America. Of course, Reagan was aided by willing Russian leaders—Gorbachev and Yeltsin. Lithuania's freedom came too late for my parents. They died before the fall of the Berlin wall.

For most of my life, I lived under the impression that I was born in Memel during the time it was occupied by Nazi Germany. My original birth certificate was "lost" during the war. When we arrived in Munich in 1945, my mother procured an affidavit supplied by the papal nuncio that I was, indeed, born in Memel. This established me as a German citizen and would make life easier for me once I grew up in that country. In fact, I was not born in Memel, as I found out when I was in my mid-sixties. After my parents died, rumors abounded that my mother did not want me to be born under the Nazi flag. When she entered labor my father was hiding in Lithuania. So my mother asked a couple of male friends to secretly escort her to the resort town of Palanga, fifteen kilometers to the north and just across the border in Lithuania. During the summer of 2005, my son Tomas was visiting Lithuania. I asked him to check out the hospital records in Palanga in hopes of finding my original birth certificate. The resu lt was negative, but the hospital records showed that I was baptized in a nearby town called Kretinga. My dutiful son went there to investigate and found the baptismal papers, as well as a document indicating that I was born at a hospital in this town. A search of hospital records revealed my original birth certificate, which my son delivered to me (an official copy) when he returned to Seattle. It was good to know where I was really born, but I have to wonder whether there are other secrets that my mother kept from me.

On June 8, 1956, I drove to the federal courthouse downtown and rushed into the judge's courtroom. I was late. The room was packed full with immigrants waiting to be sworn in as citizens of the United States of America. I had barely squeezed inside the door when I heard it open again and someone else entered. Then a wave of very distinct perfume overcame me just as the swearing-in procedure was about to begin. I looked over my shoulder and my heart skipped a beat. Standing directly behind me were two of my favorite movie stars: Stewart Granger and his wife, Jean Simmons. They looked as glamorous as on the big screen. Jean Simmons was wearing an elegant, broad-brimmed black hat. Both were being sworn in as US citizens with the rest of us.

My parents had some very good friends who reminded me of the aforementioned movie stars. Mr. and Mrs. Vasilauskas were glamorous people in the real sense. The wife also looked good in a broad-brimmed black hat. They had one daughter who was about my age and we often played together. During my last visit to their home in Chicago, the daughter and I were both fourteen and our play was more on the flirtatious side. She was developing into a beautiful young woman, taking after her mother. A few years later, we received photos from the parents showing their daughter's entry into the Catholic sisterhood. The novice looked very beautiful and serene. The parents were shown escorting their only child down the church aisle. They looked as glamorous as ever, but they did not look happy. *Why would an only child choose to become a nun?* I wondered.

*BOY SCOUTS*

Troop 604 of the Boy Scouts of America was located in our neighborhood, and I joined it when I was twelve years old. The scoutmaster, Mr. Shannon, was a congenial type and a dedicated instructor. He was assisted by numerous volunteer fathers in the task of teaching us the basic essentials boys need to know in order to grow up into upstanding and productive citizens. Scouts earned merit badges for successfully completing various courses such as swimming, first aid, map reading, etc. With the attainment of a certain number of badges, the scout would get promoted in rank: from Tenderfoot to Second Class, then to First Class, Star, Life, and finally to Eagle Scout (a high honor). I made it to First Class in the two years that I was a member.

Joining this troop also gave me the opportunity to go into the mountains and be one with nature again. In Germany, the Alps were so close, while here in California, the Sierras were many hours away. My first camping trip took us into the southern Sierras (Kings Canyon National Park). I did not have a sleeping bag and was confident that a warm blanket would suffice for the sojourn. When I unpacked my gear in our base camp, the chaperones of our troop were aghast. "You'll freeze to death!" they warned me. I argued that I had lots of camping experience in the Alps (an exaggeration) and never needed a sleeping bag. The truth was I could not afford one. The Alps do stay relatively warm at night and I did not realize how cold the High Sierra could get. The men were right: I froze! I did not get a wink of sleep lying on the bare ground with only one blanket. My body shivered, my teeth chattered; this was one long and miserable night. I was greatly relieved when dawn broke over the horizon and sun rays began to reconstitute my body temperature. When asked how I fared during the night, I lied, "Oh, no problem. A bit on the chilly side, maybe." The following week, I went to a sporting goods store and bought a Dacron sleeping bag for ten dollars.

The best trips were to Yosemite Valley. It was a six-hour drive in an open truck, but it was worth it. What a magnificent miracle of nature this place is, I thought. I wished I could have scrambled up the granite rocks, but I could not find a friend who had any climbing experience to join me. We did go on terrific hikes.

Early one morning, we were scheduled to hike up to Glacier Point, have lunch up there, and come back down into the Valley by the end of the day. Several of the more ambitious scouts decided to make the trip more challenging by having a race. The proposed route would take us up the precipitous trail to Glacier Point, down the other side, around Half Dome, over Vernal Falls, and back to camp in the Valley. More than a dozen of us kids agreed to join the race. We started at six in the morning, and by the time we reached Glacier Point, only six scouts were willing to continue the demanding trek. Six of us ran down the trail leading toward Nevada Falls and around the back side of Half Dome. It was a race, and to stay in the competition, *we ran most of the time!* By mid-afternoon, the leaders were passing the majestic Vernal Falls; I was in hot pursuit. The survivors started arriving in camp well before dinnertime, exhausted but triumphant. I did not come in first, but I was happy to have been among the six finishers.

My experience with the Boy Scouts was a positive one. I met decent people and made good friends. The organization serves a constructive purpose by giving inner-city kids an opportunity to appreciate nature and learn a better value system than they would out on the streets, where delinquency is the norm.

## THE QUEST FOR WORK

My parents were happy to find work that enabled them to save money for a new future. America truly was, and still is, a land of opportunity. Within three years of our arrival in America, my parents were able to make a down payment of $1,000 on a two-bedroom house in a middle-class neighborhood. The price of the house was $10,000. The interest rate for mortgages was at 4%. It was a typical tract house (vintage 1945) in the pseudo-Spanish style, with a stucco exterior and a fake fireplace in the living room. It had two bedrooms, one for my mother and one for my father. I slept on a pull-out sofa in the living room. There was a detached two-car garage and a roomy backyard. In the back was a grape arbor supporting vines of climbing roses, a banana palm, and an orange tree. My mother was happy here. We were half a block from the intersection of Century Boulevard and Western Avenue (10040 Hobart Boulevard). On the other side of Western Avenue was Inglewood. It was a straight shot down Century Boulevard to Los Angeles International Airport (now LAX). On the downside, we were in the flight path of planes landing at LAX; we could see the underbellies of the planes close up. It did not take us long to tune out the noise of approaching planes.

I was a member of the high school gymnastic team and used my backyard to supplement my workouts. The rear patio contained two rusty T-shaped poles with laundry lines strung between them. I used one of them to do my daily chin-ups from the crossbar. The backyard was large enough for me to practice tumbling on the grass. One time I performed a forward flip in the pike position. I landed incorrectly and broke my heel. My mother called our family doctor (a Russian immigrant who was probably unlicensed). He examined my swollen ankle and concluded that I had burst a vein. "There is blood in there and I will get it out so that the swelling goes down," he said with a heavy Russian accent. He then pulled a large syringe out of his bag and proceeded to poke the needle into the swelling area. I screamed with pain. When no blood was extracted, he would poke into another spot. This was crazy, I thought. After several pokes, he gave up trying to extract blood. I insisted that my mother take me to the hospital and get my foot x-rayed. Sure enough, my heel showed a crack all the way through. The ER doctor put me in a cast and, in a few weeks, my injury was healed.

Southern California is famous for its oil fields. The city of San Pedro is sinking, they say, because so much oil has been extracted over the years. It was not surprising that our neighborhood lay above a large oil field. Oil contracts were consummated long before these houses were built here. Nonetheless, we did get an oil royalty of about fifteen dollars each month.

Before my parents bought this house, we were in a saving mode for the $1,000 down payment. Not a penny was wasted on frivolous items or activities. I wanted to help. A Lithuanian entrepreneur named Antanas Skirius had arrived from Europe a few years earlier and managed to start a publishing business. His main production was the publication of *Lithuanian Days*, a national journal of Lithuanian affairs, formatted along the lines of *Life* magazine. His offices were located on Figueroa Street (in Watts), and he was more than happy to employ any Lithuanian refugee willing to work for less than minimum wage. I did not care how little I was paid; *I wanted to work and earn money by the hour!* My mother relented and let me work for Skirius for a starting wage of fifty cents an hour. My job included stapling the collated pages of the magazine together, trimming the edges with a huge guillotine that required considerable manpower, and then stuffing the individual issues into envelopes addressed to thousands of Lithuanians across America. The sorting of envelopes gave me a good indication where the concentrations of Lithuanian colonies were: Chicago, New York, New Haven, Brooklyn, Cleveland, Pittsburg, etc.

One of the regulars at his print shop was a highly regarded Lithuanian poet by the name of Bernardas Brazdžionis.[36] He must have been in his late sixties and he had no other profession. Mr. Skirius taught him how to operate the Linotype and he became expert at it. I never stopped marveling at this machine that printed texts for newspapers and magazines. It was so big that it took up enough space for a small room. It had so many complicated parts that it defied imagination. The linotypist would sit at a keyboard and compose the script for printing. This effort would result in several word-long dies cast in a lead/zinc alloy. These dies would then be (automatically) placed into trays that produced the printed page. Once this was accomplished, the dies would be melted down and reproduced by the Linotype machine for new printing dies. With the advent of computers, the dark ages of printing with such manual methods have become a distant memory.

Despite his advanced age, Mr. Brazdžionis wanted to buy a car and learn to drive it. I had just turned seventeen and was a licensed driver. He hired me to help him buy a new car and to teach him how to drive it.

One Saturday afternoon, during the late fall of 1956, we set out to buy the new car. He needed me, mainly because I was fluent in English and he was not. Our strategy was to scout out several dealerships and investigate several makes of cars. We agreed that, no matter what, we would not buy the first car that was offered to us. After all, we were not dummies (we thought). The

[36]He later became poet laureate of Lithuania.

first dealership that we entered had an array of new Chevrolets. The salesman was accommodating and showed us the different models. Mr. Brazdžionis narrowed the field of choice to a four-door sedan with no frills. We thanked the salesman and started to leave. At this point, the salesman asked us to sit down with him to pencil out a price. "With no obligation," he said. OK, the price he came up with was educational, but we reminded ourselves (in Lithuanian) that we had agreed to shop around before making a purchase.

Once again, we headed for the door, but the salesman called us back with an enticement that he could lower the price considerably. We sat down with him again and I translated all the new information. At the end of the presentation, we thanked the salesman and proceeded to leave. Once more, he stopped us and asked us to wait until he could talk to his manager in order to get "approval" for an extra-low price for us. He disappeared for ten or fifteen minutes and came back with a newly typed offer of an "incredibly low price." He also threw in extras, such as the radio and air conditioning, "for free." All Mr. Brazdžionis had to do was sign on the dotted line and he could drive his dream car out of the showroom in five minutes. By now, Mr. Brazdžionis was no longer listening to me. He was convinced that such a deal would never be offered again. He signed on the dotted line. As I drove that car away from the dealership, we both sat in silence, wondering what had happened. I was embarrassed to admit that yes, we had been duped.

Then came the lessons. I chose Vermont Avenue on Sunday morning, since it would be a roomy boulevard with minimal traffic. I demonstrated how this new car operated and showed him how to shift gears by using the clutch and how to use the brakes. The rest would be easy, I thought. When it came to his turn to drive, he started out reasonably well in first gear. When he had to shift into second, he got a little confused and lost focus as to where he was heading. Before I could stop him, he swerved up onto the median and took out half a dozen No Parking signs. They flew to the side like so many matchsticks. I got him to stop halfway across the median and took over the driving as quickly as I could. We got out of there before any witnesses could report us. The following weekend, I found a large asphalt play field for his driving lessons.

When I was about thirteen, my mother sent me to apprentice under a car mechanic. This was at an auto repair shop on Western Avenue owned by a prewar Lithuanian immigrant. His shop was typical—greasy, dirty, and very messy. Most of the cars were prewar relics. This was good since the engines were simple and easy to understand. I learned how to take a four-cylinder motor apart, overhaul it, and put it together again. It was low-tech work by today's standards. I saw the guts of an internal combustion engine and understood what made it function. Old pistons would get new rings. Leaky intake and exhaust valves would get ground by hand until they fit snugly in their seats. This experience helped me with future repair problems of vehicles I acquired. Before long, fuel injectors replaced carburetors and the engines became computerized. My expertise with old engines became outdated, but my mechanical skills did not.

Our neighborhood had standard lots where the recessed houses had lots of green lawns in front, and often in the rear, as well. People were happy when I offered to cut their lawn for a nominal price. Pushing a lawnmower was tedious work but it provided for good pocket money.

On the corner of Century and Western was a small commercial district. It contained Karg's Grocery Store, where we did most of our shopping. Mr. Karg was a genial, old-fashioned businessman. He hired me to stock the shelves. Once a month he would have "specials," and I offered to paint the posters (which he would display in his storefront windows). At fifteen I already showed skills as a commercial artist. My posters did not simply describe what the specials were; I used color and varying-sized lettering to emphasize a product. Mr. Karg was not impressed and refused to display some of my more imaginative posters. I continued to stock the shelves, but at a rate that exceeded expectations. Mr. Karg was duly impressed and complimented my efficiency. Since I was performing more work than he expected of me, I asked for a raise. He declined, stating that he would just as well have me work at a slower pace. I thanked him for his kindness and quit. He was a little baffled by my decision; he did not understand that I was keen on doing more and better work, but the compensation had to be commensurate with my production level.

The following year, a new store opened next door to Karg's Grocery. It was called Valley Furniture. Their motto was "We'll feather your nest for a little down." I wasted no time offering my services and was given a part-time job in the delivery department (I was still in high school). The owner was an elderly gentleman by the name of Don Thomason. He had a beautiful trophy wife who would come in on occasion—bejeweled and fashionably dressed. He had a son, Donny, who was a little older than I. Mr. Thomason also had a daughter who was a stunning beauty—with a perfect body (enhanced through bodybuilding). Donny was a down-to-earth, no-nonsense type of guy and he did not like his flamboyant sister. I liked her, of course, and I enjoyed her stories of dating Hollywood luminaries. A few years later, she married Mickey Rooney (the movie star). While married to him, she got involved with a young lover who, in a fit of jealousy killed her and himself.

Delivering furniture with Donny was good hard work and I got paid reasonably well. When no deliveries were needed, I often stood by as a backup floor salesman. I was taught how to read the coded numbers on price tags, which indicated how low the price of a specific item could be bargained down to (tricks of the trade).

For a while I found part-time employment with the largest department store in the United States: Sears, Roebuck & Co. I was hired as a floor salesman in the sporting goods department. Sometimes, I filled in for absent salesmen in other departments, such as men's clothing, automotive supplies, etc. The location of the store was in Inglewood (on Manchester). The salesmen in this store were paid a small salary in addition to a commission. I would record each sale on a little scorecard and submit it to my boss at the end of each day. There was a lot of pressure to sell as much as possible. In other words, the "hard sell" was encouraged. I did not like it. One time, an attractive couple with two young children came in, interested in buying a complete camping outfit. This would have meant a big commission for me. They wanted to go family camping and had set a generous budget for good-quality equipment. I did not think highly of Sears & Roebuck camping gear. I thought it was cheap and poorly manufactured. I asked if the couple was willing to pay for higher-quality gear. When they answered in the affirmative, I gave them directions to a sporting goods store specializing in quality gear. They were very thankful and left for the other store. Somehow, my supervisor found out about my sending these potential customers to a competitor, and I was fired. I did not enjoy working for this giant company and did not regret leaving.

Most neighborhoods in Los Angeles had local papers that came out once a week. They would print only local news and were heavy on advertising. For several months, I had a job with

*Southwest Wave* doing ad layouts. I would cut and paste pictures of products that were being advertised onto mock-up sheets. My artistic imagination, this time, was appreciated without restrictions. There were deadlines that had to be met before press time. It was a demanding schedule and I really enjoyed the challenge. The job did not last very long due to budget cuts. When my job was terminated, I received a glowing letter of recommendation.[37] It made me look like I was practically running the whole operation.

## DELIVERING NEWSPAPERS

My parents were working hard (even overtime) to make ends meet. I wanted to help. I managed to get a job with the *Los Angeles Times*, selling newspapers at the intersection of Western Avenue and Imperial Highway. It was a busy crossroads and business was brisk, though a little hazardous—walking between long rows of cars and darting in and out of traffic. The few dollars I made each afternoon helped offset minor expenses at home, i.e., I was able to buy a few groceries and lunch at school. I wanted to help more and asked my mother if I could get a job as a newspaper delivery boy. This would require me to get up at three thirty every morning, seven days a week (with only two weeks off a year). I was getting by at school with a C+ average—not good enough for my mother. "Get your average up to a B or better, and I'll let you apply for a paper route." The following semester, I brought home a report card showing a B+ grade average. The *Los Angeles Examiner* hired me and I was assigned a small route not far from home. I was delighted.

---

[37] Excerpt from a letter by Robert C. Clements, Advertising Manager, Wave Publications. May 23, 1958:

*"Mr. Bertulis is very quick to learn, he does what he is told, and if work slacks, he is alert to find wha needs doing, and does it. He pays no attention to the hour of five, and has often stayed on late into the evening to finish the job..."*

Getting up at three thirty, rain or shine, was no easy task, but I got used to it. I would ride my bicycle to the distribution center located in an empty storeroom on the corner of Manchester and Budlong. Several boys would meet there to prepare the papers for delivery. On weekdays, the papers would arrive in stacks and we had to bundle them tightly with a rubber band or a string, so that we could toss them onto the subscriber's porches while riding our bikes along the sidewalk. On rainy days, we would wrap the newspapers in wax paper. Canvas saddlebags full of newspapers would straddle the rear of the bike. This load must have weighed a good fifty pounds, and riding the bike with so much weight was not easy. Several trips back to the distribution center were necessary to complete the route. There was a Big Donut drive-in bakery on the corner of Century Boulevard and Normandie Avenue. The smell of fresh donuts would draw us delivery boys into this place, where we treated ourselves to pastry delights for breakfast. Then came the race to Bret Harte Junior High School, several miles away. School started at 8:00 a.m. and ended around three in the afternoon. The delivery of the Sunday paper was a much bigger undertaking. The bulk of the paper would arrive the day before (advertisements, comics, magazines, etc.). The sections with time-sensitive material would arrive on Sunday morning. We would first collate the paper into one huge unit. There was a simple machine that quickly tied the paper into a bundle. I would usually finish the deliveries by around nine or ten in the morning, then go home for some more sleep.

On my fourteenth birthday, I became old enough to ride a motor scooter legally. I bought an old Cushman (for sixty dollars) so that I could take greater loads and deliver the papers much faster. I was also able to expand the size of my paper route, thereby increasing my earnings. But first, I had to make the old clunker I bought operational. I took the engine completely apart and overhauled it (having learned the skill in the auto shop a year earlier). Rebuilding the clutch was a new experience, since its operation is centripetal, while a car's is centrifugal. The carburetor needed revamping as well. Cushman scooters have metal body enclosures (hiding the engine and gas tank) and this body was in poor shape. I repaired all the dents and sanded out the rust spots. Then I painted it fire-engine red. When I was done, it looked like new and it ran like a Swiss watch. This machine was hot!

With the expanded paper route, I was finally making more than just pocket money. I was so proud when I was able to make a full month's mortgage payment on our house, taking the pressure off my parents.

Before I acquired the scooter, my primary mode of transportation was my thumb, i.e., hitchhiking. Now I was able to get around town quickly and conveniently with my own vehicle. Late one evening, I was returning from a movie when I decided to take a shortcut through a residential area unfamiliar to me. While I was driving down a dark street, a young boy standing on the curb suddenly shone a powerful flashlight in my face. I was temporarily blinded. Before I could recover, I collided head-on with a chain-link fence that was straddling the street. Apparently, it was the entry to a school or a playground. I was propelled face-first into this barrier—shearing the handlebars off the scooter in the process. The fence made a rather distinct imprint on my face, puncturing the skin in several places. Hurt and bleeding, I managed to jury-rig the damaged steering mechanism on my scooter and drive back home. I was more concerned about my mother's anger over allowing myself to get involved in such an accident than the consequences of my facial injuries (permanent scars?). However, when I arrived at our house, my mother let out a shriek when she saw my mangled face. Rather than reprimanding me, as I expected, she was most sympathetic. She gave me first aid and drove me to the nearest hospital. In the emergency ward, the attending nurse for registration received us. The nurse took a good look at me. Then, to add insult to injury, she asked my mother, "Is your son over twelve or under twelve?" *I was sixteen!*

When I retired from the paper route, I sold the scooter to a friend down the street. He did not have a paper route or a job; he just wanted the scooter to run around in. We agreed on a price of two hundred dollars. Since he only had fifty dollars, I accepted it as a down payment with an agreement that he would make three fifty-dollar monthly payments. Then I made a huge mistake: I signed the "pink slip" transferring the ownership to him. Nobody told me that it is customary to sign over the ownership *after* payment in full is received. My friend Dale never made any more installment payments and drove the scooter into the ground. A few months later I saw it abandoned and completely trashed. I was heartbroken.

*SOLICITING*

Another opportunity to earn money with the *Los Angeles Examiner* came in the form of an evening job called "soliciting." The key to every newspaper's survival is a strong customer base. So, getting new subscriptions is a high priority with any paper, and successful solicitors are well rewarded. I was small for my age but articulate in my sales pitch. Our boss (the dealer) would take our team of solicitors into neighborhoods that were identified as being undersubscribed. For new subscriptions, we were rewarded with money and credits for gifts from a catalog. These included a variety of household goods, toys, appliances, and so forth. We had an old stove range that was hardly functioning. I was so successful with my solicitations that it did not take me long to earn enough credits for a new (state-of-the-art) gas stove. My parents were delighted. I also obtained other appliances and household goods such as an iron, a toaster, a mixer, tableware, an alarm clock radio, and a fourteen-volume encyclopedia.

Our team of solicitors would be invited on field trips. A day at the amusement park in Long Beach was always popular (we would also get a handful of free passes). Once, we took a three-day trip to March Air Force Base and got to see fighter jets close up. Another time, we took a three-day trip to San Francisco. We stayed at a hotel and got to eat in nice restaurants; both were new experiences for many of us inner-city kids. I remember going out to the famous Cliff House on the north shore and having lunch there. The Golden Gate Bridge was awe-inspiring.

Then there was an annual citywide competition, where the solicitors with the most subscriptions to their credit would be rewarded with a free trip to Hawaii. Fifteen kids and I from the greater metropolitan area (including the San Fernando Valley) boarded a United Airlines DC-6 and flew to Honolulu. The year was 1953 and I was fourteen. We were greeted by hula girls who placed fragrant leis around our shoulders. Newspaper reporters took our pictures and interviewed some of us. Then we were chauffeured to the Moana Hotel at the premier location of Waikiki Beach. However, we were not given rooms in the famous high-rise on the beach. The Moana had garden bungalows across the street and we were assigned comfortable accommodations there. There were ample opportunities to join tours around the island. I went on a couple, the Dole pineapple factory and Coconut Island. Of course, we participated in the traditional luau, where we got a taste of that strange paste called *poi*. A pig was baked under ground and was truly succulent. Male and female performers danced the hula to beating drums. Then I focused on what to some of us was the main attraction: surfing!

Those of us with a more adventurous attitude decided to learn how to surf and spent every available moment doing so. The surfboards in those days were big (ten feet long?), built of wood, and heavy. I was barely five feet tall, but lack of height did not slow me down. We were all in very good physical shape and had no trouble getting past the big waves. We learned to catch a wave by watching the "regulars." Then came the thrill of riding a wave into the beach without falling off. If I fell off, as was frequently the case, the surfboard would continue to the beach without me. It was a long swim to retrieve the board. After a few days, some of us were able to stand up on the board while riding a wave. Keeping our balance while standing on a speeding board for any length of time was difficult for even the best of us.

The waves were big (by California standards) and the break was a long way out. I learned to ride the board pretty well while in the prone position. The challenge was to do so standing up. More often than not, I would wipe out  and the board would coast into the beach. The wipeout I dreaded the most was when I was standing up and my location on the board was too far forward. With horror, I would watch the tip of the board begin to slip under the surface of the water. I would try to maneuver aft. But by then it was too late—the water's grip on the tip of the board was too strong as it continued slipping below the surface. While rapidly gliding down the face of the moving wave, the board would abruptly dive straight down, catapulting the hapless rider (me) forward. The ten-foot-plus wave would crash over me and keep me submerged, as if in a washing machine set to "high agitation" mode. Holding my breath until I could surface was one concern. Once I surfaced, another concern arose: my board had taken a deep dive and was now on its way up. Its buoyancy propelled it to the surface with such force that it would shoot five or ten feet up into the air, sometimes missing my body by only inches. A collision would mean broken ribs at best, or a knockout at worst. The consequences could be tragic. Numerous times I would tread water at the surface, anxiously waiting for the board to shoot past me. Fortunately, I never got hit.

If my board did not nosedive, it would coast into the beach—very far away, it seemed, while I remained trapped in the breaker zone. I would start to swim, but another big wave would overtake me and I would go through the "high agitation" mode again. Just as I would manage to surface, grabbing that life-saving breath of air, I would look up into the face of another ten-footer breaking over me. I would have just enough time to take a deep breath, and down I would go again. Once, this cycle of waves hit me several times in succession. I became exhausted and felt my strength ebbing. I knew I would not last long enough to make it into shallow water. I looked for a life-saving alternative. Near me was a man lying on his board, waiting for the right wave to catch. I swam over to him and simply latched onto his board. He must have noticed my desperate state of exhaustion. Without a word, he paddled to shore with me hanging on like a wet rag. I took the rest of the day off.

ood
rvice
'ays

# The Junior Examiner

CHARACTER QUALITY — AMERICA FIRST! — ENTERPRISE ACCURACY

THE CARRIER PUBLICATION OF THE EXAMINER — A LIVE NEWSPAPER FOR LIVE CARRIER-SALESMEN

L. A. Examiner Educational Div.

Phone Richmond 1212, Sta. 505

L. XIV, NO. 4      JULY, 1953      Price, Yc

# AWAII GREETING THRILLS CARR

## Francisco Makes Hit

nine happy, carefree
carriers, winners in
it Hawaii-San Fran-
ntest, assembled at
s Lockheed Air Termi-
ird the big United Air
-6 planes on the first
ie San Francisco-Ha-
After a smooth and
flight the big plane
to the San Francisco
ind the g r o u p was
i to begin their tour
iited Air Lines main-
ase.

tours concluded, the
injoyed a good lunch-
d in the base cafeteria
ch they boarded spe-
s for the Pickwick
an Francisco. Prompt-
p. m. Grayline Buses
the group for their
fabled Fisherman's
here they enjoyed a
od dinner at Sabella's
to.
with $2.00 spending
id a free evening the
de a bee line for the
s to return to down-
Francisco. Later in
ng the boys returned
tel, each with a report
seeing tour or a com-
ew of a good movie.

## ay City

Wednesday morning
visors passed out the
cash and the boys
heir morning meal at
f their own choosing.
akfast they boarded
ises for a tour of San

EXAMINER CARRIER BOYS IN HAWAII: Arriving by United Air Lines were these winners of the Examiner Carrier Contest. The boys were thrilled with the terrific island welcome. (Front row, left to right): Alex Bartulis, Jim Clark, Don Bales, Joe Dominguez, Gary Shefflin, Jerry Spunt, Jon Nichols, Louis Valkay; (back row, left to right): K. Riding, J. Lee, A. Calzada, Allison Polk, V. McConnell, T. Dewing and J. Otten

## Retur Islan

"Aloha Nui
the friendly
15 outstandir
riers as they
lulu aboard a
DC-6, July 9tl
ful days in S
a sleepy trip :
the boys were
ception. Hav
and hula girl:
as they were
sented leis by
Circulating
Honolulu Star
Chapman, Pr
Robert L. Fer
Gouvea, Area
Star Bulletin
Sano and Joh
Air Lines an
of the Hawai

The group t
for the Moana
Guslander, a
carrier and m
received then
mediately wer
arrangements
stay on the is
rable one.

## Tour Plan

A tour th
apple plant
breakfast pro
the boys. The
juice from a
treated to as
apple as the:
completion c
Pincetich, th
manager for
through the

"Winning" a trip Hawaii was the result of hard work soliciting subscriptions for the *Los Angeles Examiner*. Alex is standing on the far left just after arriving in Honolulu with fourteen other carriers from the Los Angeles metropolitan area.

# THE 1950s

The decade starting with 1950 was remarkable for its economic success and social optimism. Today, we look back with nostalgia at a period in American history that had it ups and downs, but one that was also full of vitality. It was a remarkable time to grow up in as a child.

Eisenhower was elected president for two terms. The on-going joke was that he was spending more time on the golf course than in the Oval Office. America was enjoying a post war boom. Unemployment was at an all time low. The prime rate was hovering at around 2%. Real estate was cheap and just about anyone could afford to buy a house if they set their mind to it. Huge developments with thousands of cookie-cutter (design variation) houses were being built in the San Fernando Valley (east of LA), displacing vast orange groves in the process.

The price of gasoline was 25 cents per gallon. Detroit produced automobiles that were big, unwieldy, and huge gas-guzzlers. These cars sported lots of chrome and no seat belts. A phone call cost 5 cents and you had to be careful what you said because there were party lines (people sharing the same line when opting for a cheaper rate). Television sets were becoming affordable and the movie industry was concerned that it would be driven out of business (never came close). TV transmissions were in black & white, but movies had a breakthrough when "Technicolor" was introduced. During the summer people watched movies in drive-ins; you never had to leave your car (teenagers loved it for other reasons).

Hollywood was on a roll, turning out big budget films with popular movie stars whose names will remain in our memories forever. Marilyn Monroe, Clark Gable, Katharine Hepburn, Gary Cooper, David Niven, William Holden and James Stewart were among my favorite. I cried when James Dean died in a car crash (driving his Porsche). The world mourned Albert Einstein's death. The Guggenheim Museum was completed in New York, but its architect, Frank Lloyd Wright, did not live long enough to see it completed. Children could choose from an unending selection of comic books, while young adults were introduced to a new magazine called, *"Playboy."*

Disneyland attracted entire families, not only from California, but from all over the World. Jack Kerouac's writing created a generation of "beatniks," which evolved into a generation of "hippies" during the next decade. Elvis Presley gave us a form of rock & roll that shocked the more prudish members of society. But, he had a remarkable voice and good songwriters. Teeny-boppers went wild at his performances. Music was no longer recorded on fragile 78 rpm records, but on pliable 45s. Then came the breakthrough in Hi-Fidelity: "Long Playing" records made of vinyl (referred to as LPs). Their popularity did not last that long, for they were replaced by 7 inch reel to reel tapes, which could be erased and re-recorded on (they did not last that long either).

The richest man in the world at that time was an eccentric Texan named Howard Hughes. His start up wealth came from his father's tool company. His ambition knew no bounds: he soon became a movie mogul, airplane builder, record breaking pilot, and the major owner of Las Vegas casinos (dispossessing the Mafia land lords). He was also known to associate with aspiring movie starlets (under contract with him). He married two of them, first Terry Moore and then Jean Peters, though they were not traditional marriages.

The price of gold was fixed at $35 per ounce, but you could only sell it to the government (if you mined it). The price of crude oil was fixed at $3.50 a barrel (the Arab oil cartel changed that when they took over ownership of ARAMCO and allowed the price of oil to meet market conditions).

Dr. Jonas Salk introduced a vaccine that brought the scourge of polio under control. Yet, cigarette companies were placing ads, which claimed: *"Four out of five doctors prefer to smoke Chesterfields."* It was not long afterwards that the government enacted "Truth in Advertising Laws." (One of my climbing friends was paid a hefty fee to endorse *Camel* cigarettes after he reached the summit of Mt. Everest. He had never smoked a cigarette in his life.)

America was testing atomic and hydrogen bombs in Nevada and the Pacific Ocean. The Russians were doing the same. School children had practice drills where the teacher would suddenly yell "drop!" and everyone in class would hide under the nearest desk. I did that many times, wondering if my experiences of air raids in Germany would be relived again. The "Cold War" was in full swing.

Social injustice continued in the South. "Jim Crow" policies remained in effect. Dr. Martin Luther King, Jr. and his followers were on the march. Desegregation was gaining momentum throughout the United States. Universities in the South were forced to admit black students to attend all white schools — with the help of the National Guard.

Even though the War in Europe had ended, international events still had a significant effect on life in America. Communist Chinese ambitions in Asia resulted in America's participation in the Korean War. The draft was revived and many young American men died fighting in that conflict. President Truman rejected General MacArthur's preemptive attempt to stop the Chinese invasion of Korea and opted for a policy of appeasement. Today, we are still living with a divided Korea and the ever-present threat from a communist government whose policies border on lunacy and the cruel oppression of its own people.

Communist ambitions throughout the world resulted in paranoid reactions in America. Senator Joseph McCarthy went on a witch-hunt of communist sympathizers (real and imagined). Julius and Ethel Rosenberg were executed for handing atomic bomb secrets over to agents of the USSR. Stalin died - in a coup perpetrated by his politburo and lead by Nikita Khrushchev. Boris Pasternak's epic novel of the Russian revolution, "Dr. Zhivago," was published in Italy. He was awarded the Nobel Prize for literature, but was forced to reject it by an outraged Kremlin.

Egypt's Gamal Nasser made a grab for the Suez Canal and England threatened to retake it by military force. President Eisenhower told the British to back off, in no uncertain terms. An international crisis was averted by a former general with fortitude. Fidel Castro succeeded in overthrowing the corrupt regime of Fulgencio Bautista. America's approval is short-lived when it becomes clear that Castro is turning Cuba into a communist dictatorship (with Soviet help).

The USSR launched "Sputnik," the first ever satellite to travel in outer space. America was upset to be outperformed in the race for outer space by a country that most people considered backward (in the field of science). Humiliated, the USA increased its efforts to regain its dominance by financing rocket research and generous scholarships to aspiring young scientists. We regained our dominance by landing men on the moon a few years later.

The 1950s were formative years in my life. I was a teenager and the events of those years shaped my life, to a large degree. I learned to appreciate what America was and the ideals it stood for. Freedom is not to be taken for granted. I became a US citizen in 1956.

# Chapter VI: HIGH SCHOOL YEARS

*SPORTS AND ACADEMICS*
Most of the white students from Bret Harte (including me) graduated to an all-white school farther west. Washington High School was located at Denker Avenue and 108th Street. Our class had about 450 students. Most of the black kids were assigned to Fremont or Jefferson High School. These were major schools in the Los Angeles school district. Washington had a stellar reputation when it came to sports. Luminaries such as Esther Williams (Hollywood movie star) and Hugh McElhenny (football legend) were among its alumni.

Jefferson HS was all black and had a good reputation for academic achievement. It did not suffer from any notable racial problems. Fremont HS, on the other hand, was racially mixed and had a reputation for racial strife. Washington and Fremont were arch-rivals when it came to football. After one fierce football game, which I attended, a fight broke out on the field. It was eventually quelled, but both schools were suspended from further competition that year.

Having experienced the gymnastics sandpit at Bret Harte, I signed up for the high school gymnastics team. That first year (tenth grade), we were blessed with an excellent coach, Mr. Perry, who knew how to teach his team the skills necessary for success. I showed good potential in this sport and entered every event (all-around). My favorite events were the parallel bars, high bar, rings, and free exercise. We had a strong team and did well in city tournaments. One upperclassman named Luigi was a phenomenon. He placed third *nationally* in the long horse as a junior. He was an amazing tumbler and fearless on the swinging rings (now no longer an event). I think he later had a successful career as a Hollywood stuntman.

I was a dedicated competitor. Our team worked out for two hours every afternoon. In addition, I developed a workout routine at home. I would do two hundred pull-ups (twenty at a time) before dinner every day. Not only was I strong, I had developed a good physique. Every year there was a Mr. Washington competition at our school for the boys who were into weight lifting and bodybuilding. One student would always excuse himself from the competition (Patrick

Casey)[38] because he was already semiprofessional and built well enough to win major competitions. Instead, he honored us by being one of the judges. Most of the entrants were aspiring "Mr. Charles Atlas" types. I was not a weight lifter and had no aspirations for bodybuilding. However, someone with a good sense of humor dared me to join the competition. On a lark, I decided to take on the dare (I too had a sense of humor).

The competition was to be held in the school auditorium at noon. I knew I could not come even close to the physiques of practicing weight lifters. However, since the competition would be held during lunch break, I figured that none of the competitors would have the opportunity to get pumped before the competition (the school did not have a weight room). My strategy was simply "brain over brawn." I skipped the period before lunch and went to the outdoor sandpit that contained a high bar and other apparatus. For an hour or so, I did hundreds of chin-ups and push-ups. I got pumped! At the right moment, I went over to the auditorium and greased my body with olive oil (to accentuate my muscles). As I expected, none of the other competitors had the opportunity to get pumped up. When my turn came to go on stage and display my physique, I flexed my muscles and got a surprisingly loud round of applause (the applause meter was a factor in judging the winners). To this day, I am not sure whether the students were applauding me because I impressed them with my muscles, or because I looked so funny and had the chutzpah to enter the competition. I was awarded third place!

---

[38]Guinness Book World Record holder in weight lifting.

Mr. Perry was such a good gymnastics coach that we lost him to Pepperdine College. Subsequent coaches did not have a clue about gymnastics, and the quality of our team declined. Without a coach who could teach us proper gymnastics technique, we were left to our own devices. Historically, our high school had always done well in city competitions. When I was a senior, I was the ranking gymnast on our team. I failed to place in any event in city finals. It was a humiliation noted in our school paper.

I liked history as an academic subject. The sciences were low on my list of favorites. I did well in math and I excelled in architectural drawing classes, which I took during all three years of high school.

My mother had destined me to be an architect since before I was born. She knew that she was carrying a son when she was pregnant, or so she claimed. She did not want to raise a boy to become a soldier, a politician, a lawyer, or a doctor. The former two professions were profuse in her family tree and most of those men died prematurely; the latter two did not meet her "creativity" agenda. She wanted an artist. And what could be more creative than the fields of art or architecture? I think that attitude might explain why she was drawn to my father—the musician. After I was born, she gave me building-block type toys with which to construct projects. Fortunately, I showed a distinct aptitude for architecture. Was it an accident or was it my mother's predestined influence? During a high school aptitude test, I scored in the 99th percentile in the spatial comprehension section (off the chart!). I never doubted that someday I would become an architect, even before I understood what it was that an architect did.


## A DOG NAMED RUDIS

Our neighbor on Hobart Boulevard had a dog named Ginger. It was a pedigreed Doberman pinscher and a serious guard dog. I had a little kitten that was either fearless or very dumb (or both). Once this little kitten simply walked through the fence into Ginger's yard, and I fully expected the dog to tear it to pieces. It did no such thing; the dog was not pleased, but it simply kept a wary eye on the intruder. Then the kitten walked over to the dog while it was busy eating dog food out of its dish. The little cat did not hesitate to delve into the meal as the dog backed off, snarling and growling. Kitten continued to eat nonchalantly. Ginger was a good dog.

Once Ginger escaped into the street when she was in heat. She mated with a German shepherd and became pregnant. She had a litter of pups and I was delighted when my mother allowed me to adopt one. The puppy was reddish in color and I called her Rudis (Lithuanian for "Rusty"). I loved this dog. She was small in stature and looked like a dog that was a half shepherd and half Doberman. She was smart and I had no trouble teaching her anything. My first rule was to speak to her in Lithuanian. This way only my parents and I could give her orders she could understand. She would accompany me out into the street and would heel obediently. I never needed a leash with her. Since there were potential "enemies" all around us, I would make her aware that there was danger by saying, "puff" (a word I invented). Whenever I said "puff," she would stop whatever she was doing and start growling; the hair on her back would rise and her eyes would start scanning for danger. Fortunately, I never had to use this command when there was real danger, like being accosted by some bully. She understood everything I said, it seemed. I would show off her obedience by putting her to a test: I would place a piece of raw meat on a plate on our back porch floor. We would leave Rudis alone with the dish, instructing her not to touch it. Through a side window, we would observe the dog lying on the floor with her nose an inch from the plate as if mesmerized, but she would not touch the meat. Of course, I would reward her obedience with a morsel of leftover food.

One day while I was at school, Rudis escaped into the street and mated with another dog. The result was a large litter of puppies. My mother decided to have her spayed. Sadly, Rudis died during the procedure. I was devastated. She was my bodyguard and my best friend since the days of Guzhinas, ten years earlier.

*STRANGE HAPPENINGS*
One day I overheard some college students talking about a lecture they had attended on hypnosis. What I overheard fascinated me. The students were describing how to undergo self-hypnosis. I listened carefully and then went home to try out what I had learned. It was midday and no one was home. I lay down on the living room couch and just relaxed, at first. Then I focused on my toes and mentally ordered them to "sleep." I mentally moved my focus

up from my toes, a couple of inches at a time, and ordered that part of my body to sleep. I continued this process over the full extent of my body until I reached my head. I noticed that now I still had my full faculties, but my body was weightless. I could not tell which side of my body I was lying on. With my right hand, I pinched my left forearm. I felt nothing.

Then I continued to coax my head to sleep. A strange sensation overcame me: I started losing consciousness, and psychedelic colors began whirling around in my head. The further I went into the trance, the tighter the psychedelic ring became, and the darker my consciousness. I was able to toy with going in and out of this psychedelic state. I felt safe while I was still in control. Once my mind shut down into darkness, I suspected I would no longer have any conscious control, i.e., I would be "out." The idea scared me and I never allowed myself to go that far.

Over the next few months, I toyed with self-hypnosis a few more times. When I met with some professional hypnotists, I shared my experience with them. They admitted that I was an unusually good subject and invited me to participate in their sessions (I declined to go). They agreed that I was wise not to have gone "all the way" by myself. "It may have been hard to bring you back out," they said. Many years later, I tried self-hypnosis again but was not successful. I lacked the focus and concentration of my early years. However, when in 1973 my wife was in hard labor while trying to deliver our first son (Tomas), I used my hypnosis technique on her. I succeeded in alleviating her pain, which made her relax and deliver the baby naturally,

*MY OWN CAR*
During my senior year in high school, I finally bought my own car. It was a French Citroën, model 2CV. I was attracted to this car because of its unique features and ingenious design. First of all, it was extremely economical: it got fifty-four miles per gallon! The reason for this remarkable economy was that the engine had only two cylinders, albeit large ones. If the battery died, I could start the engine with an old-fashioned crank handle. It was so low-tech that I could not help but love it. Instead of a gas gauge, it had a long dipstick. When I was down to the last gallon of gas, the engine would stop and I would turn a lever that would allow the last of the gas to be consumed. This allowed me to drive about fifty more miles to find a gas station.

The windshield wipers did not have a separate motor; they were connected to the car's driveshaft, and if I stopped at a red light, the wipers would stop also. However, if needed, I could continue to operate them manually. The windows would not roll down: they would simply flip open. The four doors could be easily unhinged and removed. The seats were similar to deck chairs and could also be removed. After a dusty ride in the desert, I could wash the interior with a garden hose. The engine weighed less than a hundred pounds and two people could lift it. The car was so light that when I got stuck in some soft sand or mud, I simply lifted one end or the other out of the rut. It was a perfect car for exploring the desert—I could go anywhere.

The 2CV did have a limitation: its maximum speed was about sixty-five miles per hour, and slower on inclines. That was OK with me. I did not have an ego that required hot-rod performance.

Disaster struck one night. I was coming home late one evening and neglected to fill the tank with gas when the warning came on. Two blocks short of my house, I was forced to park my car on the main thoroughfare (Century Boulevard). So late at night, there was little or no traffic. Around three in the morning, there was a knock at the door. It was two policemen. They asked me if I was the owner of a green Citroën 2CV. I replied yes. They informed me that it had been struck by another vehicle and had been badly damaged. They drove me to the site where I had parked it a few hours earlier, and I saw that it had been rammed from behind. It was now straddling the sidewalk. A truck must have hit it at high speed. It was not just damaged—it was totaled! There were remnants of bright-yellow paint left behind by the vehicle that struck my car. I kept samples of it in case I would ever come across a damaged truck matching this color. To no avail. The police had no interest in tracking the perpetrator down. "No death or injury was involved," they said. My insurance would not pay for the damage because I did not have collision coverage.

I was going to school and working at this time. I needed a car; public transportation during those days was notoriously deficient. I was saving money for college tuition and I used these funds to buy myself another 2CV. I dropped out of school for a year in order to make up the money lost by this accident.


## THE PREDATOR

I was fourteen when we moved into our new home on Hobart Boulevard. A twenty-six-year-old man who lived with his mother across the street welcomed us into the neighborhood. He was charming and flirtatious. My mother adored him. Over the next few weeks, he became a buddy to me. He regaled me with stories about going fishing with famous movie stars and promised to take me along sometime. He would invite me over to his house to watch television (we did not have one at our house). While we were sitting on the couch, he tried to get intimate with me; I resisted. He would invite me to shower with him, but I found his naked body disgusting. I began to reject his friendship, but he would force himself upon me physically. I did not realize that he was a pedophile because I knew nothing about sex. I was too young.

I complained to my mother, but she did not take my concerns seriously. When he invited me to spend a weekend at his aunt's cabin at Lake Elsinore, I declined. My mother thought I was being impolite and insisted I accept the invitation. It was a one-room cabin and I refused to sleep in the same bed with him. I slept on the couch and was prepared to fight him if he tried to accost me.

Again, I went to my mother and tried to explain that Ralph showed a great interest in my genitalia and would shamelessly expose his. My mother would only giggle at these descriptions of perversion. I was dismayed with her lack of concern. What was it that she did not understand? If I were a young girl and a man tried to molest me, she would have been outraged, I'm sure. Why can't women understand that boys are equally vulnerable to sexual abuse as girls, I later wondered?

I did not approach my father with this issue since I never discussed my personal problems with him. He always showed concern but could not empathize with me on an emotional level.

The dilemma with Ralph reached a crisis and caused a rift between my mother and me. This was the main reason I eventually moved out of our house and into my own apartment. My mother was saddened by this decision and did not fully comprehend my motives, I'm sure.

I would visit her on occasion over the intervening years. Once, when I showed up at her house, Ralph found out and came over to greet me. I was not happy to see him but I restrained myself from showing my disaffection. He had "wonderful" news to tell me: he was now an assistant Boy Scout leader and was having a great time with all the boys! I shuddered at the thought.

## A LOVE FOR THE HUNT

During our early immigrant years, money was tight and medical expenses could be high. There were many doctors and dentists from Europe who were perfectly qualified in their professions but could not practice because they lacked an American license. During the day, they might work as assistants for licensed practitioners, but at night they would often moonlight on their own. One such immigrant from Germany became our dentist. Dr. Richard Fehr opened shop in his living room at home. I overheard him tell tales of his weekend trips hunting jackrabbits in the Mojave Desert. I had always wanted to go hunting—ever since I heard tales of my great-grandfather's exploits in the forests of Poland and Russia. I was only fourteen, but I asked if he would take me along on one of these hunts. Thus I was introduced to hunting. A young man named Georg Hoenig, an immigrant with Hungarian and German roots, was a friend of the dentist and joined us on these trips.

Georg was eighteen years old and had a passion for hunting. He was already well on his way to becoming a professional gunsmith. In his high school metal shop, he hand built a pair of .22-caliber revolvers machined from a single block of aluminum. These revolvers were operational and could shoot accurately. He won national recognition for this project. After graduating from high school, he became a gunsmith at a highly regarded gun store called Pachmayr & Co. There he worked until he moved to Boise, Idaho, where he opened his own shop. He catered to an exclusive clientele that demanded nothing less than the best for their fine guns. More recently, he developed a revolutionary style of shotgun (and combination gun) that breaks open rotationally. They sell for about $30,000 each, and they are masterpieces.

Georg became my mentor—an "older brother" I could

trust. Not only did he teach me how to hunt small game (rabbits, ground squirrels, quail, dove, etc.), he taught me gun safety and gun care. He introduced me to classical music (like my father never could), and he showed me how to be a free thinker. On many weekends, I would join Georg on hunting trips, mostly to the Mojave Desert. Somewhere between the towns of Lancaster and Mojave, we would hunt jackrabbits. Some years these critters became prolific and the farmers would poison them (not good for the environment). Other years, we hardly saw one. Their population was cyclical. Jackrabbit meat is tough and not very tasty. I would bring some home for my dog to eat. To me, the desert was always beautiful and fascinating. I got to know the flora and fauna and developed a strong kinship with this harsh environment.

I always had to borrow other people's rifles in order to go hunting and I really wanted my own gun. My mother would have none of it. "I'll let you buy your own gun when you turn sixteen and not a day before," she insisted. When my sixteenth birthday arrived, I wasted no time in buying my first gun: a semiautomatic .22-caliber rifle, Winchester Model 63. I used this classic rifle for many years and today it is still in almost mint condition. A few months later, I bought my first shotgun, a Remington Sportsman 58 (12 gauge). I was bringing it home, driving my mother's big Buick up Western Avenue, when a police car pulled me over. The policemen suspected I was too young to drive, since I could barely see over the dashboard. My driver's license proved I was of legal age. Then they noticed the new shotgun on the back seat and several boxes of ammunition on the floor. I explained to them that I enjoyed hunting and had just purchased this weapon. They believed me. As luck would have it, these two policemen were also hunters. They were fascinated by the newly released Sportsman 58 and spent time admiring it. Then they waved me on, wishing me good luck hunting.

Most of my hunts involved small game; sometimes, I tried my hand at big game. Bear and mountain lions (cougars) were always high on my list. I've seen black bear during my jaunts through the forest, but never when I had a gun with me during hunting season. Cougars I never saw in or off-season, though on numerous occasions, I saw cougar tracks and had the eerie feeling I was being watched by one of these big cats. Once, while hunting deer in Northern California, I nearly got shot by another hunter. It was midday and I knew that the deer would be bedded down for their midday nap. So I tried the old Indian trick of slowly walking through the dense undergrowth, a few steps at a time (just like a deer would) in the hopes of stumbling onto a napping deer. Well, I must have been very convincing, because as I emerged from a dense clump of brush, I found myself staring straight into the end of a rifle barrel. The hunter holding the gun in my face was trembling with excitement. He had been listening to the deer-like rustling I was making and was sure I was his deer. Fortunately, he refrained from pulling the trigger before realizing that I was a fellow hunter.

During one of these hunting trips, I came across a landfill (dump) deep in the foothills of the Sierras. I was not surprised to see a dozen or so crows scavenging for food. I did not expect to see people scavenging through the refuse. These were unusual people—they were Gypsy women, five of them. They were dressed in many layers of colorful skirts and blouses, as if still living in the nineteenth century. There was no car or pickup truck around, so their men must have dropped them off. I was impressed by the similarities between the crows and Gypsies: both live by their wits on the outskirts of society and both have strong family networks. In Lithuanian folklore, crows (and ravens) are associated with good omens.


## RIDING WITH COSSACKS

Jurgis Peteris was the husband of Jone, one of my mother's closest friends. They were frequent guests at our home on the Baltic coast. They immigrated to the USA and settled in Cleveland. While there, Mr. Peteris succumbed to a severe form of arthritic rheumatism. He lost half his body weight in a rather short period of time and was told he did not have much longer to live. His doctors told him that his only chance for survival was to move to the desert of the Southwest. His family could not afford such a move. My mother offered to take him in with us in Los Angeles. After all, the climate here was dry and warm. My father and I constructed a small bedroom attached to the rear of our garage. It was roughly five feet wide and eighteen feet long. This became Mr. Peteris's bedroom for the next two years.

When he arrived, we hardly recognized him. He was no more than skin and bones and looked thirty years older than his fifty-eight years. His tenure in our household greatly affected my life. Whereas my father worked long hours and spent the rest of the time at the piano, Mr. Peteris had little to do except read various newspapers and the books he loved. He soon started to enjoy my company and I found him a most fascinating human being.

When he was a young man and Lithuania was still under the rule of the czars, he joined the Russian army. The Russian Revolution broke out and he volunteered to fight with the Imperial Cossack cavalry. He was an expert horseman. The Cossack tribes were famous horsemen and fierce fighters. They were part of the Imperial army but never integrated with Russian army regulars. They had their own military hierarchy, which the Russian officers respected. It was highly unusual for an outsider to fight alongside these legendary horsemen, and young Mr. Peteris was such an exception.

Of course I was only too eager to hear all about his military exploits. He explained to me that when two opposing cavalry units would spot one another on an open field, they would attack in formation, sabers drawn. Then, as the horsemen would surge through each other's lines, they had only one chance to take a swing at their opponent. The idea was to kill or disable the rider who was confronting you. However, because of the high speed involved, a disabling blow was hard to execute. When one or more horsemen were hit (that is, injured or killed), the skirmish was terminated and each side rode off to lick its wounds (so to speak). I asked the inevitable question, "Did you ever kill an opponent?" He raised his right hand and showed me an old long scar. "Here is where a falling saber sliced me when I struck an opponent across the small of his neck." I was impressed.

Mr. Peteris was an old-fashioned gentlemen, the kind we associate with the Old South. I never saw him without a white shirt and tie. He adored my mother and there was nothing he would not do for her. Even though they had known each other for over thirty years, they addressed each other formally, by their respective titles (Mr. or Mrs.). During family parties, he would spend a limited amount of time with the "older generation" before deftly drifting over to where the youngsters were gathered. He was welcome company with us because he was young in spirit and full of humor. He had one bad habit: he smoked cigarettes, but only outdoors.

Mr. Peteris was a master chess player and he offered to teach me the game. I caught on fast and he noticed that I had a natural aptitude for the game. At first, he would play me minus his queen. That would be his handicap in order to make the game interesting for him and give me a fighting chance. After a few months, I became good enough so that he would play me without a rook, and later without a bishop. That's about as good as I got. I would never be able to beat him without some handicap.

During my junior year, I tried out for the high school chess team and won a spot on the four-man team. In tournaments, I played position number four. The top three positions were taken by senior class-men. This meant that I was destined to be the number-one player the following year, a position then occupied by a talented player from Cuba named Raul.

Our first inter-mural game was against Jefferson High School. My opponent was an intelligent black student who played a good game. I barely fought off his attacks and was greatly relieved when the game was over. Future games that season were not nearly as hard for me as that first game against the kid from Jefferson High School. I remained undefeated and we won first place in our league. This victory qualified us for the city championship game. Unfortunately, Raul got sick and could not participate. Our coach, Mr. Hertzl, knew that our chances for winning were slim. His strategy was to sacrifice position number one and hope to win the other three boards. I became the sacrificial lamb. I was not happy about it. After all, I wanted to maintain an undefeated track record.

This time my opponent was a jovial senior of Mexican descent. He was a superior player and displayed his confidence with lots of humor. I was not in a mood for jokes. I played hard with an aggressive strategy, intent on winning. In the end, I lost my nerve and caved in. It was a loss that shattered my confidence. The following year, I declined to join the team, much to Mr. Hertzl's disappointment. I would have been his best player. I did not play chess again for many years. I was burned out.

## SEX EDUCATION

When it came to sex, I was a late bloomer. Sure, I experienced my first kiss in Munich when I was about nine. I held hands at a movie with a fourteen-year-old girl once. I went on a date once or twice while in high school. However, none of these experiences ever aroused any interest in the opposite sex. Why waste time with girls when there was hardly time to do exciting things like hunting, mountain climbing, skiing, surfing, etc.?

So, when some of my streetwise friends started talking about how babies are made (by intercourse), I just laughed. "No way!" I said. "That's the silliest thing I ever heard of. What...? Roosters do it with hens? Ha, ha! Every animal does it? You guys are putting me on!" But then I started noticing that dogs would meet in a sexual way. I had just never put two and two together. Then a horrible thought struck me: Do my parents have sex? Well, I was here, so it must have happened at least once. I never saw my parents sleep in the same bed. For that matter, they usually had separate bedrooms. I guess they were old-fashioned when it came to their privacy. When I accidentally came upon some condoms stashed away in my father's drawer, I was shocked. *Do they still do it? Why?*

My buddies were bragging about conquests that they had made with girls. Once was not enough. A handsome guy named Chuck claimed to have had sex with various girls—fourteen times! The rest of us admired him for this accomplishment as if he were some sort of noble gladiator. I now doubt if half of these stories had any truth to them. I too started telling stories of conquests. It was the manly thing to do. They were face-saving lies, of course. Just to sound more convincing, I carried a condom in my wallet, so that I could say I was ready for any opportunity. This impressed my buddies to no end.

During the mid-fifties, there was a dance hall in downtown LA where young men could find clean-cut young women to dance with—no strings attached. You simply bought a string of tickets at the entrance door for twenty-five cents apiece. The music was provided by a gramophone. When you felt confident that you could dance to the music being played, you walked over to where a selection of young ladies were sitting (usually young college girls) and asked for a dance by giving her one of the tickets you purchased at the door. The whole affair was kind of sterile and boring, and I did not attend the event again. A better option was to sign up for Arthur Murray's Dance Lessons, which was not cheap. But at least I learned to dance properly.

I did some dating during my college years. I even fell madly in love once. These women were always attractive and I was sexually awakened. Nonetheless, the women I dated remained virgins, and so did I.

*AMERICA'S HEARTLAND*
During the summer of 1955, I turned sixteen and my mother was concerned about the growing number of delinquents in our neighborhood. Some of my friends started smoking, not just cigarettes but cannabis. Gang activity was on the rise, and vandalism was becoming more prevalent. My mother decided to send me off to work on a farm in Indiana. The Carter family had been our original sponsor when we first arrived in America, but then they reneged. Nevertheless, my mother kept in touch with them and now wanted to know if these farmers would allow me to work for them that summer in exchange for room and

board. It seemed like a fair deal and they accepted.

Carter Farms is a five-hundred-acre ranch near the town of Gaston in central Indiana. The owners, Urban Carter and his wife, were your archetypal all-American farmers: hardworking, patriotic, generous, proud, and down-to-earth. Their son (Gordon) and his wife followed in the footsteps of the elders. Gordon was a bright and handsome young man around thirty years old. He graduated from Ball State University with a perfect 4.0 grade point average. His hobbies included performing at rodeos; he was an expert with the lariat and the sixteen-foot bullwhip. He became my mentor. Urban had a younger brother who was mentally disabled, the result of chicken pox during early childhood. Gordon would wash and shave his uncle every morning before breakfast.

My daily chores included feeding the chickens and collecting their eggs (about two hundred) from the henhouse before breakfast every morning. I would also clean the eggs and sort them according to size. In the evening, I would shovel out the manure in the horse stall and spread out a layer of straw. The horse was named Major. He was a beautiful quarter horse stallion, about ten years old. Gordon led every local parade riding this magnificent animal. Since he was a stallion (stud), Major had to be kept locked up in the barn all day so that he would not go after the mares grazing in the pastures. After all my chores were done, I would saddle Major up and take him for a run. By the end of the day, Major was keen to go.

At the local general store, I was outfitted with a straw cowboy hat (the sun was intense) and a pair of cowboy boots (so my feet would stay in the stirrups). I received riding lessons from Gordon, but they were hardly sufficient to make me a skilled horseman. Quarter horses are bred to herd cattle. They accelerate quickly and they can turn on a dime in order to cut a steer from the herd. While in the saddle, I could feel the muscles of the big beast beneath me straining to let loose with all his power. I would always rein him in and he would respond like a true champion, which he was. Early on, I made the mistake of turning my head to the left or right to glance at something. Major took this as a signal and turned ninety degrees on a dime, while I kept on going straight, head over heels! I managed to avoid such mistakes in the future. Sometimes, I would allow Major to accelerate without restraining him. It was a thrill to feel such power! But I never had the nerve to let him reach full speed. I feared I might lose control.

Between breakfast and dinner, I would join the men out in the fields. There were wheat fields that needed reaping, alfalfa fields that needed mowing, cattle that needed herding, and hay that had to be baled and loaded onto flatbed trucks. The latter was backbreaking work. There was a flock of sheep and the males had to be castrated. The technique was called "clamping" and was bloodless.

On weekends, we would relax and have fun. I learned to use the lariat and the bullwhip. Gordon could take the whip and flip the ashes off a cigarette at a distance of sixteen feet. At a rodeo, a beautiful cowgirl held the cigarette between her lips. I preferred to hold a piece of straw in my fingers with my arm fully extended. Gordon never missed.

There were old-fashioned picnics and swimming at a small lake. Neighbors would meet and kids of both sexes would make plans for movies, hayrides, roller-skating, etc. I met a lovely girl my age and we felt a certain attraction. With other couples, we would meet at the local A&W drive-in and order root-beer floats in ice-cold mugs. I enjoyed her company, but I was not ready for any kind of romancing. I was too focused on the many adventures that were still awaiting me.

For an inner-city kid, this was an unforgettable summer. I will always be grateful to the Carters for giving me the opportunity to experience life in the American heartland. This is where Thomas Jefferson's ideal of an American Republic still lives.

*GROWING UP*
At sixteen years of age, I was still a shrimp, barely five feet four inches tall. I would religiously measure myself against the jamb of our bathroom door. My mother would hold a ruler horizontally over my head while I tried to stretch as high as possible without lifting my heels off the floor. I complained to her that I did not like being so short in stature. She assured me that one of these days I would grow up to be tall; the gypsy had said so. "You're just a late developer," she would assure me. I did everything in my power to expedite my growth. I drank a half-gallon of milk every day because someone told me that milk contained vitamins essential for strong and healthy bones—

where the growing takes place! I would sleep at night stretched out to the fullest extent because my aunt Mura said curling up during sleep inhibits growth. Nothing seemed to make a difference.

When I was seventeen, we began to notice that the monthly lines on the bathroom door jamb demarking my height were being spaced farther apart. I was accelerating! During one twelve-month period, I grew nine inches. I reached a height of six foot one and eventually stopped growing at six foot two. It seemed like a miracle. Girls in my class started noticing me.

*OUTDOOR ACTIVITIES*

The fashionable thing to do while in high school was to see who had the most souped-up hot-rod and who was seen with the most attractive "chicks." Neither field interested me much. I liked sports and the great outdoors.

I had heard that there was a summer soccer league (Fussball!) at a park called Dorsey, in the west of LA. It included many foreign players of all ages, but mostly Germans. I became interested; I was seventeen. Some of my older Lithuanian friends were members of one of the soccer teams and invited me to come for a tryout. They were of drinking age, and after the games they would enjoy "replaying" them over pitchers of beer. I hitchhiked across town and participated in a scrimmage. I still possessed some of those skills that made me a standout in Munich, and the regulars on the field invited me to join their team.

After the scrimmage, I did not join my friends for a beer (I was too young). I began walking back toward Crenshaw Boulevard in order to hitch a ride back home when I noticed a bunch of black kids following me. They soon caught up and started taunting me. Then they demanded money. I emptied my pockets and showed them I had none. Before I knew it, they started attacking me. I was knocked out—cold. When I came to, the thugs were nowhere to be seen. Somewhat sore but not seriously hurt, I proceeded to hitchhike home. I decided not to attend any more games at Dorsey Park.

On some occasions, I would drive to Venice Beach (near Santa Monica) with teammates from our high school gymnastic team. There was an area called "Muscle Beach" where world-class weight lifters strutted their stuff. Most of the time, we watched these muscular men lift huge weights above their heads. Sometimes, we were more interested in watching their bikini-clad ladies, who were also bodybuilders.

The main reason for coming here was the excellent gymnastic equipment located on the beach. This included a high bar, parallel bars, and swinging rings. Some of the best gymnasts in Southern California would do their routines here, and we would learn from them. Some were stuntmen from Hollywood. Here I saw a man do a triple flip from the swinging rings—a rare feat in those days.

During the summer of 1956, my mother bought a 1953 Buick so that she would not have to hitchhike to work. On weekends, she would loan me the car. During those occasions, I would drive over the San Bernardino Mountains and into the desert. They were exploratory trips and usually I would make them without companions.

Driving eastward one weekend, I came upon Joshua Tree National Monument. It is a beautiful desert park strewn with old granite "boulders" as big as small buildings. I scrambled over them and regretted not having a climbing partner with a rope. It is now a national park, and climbers from all over the world come to test their mettle on these challenging routes.

Many a summer weekend was spent playing at one of the many beaches that line the LA coast: Manhattan, Hermosa, Santa Monica, and El Segundo were among my favorites. In wood shop at school, I built a belly board from a piece of plywood and used it to surf the waves.

Once a year, we would participate in a grunion run. The grunion is a little fish (a little bigger than a smelt) that travels all over the Pacific Ocean but lays its eggs only on the beaches around Southern California. They come in at night only during a full moon. When the tide is highest, they ride a wave onto the beach. The female digs its tail into the sand to lay its eggs while the male encircles her with his body. People come out with bags and buckets to pick the fish up before they can return to the water on the next wave. When they arrive on the beach, the glistening bodies can be seen in the moonlight. They make good eating when panfried in butter.

One evening I used my mother's car to visit a friend via

Figueroa Street. It was dark and the streets were nearly empty. I was driving at the speed limit if not a little more. The light was green ahead of me, but then I noticed that two kids were rushing to cross the intersection. I could have veered around them, but when they saw me coming at a fast clip, one of them decided to turn back while the other continued to run across. Now I had an awful dilemma: I would have to hit one or the other; there was not enough time to stop. I decided to "thread the needle" by driving in between them, hoping for the best. I barely evaded the boy on the left, but the one on the right glanced off my fender and went down.

I looked in my rearview mirror and saw that the kid was lying on the ground and not moving. I was in shock. There were cars behind me in the distance. As I coasted along at five miles per hour, I considered fleeing. My mind was in a whirl. After about a hundred yards, I pulled over and parked the car. I walked back to the accident site and found a blanket over the kid and several adults talking to him. One man came up to me and asked if I was the person driving the Buick. I nodded. He then shook my hand and congratulated me for a "splendid job maneuvering the car" to avoid hitting the two kids.

Then I noticed that the kid was trying to get up. He felt fine, he said. Bystanders insisted he stay put until the ambulance arrived. When the medics came, they checked him over and declared him healthy. Apparently, the glancing contact did not harm him. He ran off to meet up with his buddy.

Back home, I told my parents what happened. We were afraid that the kid's family might decide to concoct an injury and try to sue us. So we did the right thing: we reported the incident to the insurance company. It was one of the big national firms. They responded by canceling our policy. In those days, this was a legal (though not ethical) procedure. My parents found another insurance company that took us in the high-risk category. The cost of this policy was more than double the old one.

## THE GROSCH SAGA CONTINUES

During high school, my old friend Schurick and I drifted apart. Whereas I was active in sports, Schurick was more interested in the shadier side of social activity. There was a contingent of students who habitually smoked marijuana during class breaks. They would hang out at the far side of the gym building. Schurick was an active member of this group. He tried hard to get me to smoke a joint with him, but I resisted. I warned him that smoking marijuana could lead to more serious drugs later. He would laugh at me and shake his head. "I know better than that. I would never touch the hard stuff," he would assure me.

Schurick was a talented swimmer (breaststroke and butterfly), but he made no attempt to join the swim team. He was intelligent, but his academic efforts waned. He was tall, dark, and handsome (really!) and girls fell for him. He did not have to brag about his conquests. There were many. After high school, he served in the army for a while —in artillery, like his father. In civilian life, he learned the trade of welding and supported himself that way.

With his dark complexion, he could easily pass as a Mexican (except for his blue eyes). Eventually, he integrated into the Latino community and they kept him well supplied with marijuana. He married a lovely girl of Mexican descent and they had a baby girl. Unfortunately, by then Schurick was a heroin addict. He went to prison. From San Quentin, he would write me letters, but I declined to respond. Heroin addicts have a reputation for leaning on their friends to pay for their addiction, and I did not want him coming to me. Then tragedy struck. His wife committed suicide by jumping out of the window of an office building where she worked. Mr. and Mrs. Grosch adopted their little grandchild. They were living on a small pension and could hardly make ends meet. I would discreetly send them money when I could afford it.

Then tragedy struck again. While driving home one night, the grandparents did not notice a railroad warning, and their car collided with a train. They were both killed instantly. In a way, I thought this may have been a blessing. If one of them had died before the other, the survivor would have had a tough time living alone. Their granddaughter was put up for adoption.

My mother often argued with her best friend Mura over the wisdom of using corporal punishment with their respective boys. Mura was adamantly opposed to spankings of any kind and the parents never did so with Schurick. On the other hand, I got spanked plenty. I am not sure that this is a good example to use, but in my case the spanking did not seem wasted.

## GRADUATION

In June of 1957, I graduated from high school. Dr. Fisher, the principal, called me into his office to hand me my diploma personally. I had an overall grade average of B+, but that was disappointing to him. He delivered a harsh lecture: "Alex, you have the talent and brains to have been an A student. This B average is a poor showing of your potential. You did not take academics here seriously and you did not apply yourself fully. I know that you plan to go to college, but if you continue in this way, you'll never succeed." I apologized to him and promised to try harder in college.

It was senior prom time. For many, especially the girls, this was the big event where they would dress up formally and celebrate graduation with a romantic date. For many of us boys, even if we had a date, it was a compulsory event that was to be tolerated at best. The classmates I hung out with did not date very much. So, with my best buddy, Terry Blackstad, and some friends, I participated in the senior prom to a limited degree. We did not attend the dance (we would have been wallflowers), but we did go to the dinner show. The latter was held at a famous nightclub called the Cocoanut Grove (on Wilshire Boulevard). The main attraction was a musician by the name of Louis Armstrong (yes, Satchmo!). It was a memorable evening. The next time that I saw any of my high school classmates again was at the twenty-five-year reunion.

Dove hunting in central California with friends employed by Pachmayr Gun Works, Los Angeles. Georg Hoenig (second from right) was 18 years old at the time. Alex (right) was 15. Georg later moved to Idaho and became a renown gunsmith.

Alex is the shortest guy in this 9th grade class picture at Bret Harte Junior High School. Three years later he grew to be over 6 feet tall and the girls began to notice him.

Viktor Peteris was like a brother to Alex, going back to the days in Lithuania. At left he is taking cigarette break while in the army during the Korean war. He became a successful architect and married Ilona - the beautiful and talented Lithuanian artist. More recently, they celebrated their 50th wedding anniversary, which Alex was able to attend.

# A GOOD HUNT

I love a good hunt.  But, as Robert Service said so well about "...just finding the gold" and not really wanting it, I can relate the same sentiment about hunting.  Our ancestors hunted for food and some of that instinct must still be lurking deep down inside of us.  Most modern hunters enjoy it as a hobby because of a basic love for nature (including animals!). There is also the opportunity to interact with companions on a more basic level which civilization and city life seem to deny.  The psychological term for this is called "male bonding" (and applies to women, as well).  Just as often I would enjoy the hunt alone.  In a way, I may have been bonding with myself (if that's possible) or, more likely, I was bonding with nature and the animal I was hunting.

Animals in the wild expect to be hunted.  In the big "food chain" is there an animal that is exempt from a predator of some kind?  I don't think so.  The only exception may be:  modern man.

I was barely sixteen when my mother finally allowed me to acquire my first rifle (a Model 63 Winchester).

It held ten rounds of .22 caliber cartridges that could be shot in rapid succession — perfect for hunting jackrabbits that proliferated the Mojave Desert. Local farmers would set out poison for the rabbits, which damaged their crop during periods of overpopulation. Shooting them was more sporting and certainly more environmentally friendly.

With Georg Hoenig, who was eighteen at the time, I savored these opportunities to escape city life in Los Angeles and the crime-ridden streets where I lived as an inner-city youth. I became familiar with desert life and the flora and fauna that managed to survive there in a delicate balance. These were "poor man's hunts." We were all immigrants and hunting jackrabbits was all we could afford. Later, when I acquired a shotgun, I expanded my hunting horizons by going after desert quail and dove. Shooting a bird "on the wing" required greater skill, and they tasted a lot better than jackrabbits!

After hunting in the California desert for about three years I thought I had seen it in all its forms. One cold November morning I witnessed a rare occurrence. As we began our descent down the east slope of the San Bernardino Mountains the great expanse of the Mojave lay before us. The heavens were uniformly gray and unusually dark. By the time we reached the town of Palmdale it started snowing lightly. By the time we passed Lancaster it was snowing so hard that we realized that hunting would not be feasible with so little visibility. Georg pulled his Volkswagen camper off the highway and we began to look for a sheltered spot among some hills nearby.

We found a small cave and stashed our gear in it. Since we couldn't hunt, we set up a "trap" (a device that could throw "clay pigeons" into the air) and we spent the next couple of hours "trap shooting."

At around two in the afternoon the snowfall ended abruptly. We stopped blasting our shotguns when the setting before us opened up as if a curtain had been lifted.  The desert was totally transformed from a predominantly yellow-ochre to all white!  Everything was white:  the hills, the ground before us, the sage-brush, Joshua trees, and cacti.  There was also a silence that I had not experienced before.  It was a silence that makes you stop and listen.

We were in awe of this transformed wonderland and wandered out of the little cave, which smelled of burnt gunpowder.  Not more than two hundred feet from the cave entrance I came upon animal tracks. Not one set, but dozens.  There were several rabbit tracks meandering aimlessly, many kinds of bird tracks leading in different directions, coyote tracks skirting the brush, and tracks I could not even identify.  What astounded me most was that these tracks were made close to the time before the snow stopped falling, just a few minutes earlier. This profuse activity was happening right in front of us and we never saw it! Our prolific shooting must have had little effect on the wildlife here.  These animals must have also had supreme confidence that they were out of our sight. I stood there looking at the tracks and back at the cave, dumbfounded. "How could we not see so many wild creatures passing right under our noses?" I wondered.

It was a lesson I always remembered: you may not see any animals around you, but you can bet your bottom dollar, there are many, many of "them" watching you. As we drove back over the San Bernardino Mountains, now covered by a mantle of snow, we felt we had been treated to a rare performance in a desert more alive than we ever imagined.

Jackrabbits are challenging to hunt because they run fast. Cottontail rabbits need to be "hunted." They live in close proximity to fresh water and do not range far from their burrow hidden by lots of brush. If you surprise one at close range, he'll run so erratically that you won't hit him, unless you have a shotgun. Their meat is tasty. A more esoteric form of hunting is long-range varmint shooting. Prairie (or desert) gophers, woodchucks and other burrowing animals provide a challenge to the hunter because they don't allow you to get close. It takes patience, a steady aim, and a long-range rifle with a scope to outsmart these critters. I went one step further and custom-loaded my own high-velocity cartridges for better accuracy.

Crows also fall into this category of long-range hunting. This wily bird seems to know not only when you're hunting it, but also the range of your particular rifle and it will usually stay (just barely) out of range. The rest of the time crows will make a nuisance of themselves, flying all around you and making an awful racket.

While hunting crows northeast of Ojai (Ventura County), a huge bird landed on a fence post not a hundred feet away from me. It was bigger than any bird I had ever seen and I quickly put the cross-hairs of my scope on it. Then I realized that this was no ordinary raven, it was a California Condor. This dumb bird just sat there looking at me while I could have knocked it off with a well-aimed rock. No wonder these birds nearly became extinct.

"Upland game" includes birds that like to live and forage on dry land. All are masters of camouflage. Quail run around in coveys and when you flush them from their hiding places they explode into flight all at the same time. Pheasants, on the other hand, are solitary creatures, and when flushed make a fast and singular flight to the next hiding place. Probably the most challenging birds for a hunter are the wily chukkars (partridges). These hardy little birds like to live on hillsides where they feed by running uphill, and when flushed they fly downhill. Their drumsticks are inordinately large and savory. In hunting them you must first listen for their cackle, that's how they keep in touch with each other. You can hear them a mile away. While pursuing them (uphill) they will continue their noisy cackling, which may go on for long and exhausting distances. Sometimes, the cackling will cease and the birds will seem to have disappeared. A novice hunter will think the birds have outrun him. Then, when he least expects it, the birds will explode into flight all around him, causing a near heart attack and providing a challenging target to hit.

With time, experience, and increased ambition, I progressed to "big game" hunting. In California that meant deer, black bear, and mountain lion (for which there was a bounty). By this time I was subscribing to every hunting magazine in the country and became a full-fledged member of the National Rifle Association. There was not a book on hunting at the local library that I had not read. It was open season on mountain lions and I knew that the Sierras were full of them. I spent hundreds of hours tracking them and covered whole mountain ranges without so much as getting a glimpse of one. I did become familiar with their habits and habitat.

Bears were a little easier: I actually heard one crashing through the brush one time. The encounter almost scared me to death. Another time, I was stealthily working my way through some underbrush, behaving like a deer, I thought, when to my great surprise, I came face to face with a hunter ready to shoot me. He had a bad case of "buck fever," for his shaking rifle was aimed directly at me, just a few feet away. His anxious face betrayed his disbelief that I was not really a deer. Thank God, his rifle did not have a hair trigger. This frightful experience taught me to avoid popular hunting areas.

To get away from the throng of nature-loving hunters of Southern California, I drove about 250 miles north to Big Pine, on the eastern flanks of the Sierra Nevada Mountains. Here, I arranged with an outfitter for a horse that could take me high up into the remote mountains (and help me carry my trophy deer back). Camp was made in the lower part of the valley and I only took my rifle and a small knapsack with lunch for the day outing. The trail zigzagged up the steep mountainside as I covered terrain that would have taken me days on foot. From near timberline I enjoyed views of the beautiful High Sierras. The sun was moving toward the horizon and it was getting chilly. Seeing this wild scenery made me almost forget that I was hunting. As I started my descent into the valley the light began to fade. I noticed a herd of deer on the opposite slope — probably two hundred yards away. They were grazing, seemingly oblivious to the hunter on his horse. Such herds always have two or three young bucks among them, but with the diminishing light, I couldn't tell which deer had antlers without looking through my ten-powered scope. To do this, I needed to dismount and lean against the ground to steady the sight. Sure enough, the bucks were there. At two hundred yards my high-powered rifle could make a hit (if my heart would only stop pounding and allow a steady aim).

Just as I was holding my breath and beginning to squeeze the trigger, I noticed a movement out of the corner of my eye: the old nag was casually walking back down the trail. "Christ!" I thought, "I better catch that beast of burden before she decides to run away." Actually, her decision was already made, for every time I ran up to her and could just about reach her trailing reins, she would gallop forward. The thought of spending the next few days hiking back to camp in this cold September weather, not to mention night without fire or food, was rather discomforting. I abandoned my rifle and ran after my horse as fast as I could. The animal kept her head cocked around so she could see me with one eye and always managed to outdistance me, as if to tease me. This was not a game that I was going to win, I soon concluded. I became desperate. A new strategy had to be under-taken, after all, the beast is dumb and man is smart, right? With all the remaining strength that I could muster I began to run directly downhill, crossing the switch-back trail until I arrived in front of the surprised horse. I grabbed the reins and collapsed in a heap, gasping for air with bursting lungs. We returned to pick up my rifle and I could tell that the deer were still grazing, as before. However, there was not enough light to take a shot, and I'm sure they knew it.

The hunting season in Washington State is arranged so that the deer season is followed immediately by the elk season. This arrangement is deliberate so that you cannot hunt deer and elk at the same time. These animals know this, I'm sure. One year I took some time off to hunt both (sequentially). I found the perfect little meadow with a large slope of boulders bordering one side. It was deer season and for three days I sat comfortably hidden among the big boulders — waiting for a buck to show up. On the third day an elk with a respectable rack of antlers proceeded to graze across the meadow. Since it was still deer season I had to refrain from shooting it. It just so happened that elk season would start the following day. With great anticipation I arrived at the boulders before dawn and waited for the elk to come again. Instead, a buck with big antlers proceeded to meander across the meadow. How these animals know the hunting schedule so well is still a riddle to me. I quit the meadow in disgust and decided to hunt elk in dense woods. For hours I walked stealthily through thick pine forest. Eventually, my skill and perseverance paid off. I came across a herd of elk mingling nervously among the profusion of trees directly ahead of me. The problem was that the branches of the trees obscured anything above five feet. I could see dozens of elk legs but not their heads or antlers. Desperately, I tried to identify the male species by the organs between their hind legs. I figured a big pair of balls would be equivalent to a large set of antlers. Before I could make proper identification, the herd sensed my presence and ran off.

Later that season I was still without a deer or an elk in my bag. I decided to partake in the late elk hunt that takes place in November. The plateau between Ellensburg and Wenatchee is a well-known migration route for elk herds. By November stragglers continue to travel through here and both sexes may be hunted. This time I was determined to get my elk. Their meat is known to be tastier than the finest beef you can buy. I decided a sure thing would be to track one down. I came across two sets of tracks that appeared to belong to a bull and a cow. Like an Indian from the many books I had read, I followed the tracks until sundown forced me to bivouac under a large pine. At first sign of light I got up and followed the track to their bed nearby, which was still warm. I knew I was close. By sundown I still had not gotten a glimpse of either elk, but judging by the droppings they left, I knew they were not far away. The following day the pattern was the same. The elk seemed in no hurry. Their general direction was southerly but they tended to meander all over. I felt like I was beginning to know their habits and a certain affection for these two stragglers was beginning to develop. I woke on the third morning and saw a big bull with a large rack of antlers grazing in the grass not fifty feet away. I did not dare make a move, lest I scare it away. My rifle was next to me, but the elk was so close I am sure he would have bolted the minute I made a move. So, I just remained prone — admiring the great bull chewing the dew-covered grass, seemingly oblivious to me. I felt privileged to be in the presence of such a magnificent beast.

Many years later I was invited to hunt elk on a property belonging to a rancher who had a special permit to shoot elk (of both sexes) that were invading his apple orchard. He saved the taking of bull elks for himself and special clients. He offered to let me shoot a cow. Since I was more interested in elk meat than big trophy horns, I took him up on the invitation. I enlisted my 28-year-old son (Nik) to join me since he was in better shape to cover hilly terrain than his aging father. At one point we saw some elk disappear over a hilltop and I suggested my son sneak around to the other side and try to prod the elk to come my way.

Two hours later Nik returned empty handed, but with an interesting story. He said that the elk we saw included two bulls and several cows. It was mid-day and the elk settled down for a rest. When he approached them, the cows got up and meandered off. The two bulls, however, remained sitting on the ground. When within about a hundred yards of them, Nik also sat down. They continued to observe each other respectfully. Of course, he could not shoot the antlered elk — his permission was for shooting a cow. Unfortunately, the cows decided to relocate into the next valley while the two bulls remained within shooting range. They eyed each other for a better part of an hour before Nik decided to come back to where I was.

How did the cows know to keep out of shooting range and how did the bulls know that we were not allowed to shoot them? That is a riddle that I have not been able to answer. Though, I have experienced this uncanny phenomenon on numerous occasions.

One of the most exciting hunts of all is completely
victimless. The modern "fox hunt" is now a "drag
hunt." The scent of a fox is dragged through a prescribed obstacle course, involving fallen logs, ditches
(wet and dry) and flat terrain where the horses can
run all-out behind the hounds who are in frantic pursuit of the "fox." The rules are strict: the "huntsmen"
wear red jackets and the "master of the hunt" signals
with a French horn. A sip of sherry starts the hunt off
and Irish coffee greets the weary and dirty hunters on
their well-lathered horses at the end of the hunt. The
hounds are rewarded with a barrel full of cow gut,
which they savagely rip to pieces and devour. Now,
that's civilized hunting.

Some of my best memories of hunting involved two
old timers who honored me by including me in their
annual duck hunt. Chauncy Griggs and Joe Collins
were lifelong buddies, and every fall they would go
duck hunting in the "Pot Holes" region of Eastern
Washington. These were usually guided hunts
where decoys were expertly set out before daylight.
By dawn we would be standing in "blinds" — knee
deep along the edge of a shallow pond surrounded
by reeds. The sky would begin to turn from dark and
starry to light blue. Silently, we would watch color develop on the horizon. Ducks could be heard quacking
nervously in nearby ponds. When the official sunrise
time arrived, our guide would use his "duck call" so
convincingly that birds heading for Mexico - a thousand feet up, would make a sharp u-turn and head
straight down to our pond.

We used to stay in an old trailer, affectionately called the "Smyrna Hilton," and tell endless stories of memorable hunts, discuss Greek philosophy, and relate amusing histories of all kinds. Chauncy retired from hunting when his eyesight began to fail him. Joe literally keeled over one morning while setting decoys off the beach in front of his island home. Both were well into their eighties when they joined the happy hunting grounds in the sky.

Now that the hunting fervor has subsided in my primeval libido, I still look back at the great encounters I had with my wild brethren. Once, sitting quietly on a ridge, I spent a good hour watching a coyote trying to catch marmots. As soon as he would sneak up on a mound containing a marmot, another one would pop his head out nearby and whistle. Instantly, the coyote would charge over to the perpetrator who by then had slipped back into his hole. At that point another member of the clan would pop his head out and whistle. As this one sided game continued the coyote became frantic. Finally, the frustrated coyote trotted away from the colony of marmots — ignoring a hail of whistles.

As a father I tried to introduce Nik to the spirit of hunting. While he was still too young to carry a real gun, I gave him an air rifle. One time, while we grown ups went off to hunt pheasants nearby we left my son to "hunt" a cottontail rabbit that was living at the edge of a farm we were visiting. Nik was excited with such an opportunity and took his task seriously. When we returned we found Nik holding his air rifle in one hand and a dead rabbit in the other. His face displayed rather mixed emotions: on the one hand he was proud to have hunted down the rabbit and shot it, on the other hand, he loved little animals and could not stand the thought that he had actually hurt one. A few months later, Nikki acquired a pet rabbit which lived with us for several years, like a family member. The subject of hunting rabbits became taboo. Though, he did concede that rabbits in captivity live twice as long as in the wild. The reason: in the wild they get eaten by predators before they grow old.

# Chapter VII:
# MILITARY SERVICE

*NATIONAL GUARD*
During my senior year in high school the military draft was in effect. If called up, you served two years. That was a long time to be out of circulation, I thought. Fortunately, under the Eisenhower administration, an alternative was introduced that allowed young men to serve only six months active duty with an additional four years in the active reserves, including the National Guard. My hunting partner, Georg Hoenig, and I decided to take advantage of the latter option.

We joined a California National Guard unit located in Canoga Park (a suburb of San Fernando Valley). It was a long drive from southwest LA, but it was worth it. This unit had the reputation of being one of the best companies in

California. Officers, whose day job was working as policemen with the Los Angeles Police Department, commanded it. About half of the 80 or so soldiers in this company were of Mexican descent. The rest were Caucasians. The Mexicans were a jovial group. There were pranksters and jokesters among them. None was a troublemaker. In fact, most of them were religious family men. There was a lot of camaraderie in this company and we all got along well. Our First Sergeant ran a tight ship. He was a no-nonsense medical student at UCLA. He could have been commissioned to an officer's rank, but he loved his job as the top dog with us grunts.

Company D of the 2nd Medium Tank Battalion, 185th Armor, of the 40th Armored Division was a tank outfit. Our primary weapon was the M57 tank (later substituted by the more advanced M60 "Abrams"). This was a fifty-ton monster on tracks; we learned to use it with deadly precision. In addition to the 90mm cannon, it was mounted with a 50 cal. machine gun. Two huge Chrysler engines powered the tank. An auxiliary motor had to be used to start them up. The tanks' rate of gas consumption was about one quarter of a mile to the gallon.

The company also stocked a variety of "small arms" weapons, starting with the 45 cal pistol, 45 cal sub-machine gun, 30 cal carbine (models M1 and M2), the old "Garand Rifle" (made famous by the doughboys of WWII), the 30 cal machine gun, the Browning Automatic Rifle, and the Bazooka (which was a rocket propelled hand held cannon designed to blow up tanks). One day the company commander asked if there was anyone in his company experienced in weaponry. Of course, Georg and I were so, but Georg did not raise his hand - I did. Thus I became the Company's "Small Arms Artificer." Henceforth, I was responsible for keeping all the small arms under lock and key and making sure they remained in working order, especially during periods of war games. I was sent to special classes at various army bases and received plenty of training in the use and repair of all categories of small arms in the Army's arsenal. I liked the job; I was essentially my own boss, and it fulfilled my affinity with guns.

We would meet each Monday evening and one whole weekend every month. During the summer, we would meet at a military camp for two weeks and engage in "war games." The cannon would be fired at distant targets and the machine guns would be shot at moving targets. During these exercises many of the guns would jam or malfunction. I would run around with my repair kit and extract jammed cartridges or replace broken parts. Keeping the guns operational was crucial to getting a high score in these "games." It was dangerous work and men doing these tasks have been known to lose digits when jammed cartridges exploded in an open breach. Our company had the reputation for being a perennial winner in the statewide competitions.

Both Georg and I were expert marksmen with rifle and pistol, especially when Georg modified gun mechanisms to increase their accuracy. We made up the target shooting team and won numerous medals. Naturally, we were highly regarded by the officers of our Company and were given the freedom to do things that were not always in keeping with Army protocol.

George and I enjoyed target shooting on our own. Some-times we "requisitioned" a few crates of .30 cal cartridges left over from war game practice, ammunition that was left in my charge.  Once, I placed a crate of ammo in a duffle bag so that Georg could carry the contraband out to his car without being noticed.  As luck would have it, the Cap-tain came in to chew the rag with us.  Georg was eager to get home, so he took the loaded duffle bag and tried to swing it over his shoulder.  Gravity took over and with a loud crash it dropped to the floor.  It must have weighed close to a hundred pounds.  The Captain pretended not to notice.  Georg picked the heavy load off the floor and staggered out the door.  I'm sure that the Captain knew exactly what was going on, but chose to ignore the inci-dent.  I was hiding in a corner, splitting a gut from laughter.

On occasion, when my services were not needed during the war games (they lasted overnight sometimes), I would go hunting for wild game.  Thus I would bring back a deer or wild turkey to add variety to the military menu.  While hunting deer one time during war games, I came across a grunt in a foxhole.  He was not very bright and he asked me which side I was on.  I informed him that I was his "en-emy" but I was not going to shoot him.  Then I cocked my rifle and a cartridge with a real bullet popped out.   I showed it to him and casually informed him that our side was using real bullets (in war games you shoot blanks).  His face turned white and he retreated deep into a corner of his foxhole.

During the summer camps in the desert we would often experience extremely hot weather; 120 degrees in the shade was common. While out on overnight maneuvers, we would set up camp among the sagebrush. While clearing some brush we noticed a sidewinder rattlesnake resting in the shade. This rattlesnake is small, but its venom is among the deadliest. We dispensed it with a shovel. I cut its head off and noticed that if I squeezed its neck the jaws would pop open and his fangs would jut out, just as if it were alive. I had fun sneaking up on fellow soldiers with the snake in hand. I would tap them on the shoulder and when they turned around I would hold the snake's head, jaws open, in their face. That was good for a laugh.

One of our sergeants came across a Gila Monster. It was a big fat lizard, a little slow but with powerful jaws. Its teeth emitted deadly poison. We kept him on a leash and he became the camp mascot. Once I saw a bobcat scurry across the sand dunes. I sneaked around the other side and shot him on the run. He was a beautiful animal and I now regret that I killed it. I did skin him and tanned his hide. It made an attractive pelt.

The poor soldiers out on maneuvers in the desert had only water to drink. I had a truck at my disposal and made runs between headquarters and the outposts. On a particularly hot day, I loaded my truck with several cases of ice-cold beer and delivered the precious cargo to the grunts who were barely surviving in the sweltering heat. I was welcomed as a hero.

Most years we would encamp in the Mojave Desert on the

edge of Death Valley (Camp Irvin, near the town of Barstow). Near our headquarters was a large mesa. Its flat top was slightly depressed (it might have been a remnant of an old volcano). One day it rained so hard that it filled the depression on the summit with about five feet of water. Within a few days little prehistoric fish appeared. Looking a lot like mutant shrimp, they caught the attention of National Geographic scientists, who came out and collected a few as samples. In a later article I read that the eggs of these fish can lie dormant in the sand for decades. Then, during a deluge, the pond fills with water and the fish develop, but only for a few weeks — long enough to mature and mate. This short cycle has prevented these prehistoric critters from evolving into something more contemporary.

Near the end of my four years in the National Guard, a general recommended me for Officer Candidate School. I would have been happy to earn a commission but I was not willing to spend another four years in the National Guard. I respectfully declined the offer and pursued my academic career in architecture. Had I accepted the commission I would have ended up serving in the Viet Nam war, which was just over the horizon.

*ACTIVE DUTY*
In the fall of 1958 I was scheduled to report for active duty in the US Army. I had time for one more hunt. I drove south into Orange County to a secluded area that was always good for cottontail rabbits and doves. I parked my car at the trailhead just as the sun was rising. It was cold

but clear. I was using my trusty old Stevens 22/410 Over & Under. This little gun has two barrels, one for a shotgun shell and the other for a 22 ca. bullet. It was cold, so I proceeded down the trail at a fast clip. The trail crossed a gully, which was about fifteen feet wide and six feet deep. I decided to cross it while running full speed. As I leaped into the chasm I saw a huge rattlesnake coiled up at exactly the spot I was about to land on. It was too late to change course. All I could do was spread my legs so that I would not land on it. I fully expected the snake to strike me, but it did not move. I slammed backwards into the wall of the gully. That sudden move drew blood on the back of my upper arms, I later noticed. I was in a panic and quickly dispatched the snake with a shotgun blast. The poor snake was now severed into several pieces. The head had about ten inches of neck left on it and it started moving. I switched the gun to the .22 barrel and shot it through the head, putting it out of its misery. I estimated that the snake must have been at least five feet long.

I was still trembling as I climbed out of the gully and continued on the pathway, thanking the good Lord that I had not been bitten. Then I realized why: the snake was coiled at the bottom of the gully in the shade. It was waiting for the sun's rays to reach it. It was a cold night, probably reaching close to freezing, and this snake was stiff. It could not have struck me if it wanted to. Had I known that, I would not have killed it; it was an unusual snake and not the kind I was familiar with. It had distinctive reddish markings. When I got a chance I went to a library and read up on California snakes. This snake turned out to be rare, indeed, and found only in that part of Orange County. Then I felt twice as bad.

Georg and I took the bus to Monterey a day early and we spent it deep sea fishing from a charter boat. Neither of us ever fished in the ocean before, but we caught a ton of rockfish. We could not take them with us (two gunny sacks full) so we gave them to a homeless mission.

At the appointed hour, we checked into Fort Ord with hundreds of other recruits from all over the USA  Some had college educations. A few, primarily from the deep South, were illiterate! Georg and I were assigned to different companies. After the mandatory haircuts, we were given uniforms, bedding and a rifle.

A call went out for people who knew how to use a typewriter. Several hands went up and their "MOS" (permanent job designation in army code) became, "Clerk." I did not want a desk job in the Army. I wanted to be a front line soldier (like my forefathers) and so I did not acknowledge my typing skills.

Duties were assigned, e.g., KP, latrine duty, ground keeping, barracks cleaning, etc. If nothing else, the Army is not short on sanitation. The toilet bowls and urinals had to be so clean you could eat out of them. To pass inspection, I used a toothbrush to get into every nook and cranny. KP duty was the worst. The army used a very potent (powdered) soap. We had no rubber gloves and my hands developed lesions that tormented me for years.

We were trained in how to use and care for our rifles (the traditional .30 cal. Garand). Of course, I was already expert with this weapon and spent time helping others take the gun apart and reassemble it. Cleaning the gun became an important test. During the first formal inspection, I was the only soldier in a company of 200 who passed. Henceforth, I was the company commander's favorite. The "old man" was Captain Lopez. He was happy to have such a "gung-ho" grunt like me (I volunteered a lot).

During the first week of boot camp we were put through a physical endurance test. The purpose of this test was to see how much each soldier's physical condition improved during the two months of harsh training. This exercise included running a 50-yard dash and seeing how many pushups and pull-ups one could do. Being a gymnast, I was in outstanding physical shape when Basic Training started. My running speed was good, but my pushups and pull-up ability went off the chart. After two months of tough Army training regimen I gained weight. My running speed decreased a little, but the number of pushups and pull-ups I did declined drastically. You might say the physical training I received in the Army brought me *down* to the norm.

Both Georg and I were avid readers and we were interested in visiting the old haunts around Salinas, which were settings for some of Steinbeck's famous stories. We took the bus into town and found "Cannery Row." We were disappointed to see that it was practically a ghost town. Still, it was fun to see the old fishing harbor and dilapidated warehouses. We tried to imagine which of the old Victorian houses were used to entertain the local fishermen.

Half way through boot camp I began losing enthusiasm for the military. The drill sergeants were not only bullies, they seemed to be especially intent on using foul language to humiliate and embarrass hapless recruits. Later, I was told that during the Korean War, many US POWs succumbed to brainwashing because they could not endure harsh and humiliating treatment. I am not sure how much merit this explanation had, but I felt that this type of "training" was not good for army morale.

At the end of our two-month training session, we were reassigned to our next station (mine was Ft. Knox). First we had to return all the equipment that we were issued upon our arrival. This included each man's rifle, helmet, rain poncho, etc. It seemed that everyone's equipment had some flaws that required monetary deduction from our final paycheck. When my turn came to present my equipment, the quartermaster framed my poncho up against the storeroom window and identified many tiny little pinholes which let light through. He declared the poncho no longer waterproof and deducted $20 from my payroll. I protested. I informed the sergeant that I took very good care of this item and it was in exactly the same condition now as when it had been issued to me two months earlier. Until now, no other soldier had dared to argue with the quartermaster. They would meekly submit to whatever deduction he had deemed appropriate. I stood firm. Red with anger, the big fat sergeant sent me upstairs to the commander's office. I stood at attention as Captain Lopez berated me for my insolence. He could not persuade me to give in. Finally, he said, "Bertulis, you have been one of my best soldiers. I am very disappointed. However, I will make an exception for you and accept the damaged poncho without any deduction from your payroll, on one condition: you will not tell anyone else that I am making this exception." My answer was, "Yes sir!"

I was grinning from ear to ear as I re-entered the storeroom where all the other grunts were still in line holding their gear. They did not need to ask me what the outcome had been. They could read it on my face. A big cheer went up and I got lots of pats on the back.

A few years later, I read in the *Los Angeles Times* that an extortion racket had been uncovered at Ford Ord: a number of the cadre were charging recruits for damaged equipment and pocketing the money. Captain Lopez was identified as one of the perpetrators. He spent time in the brig and was demoted to corporal.


## *WINTER AT FORT KNOX*

Georg and I got on a Greyhound bus and traveled cross-country to Fort Knox, Kentucky. This is the main base for the Armored branch of the Army. Fort Knox, where the gold is kept, is actually located in a grassy meadow a few miles away. I was assigned to a platoon of eight soldiers, all but I were from Chicago. Six were of Greek ancestry and one of Polish descent. The Greeks and I got along well, but the Pole had it in for Lithuanians; I guess resentment over the struggle for Vilnius still lingered in his memory. I had learned my lesson in basic training: don't volunteer for anything and keep a low profile. I was so successful with this strategy that it took two weeks for our top sergeant to notice me.

Once I shared KP duty with another grunt from Alabama. He was black and had never been in close contact with whites before. Here we were all equal (the army was good that way) but he clearly had strong feelings of resentment against whites. He kept taunting me orally and physically. We were equal in size and he was just waiting for a chance to lay into me (i.e., beat me up in a fight). I got tired of his taunts and laid into him first. I got the better of him and he backed off. Thereafter, we got along without any more trouble, but we did not become friends.

There came an opportunity for good swimmers to join the Regimental swim team. I tried out for the backstroke position and won. Thereafter, I participated in numerous swimming events. I was not particularly fast in the backstroke, but was able to hold my own in relay competitions. We did not win any medals but we sure had fun and avoided a lot of work duties.

During an endurance exercise, we were required to climb a twenty-foot rope. As the sergeant was explaining how this was to be done, Georg raised his hand and announced that we had an expert rope climber amongst us who "could climb the rope in no time at all". He pointed to me. The sergeant was delighted. In college I was used to climbing a twenty-foot rope in less than five-seconds, from a sitting position, using only my arms. I walked up to the rope with about two hundred soldiers watching me. When I started up the rope I immediately realized that something was wrong. I could no longer climb the rope using only my arms. I was straining very hard and finally twisted my legs around the rope in order to continued up albeit, slowly. I made it to the top, but a lot of soldiers were laughing. This was certainly one of the most embarrassing moments of my young life. The sedentary life in the army caused me to gain substantial weight, more than I had ever wanted to. I asked Georg never to volunteer me again.

It was one of the coldest winters in the South that anyone could remember. Temperatures reached 10 degrees (F) at night. We were there for advanced tank training, i.e., lots of war games. When on tank maneuvers, the heavy vehicles soon turned the frozen ground into mud. In some cases tanks would get bogged down in the muck (up to five feet deep) and had to be rescued by other tanks. This was good training but miserable work.

Fort Knox housed one of the best war museums in the country. Georg and I spent hours studying the extensive collection of military small arms (rifles, machine guns, and pistols). There was a German MG52 machine gun too. It brought back memories of the time I fired one when I was a child.

On some weekends I would take the bus into the city of Louisville. They had an excellent little opera company, and I enjoyed attending the performances. Mozart's Don Giovanni was most memorable. While in uniform, I was able to eat meals at the local mission and spend the night in a bunk-room of the local YMCA. I was on a tight budget. When I entered the Army, I resolved to save every penny possible (for college). My salary was $110 per month. At the end of my six-month stint, I went home with $600 in my pocket.

This was the era when Jim Crow laws were still in effect. There were "WHITES ONLY" and "COLORED ONLY" signs everywhere — at drinking fountains, in bus lobbies, even at the YMCA. I wondered, "How Christian is that?" No wonder the black kid from Alabama had it in for me.

For Christmas we were allowed to go home. I had rarely been away from my parents for this important family holiday and I was determined to make it home this year as well. Being the son of UAL employees, I was allowed to fly free if there were seats available (stand-by). I had to change planes in Chicago. The flight to LAX had one empty seat and I got it. It was the 24th of December and the plane was scheduled to depart at 10 AM. It was now 8 AM. I had been up all night getting this far and I was sleepy. I decided to take a nap for a while. When I awoke, I looked at the clock and saw that it was 10:20 AM. Horrified, I ran over to the departure desk and explained that I had just missed my plane to LA. "Oh, no you didn't sir," was the reply, "your plane has been delayed. It will leave in ten minutes." Was I relieved! "There really is a guardian angel watching over me," I thought.

Georg owned a VW bus that he had converted for camping (and hunting). He had left it in Los Angeles and asked me to bring it back after Christmas. I was happy to do so and spent several days driving it across the country. Most of the time I followed the legendary "Route 66," now superseded by freeways. With a car on the base, Georg and I spent our weekends traveling and exploring the countryside. We found Kentucky full of natural wonders. Our favorite was the Mammoth Caves. Tennessee was also interesting. When we took the back roads we came across real Hillbilly country. We saw people living in primitive shacks with outhouses, right out of the cartoon pictures of Lil' Abner. I'm sure "moon shiners" were still thriving here as well.

Upon returning to Los Angeles I continued to serve in the California National Guard for three more years while going to college. I was discharged in 1961 just as the Viet Nam conflict was intensifying. My timing was fortuitous, I thought.

# THE ISSUE OF PACIFISM

Christianity teaches us to "turn the other cheek" when we have been (physically) offended. Well, Jesus was willing to do so and was crucified. During Roman times thousands of pacifistic Christians were willing to die as martyrs in Roman coliseums. Today, Christians in the Middle East are being slaughtered as "infidels" by deranged Moslem jihadists. Pope Francis has recently declared that the international community "should not look the other way," implying that physical force in the defense of unarmed Christians is justified. The head of the Catholic Church is no longer advocating pacifism, it seems.

For good reason. Pacifism works when its adherents are protected by militants. That's why many pacifist sects thrive in the USA and Canada where they are protected, and not in Europe or Asia, where they are often exposed to unscrupulous fanatics.

Some of my closest friends belong to one religious group or another that advocates pacifism and/or the rejection of modern medicine. When it comes to the latter, the government steps in and requires that medicine be used to avoid fatal results. In the former, young men have been allowed to avoid the draft in exchange for community service. That's pretty generous of the American government (during times of mandatory conscription).

The reason I oppose the institution of pacifism is because there are situations where an authoritarian power can and has incarcerated and/or killed millions of innocent people. Hitler had millions of Jews killed in German gas chambers. When (armed) Allies stepped in during WWII it was practically too little too late. I don't think you will find many pacifists among Jews. More recently, Saddam Hussein of Iraq gassed droves of his own citizens (mostly ethnic Kurds). I don't think you will find many pacifists among those people. If the ancestors of the Quakers or the Amish had remained in Europe, I don't think they would have continued to exist. They are here because America (and Canada) is strong enough to protect them (militarily). Taking refuge under the protection of military power is a little hypocritical of pacifists, in my opinion.

Lithuania, the country of my birth, was overrun by an aggressive neighbor in 1941. Thousands of innocent people were brutally murdered or sent to slave labor camps where they died. My parents and I fled the most recent wave of Soviet terror (1944) and found shelter in America. When I became of age to serve in the American military, I volunteered.

From the time of the American Revolution this country has shown a willingness to fight for justice and freedom. We have succeeded in defending liberty not only in America, but also in many other oppressed countries around the world. Pacifism is a noble ideal, though, death and destruction of civilized societies is not going to be prevented by turning the other cheek.

During "war
games" in the
Mojave Desert
of California,
bordering
Death Valley
(on the Neva-
da side).

SUMMER FIELD TRAINING     CAMP IRWIN, CALIFORNIA  1959
LENNIE -- COAST -- PHOTO

Our highly trained company of the California National Guard,
Armored Division.  Alex is in the top row, 5th from right.
Georg is in the next row down, 7th from the right.

# Chapter VIII: THE LAST YEARS IN LA

UNIVERSITY LESSONS

Upon my return from active duty in the US Army in the spring of 1959, I undertook various jobs that allowed me to save money for college tuition, rent, and meals. I lived frugally—a meal often consisted of Lipton chicken noodle soup and saltine crackers. I soon tired of this minimalist diet and graduated to a more fulfilling menu—wieners wrapped in a tortilla. I enrolled for a summer session at UCLA with plans to continue full time at Los Angeles City College in the fall. College tuition was relatively cheap in those days. Then, as today, the key was obtaining good enough grades to be accepted at the university of your choice.

Unconventional as ever, my mother had other ideas for my

education. She urged me to consider an alternative to a standard university education. She was a great admirer of Frank Lloyd Wright's architecture and offered to subsidize my education if I attended his private school in Arizona. It was a very tempting proposition and I considered the options seriously. I too admired the work of this master architect and thought that an apprenticeship under such a genius would certainly be invaluable. On the other hand, I also believed in the merits of an old-fashioned university education that would give me more exposure to liberal arts classes. I decided to forego my mother's offer and opted for the university route. In retrospect, I think I made a big mistake and regret missing the chance to study under Frank Lloyd Wright while he was still alive.

At UCLA, I took English 101, and true to predictions made during high school, it was a demanding course. Nonetheless I managed to get a B grade. My academic career was off to a respectable start. The campus was beautiful and I found the university atmosphere intoxicating. There were free lectures and frequent student gatherings where current political and social issues were debated. Even Hollywood got into the act: a major studio was using one of the campus buildings as a prop for a Jerry Lewis comedy. It had something to do with the army, I figured, since a uniformed MP was posted at the entry to the building where Jerry Lewis was to shoot a scene. Lewis himself hammed it up between takes and threw insulting jokes at his various assistants. I always enjoyed his movies, but here I found his humor vulgar. I guess he was playing to the crowd.

When fall came, I signed up for a full load of courses at

LACC—I was ambitious. All the courses that I chose qualified as prerequisites for getting into a four-year university.
One advanced English class focused on semantics—a
subject that I found most interesting. I joined the General
Semantics Society, which was presided over by the great
S. I. Hayakawa[39] (of San Francisco State University). He
would come to our campus and deliver captivating lectures.

I took various math courses, more than required since I
loved the subject. One advanced course that I found particularly enjoyable was called Computations, Permutations, and Probability. It dealt with numbers games, including gambling odds and statistical forecasting. The final
exam was given. Before the elderly professor handed back
the graded papers, he made a little speech. He said that in
his forty years of teaching this course, the average score
had been about 40 percent; 60 percent would merit an A,
and it was true this day as well. Then he added that no
one in his class had ever gotten a 100 percent score, until
today. When I received my test back, I saw a big 100 percent written in the upper corner of my paper!

I was able to enroll in the second-year architectural drafting class since my three years of high school drafting qualified for one year of college level. Our instructor was a
gray-haired gentleman who made a point of proudly letting
his students know that he was a licensed architect and not
just a drafting instructor. I doubt if he had the talent to have

---

[39]As a US senator from California he is remembered for his outspoken positions
on controversial issues. He wrote *Language in Action.*

designed anything; he was a seasoned draftsman. One day a job opening for a junior draftsman at the Los Angeles City School District headquarters was announced. Our instructor recommended me and I got the job. Apparently, I was his most qualified student.

The day of April 9, 1959, will always stick in my mind. Our drafting instructor walked into class with a big grin on his face. With apparent amusement, he announced that Frank Lloyd Wright had died. I was stunned. I laid down my drafting pencil and went home. Later, I would come to realize how reviled Mr. Wright was in academia.[40] I learned to keep my admiration of this genius to myself.

A requisite for graduating in architecture from a university is four years of architectural design. Neither LACC nor UCLA had such a curriculum. USC did offer these courses and I enrolled in Basic Design 1. Professor Merendino, the renowned industrial designer, taught the class. For the first time, I was challenged to come up with original and creative design solutions under the supervision of an accomplished master. I loved the course and thrived in it. I got the single A in the class. I was attending a university in Washington State when I received the transcript from USC showing my grade as a C. I phoned Professor Merendino. He agreed that I received an A from him and he was equally shocked that his TA (teaching assistant) had changed the grade. He assured me he would look into it

---

[40]Wright believed in a creative and progressive architecture, rooted in "form follows function" and the environment—whereas most schools were still teaching the Beaux Arts style. The latter promoted neoclassical copies of historic models. The two approaches were diametrically opposed to each other.

and have it corrected. I then remembered that his TA and I had had a "social" disagreement (he was attracted to me and I did not reciprocate). I made a mental note to be more tactful in the future.

Los Angeles City College was famous for its strong gymnastics program. I tried out for the varsity team and was accepted. We had a good coach and talented gymnasts. In the past, some of them had even qualified for the US Olympic team. We would beat most of the competitors in our league, including some four-year universities such as UCLA. I was the low man on the totem pole on such a powerful team, but I was very happy to be a member. I competed as an all-around gymnast. During practices, I did very well in executing my routines. For some reason, during competition I would often falter when attempting difficult maneuvers. Later, I realized the reason for my lack of consistency. One reason was obvious: I would often study late into the night and, as a consequence, I would be weak and tired during competition the next day. The other reason was subtler: I was under the impression that eating lots of protein (such as steaks) would give me extra strength; it did just the opposite. Carbohydrates (such as pasta) are now recognized as a food source that gives an athlete extra strength and endurance. I learned too late.

During these years, rope climbing was still an event in competitions, and I excelled at it. A two-inch-diameter rope was suspended from the gym ceiling, and a metal plate demarked the finish at exactly twenty feet off the ground. The competitor would sit on the floor and then dash up the rope as fast as he could—using only his arms to ascend. A stopwatch was used to time the competitor until he hit the metal plate with his hand. I would sometimes cover this distance in 4.2 seconds—not a world record, but respectable in college competition.

I also made some friends at this school who were interested in mountaineering. We undertook occasional trips to a popular granite cliff called Tahquitz Rock (near the town of Idyllwild). Here we learned to anchor safely into pitons, belay each other with a rope, and rappel. During the winter, we tested our survival skills by climbing easy but high peaks in the San Bernardino Mountains. The highest summit we reached one cold January day was San Gorgonio (11,499 feet).

LIFE AS A YOUNG ADULT

Feelings started stirring inside me which indicated that I should get to know people of the opposite sex a little better. I remembered that among the students who came to our house for piano lessons was an attractive girl by the name of Giedre Landsbergis. My father provided me with her phone number and I called her up. She accepted my offer to go on a date with me. She lived with her widowed mother not far from the USC campus. I arrived with a bouquet of flowers and handed it to her when she opened the door; I was red faced and insecure. She quickly put me at ease and we had a good time that evening (dinner and a movie). This relationship did not lead to a romance, but we remained good friends for a long time.

While visiting Moscow, still in the era of the USSR, I attended a diplomatic function where I was introduced to Professor Vytautas Landsbergis (a musicologist and future president of Lithuania). While shaking my hand , he asked me (in Lithuanian):

"By chance, are you related to a certain musician by the name of Juozas Bertulis?"

"Yes, I'm his son." I replied. "And by chance are you related to a certain Miss Giedre Landsbergis who lives in Los Angeles?"

"Yes, she is my niece," he said, "by way of my late brother—who was killed by the Russians during the war."

What a small world! Professor Landsbergis did not know my father personally—he was familiar with his compositions. Needless to say, he and I had many more encounters during the effort to regain Lithuania's independence, and we remained allies. Giedre went into engineering. She once entered a beauty pageant in Los Angeles and was voted Miss Engineer of the year.

By the late 1950s, the Lithuanian community in Los Angeles had grown to a healthy population of over twenty-thousand or so. The younger generation (of which I was a member) was active in various organizations, as well as attending schools of higher education. There were musical groups, theater acts, Boy Scouts and Sea Scouts troops, camping clubs, dance ensembles, etc. During the summer, there were large family picnics, and in winter there were ample opportunities to get in on ski trips. I joined a folk dancing group and we performed not only at various Lithuanian functions, but also at larger venues such as Disneyland and international festivals, and on local television. Of course, there were many parties. Lithuanians are well known for their love of dance, singing, and drinking.

Viktor Peteris, my childhood friend, moved to Los Angeles to be with his parents. He was an avid lover of the outdoors and would take me with him at times. During one trip to Tuolumne Meadows (Yosemite), we camped next to a little creek and scrambled among the beautiful granite peaks. Some of the lakes abounded with crayfish, and Viktor showed me how to catch them. It was a treat to be away from the crowds of the Valley below. The high country was sunny, cool, and peaceful.

One winter we spent a week in Yosemite Valley. It was refreshing to experience it without the summer crowds. There was snow in the high country, so I decided to pack my skis and hike/climb the face of Glacier Point to the summit. Viktor drove around Badger Pass and skied in from above. We met at the lodge[41] on top for lunch and were hosted by a retired couple that was hired by the Park Service to winter there. They were surprised and delighted to see us and served us hot tea. Then we skied back out to Viktor's car. Unbeknownst to me, the old couple at the lodge radioed the rangers that they had visitors, a rare event. They also mentioned that one of us had climbed directly up the face to reach the summit. When we returned to the Valley, the rangers were waiting for us. I was arrest-

---

[41] The lodge has since burned down and has not been replaced.

ed for "soloing," an act that was against park rules during those days. Fortunately, I did not have to spend the night in the slammer. They released me into Viktor's custody (he was ten years older) after I promised to abide by park rules, henceforth.

With another good friend, I went on water-skiing trips. Rimas Petraitis built himself a nineteen-foot runabout as a college project while attending Gonzaga University. He powered it with a five-hundred-horsepower inboard engine; it could reach speeds of seventy miles per hour in smooth water conditions. Over four-day weekends, we would drive to Lake Mead (Arizona) and have a grand time. The boat could go so fast that some of us better water-skiers could surf in our bare feet! The north end of the lake was devoid of people, and we could race around without bothering any campers. During one moonlit night, I was being towed on my slalom ski at a high speed. Rimas was behind the wheel with a lady companion at his side. After about twenty minutes or so, I was getting tired and tried to signal Rimas to stop. He was too busy talking to the lovely companion and failed to pay any attention to me. Reaching a point of exhaustion, I finally dropped the towline and watched the boat disappear into the darkness. Fortunately, the water was warm and I had a life vest on. After about half an hour, I saw the boat reappear on the horizon with two searchlights scanning the waters. An hour or so later, I was picked up by two embarrassed companions.

After my graduation from high school, Viktor Peteris and I made plans to paddle down the Sacramento River in his

Klepper kayak. The trip was delayed for ten days because my mother asked me to lay a new asphalt roof on our house and apply two new coats of paint to the stucco exterior. I did not relish this messy work, but it had to be done.

We started below Sacramento and finished a week later in San Francisco Bay. Our plan was to go with the flow of the river, thus making travel easy and fast, or so we thought. We did not count on a strong headwind. In fact, due to the constant wind, the surface of the river was flowing upstream most of the time. The paddling against the current was hard and we took more time to reach San Francisco Bay than we planned. It was a memorable trip that prepared me for many more to come.


FIRST LOVE
One of the members of our dance troupe was a beautiful eighteen-year-old by the name of Onute Sumantas. She was also attending LACC (as a pre-nursing student) and we would meet for lunch sometimes. Coincidentally, our fathers knew each other as fellow officers during Lithuania's war of independence (ca. 1917). We started dating and fell in love. It was love of the old-fashioned kind—sex was not a factor. Onute enjoyed cooking, and I was dying for some traditional Lithuanian dishes, in lieu of my Lipton soup diet. On some afternoons, she would invite me for a home-cooked meal and delight in watching me eat like the starving student that I was.

On afternoons when there were no classes, we would drive to our "secret" beach where we would lie in the sun reading or go play in the surf. This beach was located north of Malibu at a landmark called Point Dume. It was a broad cove protected by high bluffs. We found a steep trail that allowed us to climb down to the isolated stretch of paradise.

For two years we were inseparable and attended every party, camping trip and function together. It was a blissful relationship and we were happy—perhaps too happy. One day Onute asked me what my long-range intentions were. I explained that I intended to complete my education, become an architect, and then marry the woman of my dreams—which she was. Onute was twenty and ready for marriage (her mother had married at nineteen). I refused to compromise and we agreed to part.

At the time, I did not realize how deeply in love I was with this woman. I missed her terribly. The thought of seeing her at a party was unbearable, so I avoided the ones that she might be attending. Yet I was dying to see her again. She owned a light-blue Volkswagen bug, and the LA freeways were full of them, it seemed. Every time I saw one, my heart would skip a beat and my blood pressure would rise. I would weave through traffic to see if it was her car. I focused on the license plate to see if it was NPE122. It never was.

Life became meaningless without her, and yet I could not admit my weakness and beg her to take me back. The only way out was to leave Los Angeles. Eventually, I chose to live in another part of the country where I was sure I would not run into her, accidentally or otherwise, and where new attractions would take her off my mind.


DRAFTING JOBS
My first real drafting job was a part-time position with the Los Angeles City School District, Operations and Maintenance Department. The city had many schools under its jurisdiction and some of the buildings (and grounds) needed upkeep and remodeling. This entailed such mundane projects as replacing ancient double-hung windows, remodeling student toilet rooms and shower areas, adding temporary structures for classroom overflow, and other minor projects. I was the only draftsman and had to use what little I learned in class to solve real problems and draw up proper solutions. If I got stuck, carpenters came in and explained how they wanted to do the work. I drew the plans accordingly. I spent half the time out in the field measuring up existing conditions. I met with school officials, maintenance men, and janitors who would advise me how to improve physical facilities. One of these janitors was the father of Rafer Johnson, the great decathlon champion of the 1956 Olympics. The senior Mr. Johnson was proud of his son and I enjoyed listening to his stories.

The office file room was full of old drawings (some were ancient blueprints on real linen) that I could draw upon for information. It was challenging work for a beginner like me. I did the work well, and the supervisors appreciated my efforts. When I resigned in order to advance to a higher (and better paying) drafting job, the office staff gave me a send-off and presented me with a going-away present (a mechanical pen and pencil set). I was touched by their sincere expressions of wishing me a successful career in architecture.

My next job was a full-time position as a draftsman for a large developer of apartment projects. It was an impressive operation. Next to the office building that employed about thirty draftsmen was a prototype apartment structure that contained about a dozen or so model apartment units —each one different. They were fully furnished and used for display purposes only. A client would select from the prototypes the kind and quantity of units he wanted, and this information would be given to a draftsman such as me. I would then gather up the various predesigned schemes and arrange them in a manner that would fit on the particular building site. That was it! There was no opportunity to innovate or design a more attractive façade. Everything was standardized. These projects were being built up and down the Southern California coast. Some of the buildings would contain as many as two or three hundred units. I soon got bored with this job, and it became clear to me that my architectural career was not going to benefit from such an experience. I left after a couple of months.

I answered an ad in the newspaper for a senior draftsman experienced in single-family residential housing. Most of my drafting lessons in high school and at LACC were in this category, so I considered myself qualified. The pay was good and I got the job. However, this turned out to be another large-scale development operation. This time there were only two draftsmen cranking out drawings—an old-timer and me. This company had commissioned an architect who drew up six different prototypes of houses with gingerbread façades, complete with construction drawings. Each design was stamped by the licensed architect—building-permit ready. Our job was to draw up complete new sets of drawings for each design, varying the appearance by adapting the façade of one house to the plan of another. Our employers expected us to crank out one permit-ready set per each eight-hour day. To accomplish this task, we drew fast. The permutations and combinations of six façade designs adapted to six different plan designs allowed for over a thousand "original" designs (all for the price of six stamped plans). Needless to say, I left when an opportunity came to work under a respectable architect.

His name was Carl C. Lee and he came from a well-to-do Hong Kong family. He really did not have private clients, as such. He used his own money to build spec houses in the Culver City area. He was small in stature and drove a big white Cadillac. He was refined in dress and demeanor, and he treated his employees well. My job was to prepare the designs and construction drawings for single-family houses that Mr. Lee would then build and sell, hopefully for a profit. This time I had considerable leeway in creating good designs that were also functional.

When construction of his twelve-unit development started, we ran into bad luck. Most of the building site followed an old riverbed, and the earth was insufficient to support the footings we had engineered. We needed to dig deeper. Then disaster struck: oil started gushing out of our foundation digs. Normally, an owner would be happy to strike oil on his land. Unfortunately, the mineral rights already belonged to one of the major oil companies, and Mr. Lee was stuck with the burden of unwanted oil on his property. The local newspapers had fun with this story.

Mr. Lee was related to the owners of the Hang Seng banking family, who were planning to construct their new headquarters on Hong Kong's waterfront. It was to be a twenty-story high-rise office tower with state-of-the-art curtain wall design. The primary designers were Hong Kong architects, but the design of the façade was left to Mr. Lee. He handed the project to me, and I was challenged with my first commercial architecture opportunity. My design was accepted. Fifteen years later, I had the chance to view this high-rise building while on a trip to China. I was approaching the harbor by ferry, awed by the concentration of so many tall buildings. I kept an eye out for "my" tall building and finally recognized it standing on the west side of the financial district. Myriads of giant skyscrapers dwarfed my office tower. I was disappointed to see it so small and outmoded. I was crestfallen.

FRIENDSHIPS

During my last two years in Los Angeles, I lived in a historic old house located at 1417 Crenshaw Boulevard (near Pico). It had been built and occupied by Mr. Crenshaw, who was a pioneer lumberman in California. I was told that all the structural wood in the house was of first-growth redwood. I guess in those days there was no concern about depleting our finest timber.

The new owners of the house (a Lithuanian family named

Simonis) lived downstairs while two rooms upstairs were rented out. The two tenants shared a bathroom off the common hallway and a big deck overlooking the street. I was one of the tenants. The other was a sixty-seven-year-old Russian émigré by the name of Zahar Martinoff. We became great friends. Zahar was no ordinary Russian—he was a Cossack. And he was no ordinary Cossack—he came from a clan that was unusually tall. While most Cossacks averaged around five foot six, his clan was composed of six-footers. The royal families of Europe liked to impress visitors by surrounding themselves with an elite guard that was especially tall. King Frederick the Great of Prussia was famous for his honor guard of tall Lithuanians (original Prussians). This tradition was not wasted on the czars of Russia. Zahar's clan of Cossacks became the hereditary imperial guards. Zahar's duties were many. One of them was to stand at attention outside the czar's bedroom when he slept.

Zahar had a great sense of humor and he was also a good storyteller. He regaled me with tales of life with the Romanovs, fighting during WWI, the Russian Revolution, and his colorful career as a saber dancer in the nightclubs of Paris and New York.

During the First World War, Zahar left his job as the czar's bodyguard and volunteered to fight on the German front. He was a cocky twenty-four-year-old and knew no fear. He singlehandedly killed dozens of enemy soldiers and was wounded many times. When he sat on our balcony and tanned on sunny days, I could see small scars where numerous bullets had penetrated his chest and big scars where they exited through his back. He had only one lung and his left shoulder drooped somewhat. But his posture was always erect. The czar awarded him numerous medals and the Cross of St. George two times![42]

The world war ended and the Russian Revolution began. This time, Zahar fought with the White Army against the Bolsheviks. Czar Nicholas II and his family fled Moscow under the protection of Zahar and his father's clan. While they were in Yekaterinburg, the Bolshevik soldiers surrounded the city and were about to overrun it. Zahar's father pleaded with the czar to flee with his Cossacks and seek refuge in England. After all, the czar had a ship loaded and waiting in the harbor on the Baltic Sea to take him to England. Nicholas II replied that the king of England, George V, had not invited him to come: "It would be unbecoming of my position to arrive with my family without an official invitation." That night, Zahar and his clan mounted their horses and broke through the enemy lines to safety. Lenin's forces found the Romanov family unguarded and executed all of them soon thereafter. The imperial ship sailed for England with the royal treasury, but without any Romanov member on board to claim that treasure. Ironically, Czar Nicholas II and King George V were first cousins.

Most of Zahar's clan, including all immediate members of his family, died at the hands of the Bolsheviks. Zahar escaped to Turkey first; then he made his way to Paris. He

---

[42]This medal was the equivalent of America's Medal Of Honor and Britain's Victoria Cross. Few recipients had the medal pinned to their chests. They died in action.

was tall and handsome, albeit not highly educated. Women were attracted to him. One wealthy Parisian lady took him as her lover; he fathered her son. When I asked him what became of the relationship, he said, "Once she had what she wanted"—his child—"I was no longer needed, though we remained friends. She writes me occasionally to tell me how our son is faring. He became a career officer in the French army."

After a few years in Paris, he sailed across the Atlantic and joined the nightlife scene in New York. Upon retiring, he settled down in Los Angeles, where the climate was more appealing. On occasion, I would witness an old comrade of his come and visit him, and they would reminisce about the good old days over a glass of sherry. This frail old man would always come dressed formally with two or three medals hanging from his lapel—none of them of high order. Later, Zahar would chuckle, "He was the youngest general in the czar's army—very handsome, charming, and he played the piano. He was a frequent guest at the Imperial Court and the czar's daughters loved flirting with him. Now, his day job is being a janitor, but when he comes to visit me in the evening, he is still the general."

One of my most colorful friends was (and still is) a Palestinian refugee whom my mother befriended. Jamal Habib was like a member of our family. He was handsome and charming, and his good manners belied his family background. To say he was unusually bright would be an understatement. He arrived in America after fighting for his country against European Zionist occupiers.

He was accepted at Washington State University in the engineering program. However, Jamal was in a hurry, and he wanted to get his bachelor's degree in engineering sooner than the allotted five years. He challenged many of the courses by taking exams that, if he passed them, would allow him to skip the classes. One story goes that he decided to take a difficult exam in chemistry with several other students. It was a grueling four-hour test. After two hours, Jamal got up, dropped his papers on the professor's desk, and casually lit a cigarette. The professor looked up at him and said, "My poor fellow, don't give up so quickly. You still have two hours left." Jamal replied, "I'm not giving up. I finished!" Indeed, he was done and he got 100 percent on the test. The end result of successfully challenging many courses was that Jamal got his bachelor's degree in engineering in two and a half years instead of five.

He matriculated to UCLA and earned his master's degree in six months (rather than the normal one year). It took him two years to get his PhD in engineering. "Elasticity and Plasticity of Winged Structures" was his thesis. It should be noted that Jamal earned his doctoral degree in the same amount of time that a regular engineering student would get his bachelor's degree.

After brief periods working for Boeing and various brain trusts, Jamal was appointed director for the construction of two of history's biggest development projects: the new cities of Jubail and Yanbu in Saudi Arabia. After a lucrative career, he retired to the outskirts of San Diego, where he now tends to his garden of exotic plants. He shuns fiction.

Instead, he reads technical manuals to keep his mind well honed. Ironically, he has trouble getting adjusted to the world of computers, though his mind works like a computer.

During my last year living in Los Angeles (1960), a beautiful young woman arrived from Australia. Her name was Irena Verbila. She had aspirations as an actress and Twentieth Century Fox was interested enough to give her screen tests. She became part of our small group of friends that included Liudas Reivydas—the flamboyant leader of our folk dancing group. Irena and I developed a close rapport and I felt that she could become my girlfriend. She rejected my overture and suggested that she would prefer to remain uninvolved. She promised to give me advance warning if the situation changed.

We often partied together. One memorable Friday night, four of us were driving around looking for a good place to eat and drink. After failing to find a place we could all agree on, we decided to head south—to Mexico. On Saturday, we saw a bullfight in Tijuana, danced late into the night, and slept the rest of the night on a secluded ocean beach. On Sunday, we rented some horses and rode them through the surf. Only in one's youth can one endure so much drinking, dancing, and cavorting with so little sleep.

A few weeks later, Irena dropped a bomb on me: she and Liudas had gotten engaged and were planning to get married! I was crushed. I did not feel that the two were a good match. Perhaps I was simply jealous. Did her immigration status require that she marry an American citizen, I wondered? My mind was in a whirl. I decided to take action. I scraped up a few hundred dollars in cash and drove out to Irena's house in the San Fernando Valley. I knocked on her door. She was surprised to see me. I explained my feelings about her engagement to Liudas and that I felt that we were much more suited for each other. I proposed that she pack up her belongings and drive to Las Vegas with me, where we could get married without much ado. Irena embraced me warmly and confided that she loved Liudas and was committed to him. Dejected, I went back home.

That experience (Irene's rejection on top of Onute's parting) was the last straw for me. I was losing control of my senses, I felt. I decided it was time to abandon my life in California and enroll in a four-year university—full time. But which one? One thing I knew for sure: I wanted to be close to mountains. I was impressed by beautiful pictures of the Grand Tetons that I saw in an issue of National Geographic magazine. I investigated the university scene in Wyoming and found that the school in Cody did not have a school of architecture. My next choice was Washington State, where the Cascade Mountain Range held great promise. As it turned out, that state had two universities that taught architecture: the University of Washington and Washington State University.

I asked my friend Jamal for advice, since he had attended Washington State University. Jamal was unequivocal: "You will love WSU. It is a small-town university. Almost everyone lives on campus—which means you'll get to know your fellow students." Jamal convinced me. I made an appointment with the dean of architecture and took the next plane to Spokane. It was a short drive to Pullman and the campus. The deadline for enrollment for the winter semester (which starts in January) had passed. However, the dean was impressed with my high grade point average and decided to make an exception. I was allowed to enroll as a sophomore. I would have to be back in time for classes scheduled to start mid-January.

265

Alex working out on the climbing rope while training with the LACC gymnastics team. His best time was 4.2 seconds, starting from a sitting position on the floor! Not a world record, but respectable.

Lithuanian folk dancing group of Los Angeles (1958). Alex is standing, third from left. Onute is in the middle of the front row. Liudas is in the dark suit on the right.

Left: Jamal during his college days at UCLA.  Right:  Rimas
and Vitaly on Viktor's sailboat at Marina Del Ray.

Feasting on crayfish on LA.  From left to right: Indris (the
brother of Gintaras), Vitaly, Gintaras (in wheelchair), Rimas
and his wife, Giedre.  At the home of Gintaras in Palos Verdes

The end of a legend, the end of an era.

Zachar on the deck that we shared while living in adjoining rooms on Crenshaw Blvd.

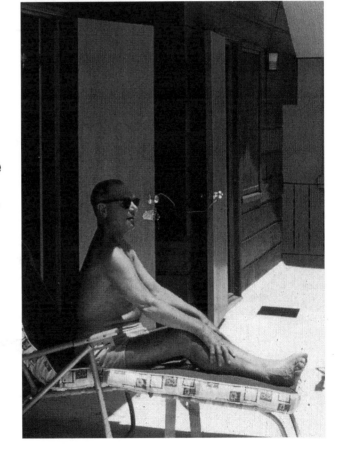

# A VISIT WITH OLD FRIENDS

RIMAS AND GIEDRE
When Rimas married Giedre in 1966 I flew down (from Seattle) for the wedding. Thirty-four years later Giedre called to inform me that her husband had just died. It was heart failure. During those years of marriage they lived in a house located on a shady lot in the middle of Los Angeles – near Silver Lake. This house was in a perpetual state of being remodeled and, somehow, it never ever got finished. Rimas was an engineer by education, but he was talented in many fields. He was a gifted designer and built his own, uniquely conceived furniture. He designed and built a 20-foot in-board runabout as a college project, which we used for thrilling rides waterskiing on various desert lakes. Engaged in numerous real estate developments, he found himself being defrauded by unscrupulous partners. During subsequent lawsuits, he found his lawyers lacking. So, he became a student of law and handily won every legal action by representing himself. I'm sure he could have excelled as a lawyer, an architect, industrial designer, mayor of a city (he aspired to run for such), general in the army (he held the rank of captain), or CEO of a major corporation. In other words, I always felt he missed his calling in becoming an engineer, and told him so.

The gains produced through his real estate investments made him financially independent. He quit his job as Chief Traffic Engineer for the City of Beverly Hills, bought himself a fifty foot Chris Craft yacht, and retired into a blissful life of inactivity. While Giedre continued with her job as grade school teacher,

Rimas seemed to be content by preoccupying himself with endless minutia on his computer, entertaining too many friends on his yacht and expounding his opinions about any subject in the universe. Rimas was one of the smartest and most talented people I ever knew. He could have launched into a new career or written best sellers (or finished remodeling his house). It bothered me to see all that talent waste away in his senior years.

Giedre was considerably younger and seemed to live in awe of her prodigious husband, until he "retired" early, that is. When he died, Giedre found herself alone for the first time in her life. She was very young when she left her parents' home to marry Rimas. Now, she wasted no time selling the Chris Craft and most of their real estate holdings. With the proceeds she bought a comfortable house on the sunny side of a hill nearby. She decorated and furnished it in ways that clearly reflected her tastes. For the first time, she was living in a home that she could think of as her own (and it was finished!).

Nonetheless, Rimas was the only man she ever loved and she missed him terribly. Fighting bouts of depression, Giedre called me frequently for emotional support. Fortunately, she had two sons, a daughter-in-law, and two little grand children who offered loving distraction. To help her get out and socialize more, I agreed to come down to Los Angeles and spend an extended weekend with her. We ended up visiting some of my old friends — all of whom she was acquainted with, to various degrees.

VITALY
When my plane hit the tarmac at LAX I pulled out my cell phone and dialed up Vitaly's number.

"Hi, Vitaly! This is Alex. How are things going?"
"Alex! I'm fine. Where are you?"

"I'm sitting in a plane at the LA airport and I am going to be in town for a few days. Do you have time to get together?"
"Sure, I would love to see you. But, I am leaving for Moscow tomorrow. Are you free tonight?"

Vitaly lives in the high hills at the southern end of the LA peninsula. We agreed to meet at a restaurant in Manhattan Beach, which was about half way between the airport and his house.

Vitaly left the USSR not as a dissident but as a member of an illustrious family that was being exiled during the Brezhnev era. With his wife and her son they ended up in Seattle. I first met him when he wandered onto our soccer field during an "old timers" game (over 30 years old) one evening. He spoke no English and my small grasp of Russian facilitated his induction into our neighborhood team. He was a good athlete and we became fast friends. Vitaly was a member of the mathematics faculty at the University of Moscow and extremely well connected to the Kremlin elite. However, he saw no future for himself in the latently anti-Semitic culture of that country. He was happy to leave when the opportunity arose.

Now, fifteen years later, Vitaly was remarried to a beautiful "all-American" girl and the proud father of two lovely daughters. He was gainfully employed in the computer industry and he still found time to "free lance" in various ventures with his former countrymen in Russia. Vitaly's humor and energy had not changed over the years. However, he no longer indulged in the liberal consumption of alcoholic beverages (Vodka). This was much to my relief since, Vitaly could and would drink me "under the table" during reunions, in the best Russian tradition. So, when the three of us sat down at the Manhattan Beach restaurant and ordered dinner, we refrained from ordering any adult beverage. After updating Vitaly's as to my family affairs, I asked him what the trip to Moscow was about.

"Well, it's a short trip — four days. I am now consultant to a Russian consortium that is going to explore for oil in the vast regions of Russia by satellite. This method is now possible with present day technology and we no longer have to drive over endless tundra and drill many holes into the ground until we hit oil. My job is to formulate the logarithms of the satellite rotations so the pictures sent to earth will be precisely located. On this trip I will just go there to exchange some information. I will also meet, briefly, with my old friend Boris (one of the controversial ogliarchs). He is due to appear in court day after tomorrow. Putin is really after these guys and I'm going to advise him to compromise. The situation is serious," he emphasized.

"Interesting," I responded, "how did you become friends with this character?"

"Well, we go back to the days when we were both professors of mathematics at the University of Moscow. It seems that even then, he had a penchant for earning some extra money. So, he decided to import some fashionable jackets from Italy for resale in the USSR. This was highly illegal during those days. It was called "spekulancia" and was punishable with five years in prison, if caught. Well, he was caught. From jail he called me to get him out with the help of my connections. I called my father-in-law and asked him to intervene. After some discussion, he agreed to call the head commissar of the region where Boris was jailed and started a friendly chat with him. He invited him to his dacha for drinks during his next visit to Moscow, etc. Then, casually, he mentioned that there was a certain 'Boris' awaiting trial in one of his jails. 'Since he is a nice guy and a friend, could you see to it that his case be dismissed?' Thus, Boris avoided 'hard time.' Of course, we had many interesting encounters since then… You might say, he owes me, big time."

[Upon my return to Seattle, I read in the papers that Boris never showed up in Moscow for the hearing and that he is still hiding in Europe someplace. Actually, he arrived in LA in his private jet and was hosted by Vitaly for various shopping sprees on Rodeo Drive, etc. The news media never found out.]

"By the way, how is you stepson, Sasha, doing?"

Vitaly's face took on a grim look. "He committed suicide last year. He was living in San Francisco and jumped off a tall building. I guess, he was depressed. We had no warning. It was very sad." I was shocked to hear this. Sasha was a teenager when they arrived in Seattle and lived at my house for a while. We were all very close.

Vitaly turned to a more upbeat subject. "What are you doing this winter? Let's go skiing again."

"OK, I responded, "I have no firm plans yet, but let me check with my kids and see what is in store."

As we settled the bill with the waitress, Vitaly joked about not indulging in any "firewater." Just as we got up to leave, the waitress brought three jiggers of tequila. Vitaly hesitated, then toasted to old times and new. I looked at my watch and was astonished to see that our brief little dinner lasted three hours.

## ONUTE AND ARVYDAS
Coincidentally, Onute and her husband, Arvydas, live four doors up the street from Giedre's new home. When I was a young college student, I fell in love. I met Onute as a fellow member of a Lithuanian folk dancing troupe. As with most "first love" cases, our relationship was pure and intense. Onute was ready for marriage; I was not. When we split up, I was so heartbroken that I

felt it would be healthier for my well being if I moved to another part of the country (Washington State was far enough away, I figured). Onute soon married a gifted scientist and, eventually, I fell in love again and married Gisela.

Fourteen years after my breakup with Onute, I was in Los Angeles attending Sunday mass at our community church. Onute was there and we met. She was as beautiful and radiant as ever. We talked for about twenty minutes and exchanged highlights of our lives. She had one daughter. I proudly showed her a picture of my third child — recently born. It was a friendly, but all too short of an encounter.

A few years later, news reached me that Onute was seriously ill. Brain surgery was required, which left her partially paralyzed and wheelchair bound. I would occasionally hear about Onute's well being through mutual friends, but I never called her.

Now, Giedre and I were invited to visit Onute and Arvydas for an evening drink. Arvydas met us at the door. He was no longer the young blond man I remembered from bachelor days. With his silver hair he now had the appearance of an elder statesman. Onute and I embraced each other warmly, though, awkwardly, since she was seated in her wheelchair. She appeared a lot thinner, very erect and her eyes sparkled with interest and excitement. My heart again seemed to melt when I beheld her. The congenial atmosphere was enhanced with the bottle of fine port Arvydas served. He was still employed by the same aerospace firm and his current project involved the exploration of Mars with land robots. Arvydas was scheduled to depart for London the next day. Trying to be funny, I remarked that, should he meet up with Vitaly along the way, they should collaborate on strategic secrets for outer space activity. We laughed a little nervously at that one.

Onute and I talked about our mutual families and friends. I had
a tough time contributing much to the general conversations
since I was in a trance. Before me was a woman with whom I
was once very much in love. Forty years had passed and feelings for her still ran deep.

GRAZINA AND JONAS
For Saturday Giedre and I were invited to the home of my
cousin, and closest relative in the USA, Grazina and her husband, Jonas. This remarkable couple recently celebrated their
fiftieth wedding anniversary. On that occasion Jonas declared,
with a toast, that he had not known an unhappy day in his life.
I'm sure that was an exaggeration — poetic license, one might
say. Grazina and Jonas are ageless, visibly in love, and infectious with their good humor and warm dispositions. She is the
consummate hostess — elegant in style and unsurpassed in the
fine art of cooking. Their condo in Santa Monica was designed
and built by Jonas, while Grazina tastefully decorated it with
furnishings and artwork. I was flattered to see one of my watercolors hanging amongst their fine collection of paintings.

Giedre and I arrived fashionably late. Jonas popped a bottle of
French champagne and Grazina offered homemade hors
d'oeuvres. Their granddaughter, Ramona, was helping in the
kitchen. She looked as young and beautiful as when I last saw
her — about a dozen years ago. She was now married and had
two children of her own. She lived across the street and insisted
that I come over to meet her family. When we entered her house
her husband, their son (1 1/2) and daughter (3), greeted us.
Both kids vied for my attention and led me into their playroom
to show off their favorite toys. The little girl picked up a picture
book and begged me to read it to her. When I demurred, she began to cry. I picked her up and, as she hugged me tightly, I
promised to come back sometime and read the whole book to

her. With that promise she stopped crying and I returned to my dinner party.

Jonas and Grazina have had a rich life together. Like most of us, they came here as immigrants from war torn Europe. Jonas got a degree in engineering, but his good business acumen allowed him to become rich through real estate developments in Illinois. They lived in a beautiful home on the shore of Lake Michigan, traveled in their own airplane and became active in US politics. Albeit, Jonas never won elective office. Then, on the eve of the 1982 recession, disaster struck. The bank called a $3,000,000 unsecured note which he could not pay. Foreclosure proceedings caused his real estate empire to collapse. Almost broke, they relocated to California and started all over. Now, after fifteen years of hard work and modest living, they are not rich, but living comfortably. "In this booming economy I could roll the dice and speculate with major developments again," Jonas observed. "The opportunities are there. But, I won't do it. I'm quite pleased with the modest projects that I now have and I'm not in danger of going broke. It's nice to sleep in peace at night."

Grazina kept bringing more good food out of her kitchen. After the two bottles of fine wine were emptied, Jonas brought out two kinds of homemade liquors. One was cherry based (made by Grazina) and the other was a type of Mead (made by Jonas). The taste contest ended in a tie. Of course, it took many tests to affirm the votes. With good food and drinks flowing, we discussed topics including, our common ancestry, history, politics, hunting, fishing, and the true meaning of life. Time flew by. It was about 2:30 in the morning when Giedre gave me a look that reminded me it was past my bedtime. Reluctantly, I parted from these friends whose humor, affection and sparks of love still resonated as if they were youngsters.

JAMAL

I did have a little headache when I arose from bed just a few hours later. Giedre served me a nourishing breakfast, including a couple of aspirin, before departing. We were scheduled to meet Jamal in the outskirts of San Diego at noon and the Peteris in nearby Vista later that evening. I carefully wrote the directions to each place on separate slips of paper.

After leaving the main freeway, the roads led through suburban foothills. Soon we were negotiating many twists and turns along inclining roadways. We arrived at a mountaintop dominated by a beautiful new house. I commented to Giedre that Jamal must have hired a good architect for his home. We rang the bell and waited. No one came. We tried again a few times with the same result. I got on my cell phone and dialed Jamal's number.

"Guess where we are?" I said cheerfully.
"Where?" answered Jamal.
"At your front door!"
"I did not hear the bell ring. You have to press it real hard and hold it down longer."

So, I held the button down longer. I could hear the bell ring distinctly. Still, no one came to the door. Frustrated, I phoned Jamal again.

"Where are you?" we both exclaimed.
"I am looking all over for you but I don't see you," he said.
"Well, I don't understand..." I puzzled.
"What is the address on the house?" he asked.
I read him the number: "3688."
"That's not my address. I'm at 18520. Where are you? What's the name of the street?"
"Uh, I don't remember."

"What's the name of the town?"
"I think we're in Vista."
"I'm in San Diego. Vista is about 25 miles west of me."

Suddenly, I realized my mistake. I had followed the instructions to the Peteris house. It's a good thing they're not home, I thought. This is so embarrassing.

"Sorry Jamal. My mistake. See you in half an hour," I said humbly. Giedre was thoroughly amused, I could tell.

Jamal was waiting for us in front of his home — an attractive one story rambler located on a sloping lot of over three acres. It was handsomely landscaped. An artificial stream and waterfall interconnected two large pools in the back yard. The 5,000 square foot house was roomy, with cathedral ceilings and it was a mess. It looked like Jamal never finished moving in. Actually, he hadn't. There were various things piled everywhere. A consummate collector and veteran hunter, he had numerous displays of stuffed game birds in glass cages. The bar and pantry were overflowing with bottles of fine wine and liquor. His latest interest in exotic Vodkas was well represented. Two large safes contained his arsenal of guns. Books overflowed every shelf and counter. Proudly, he pointed to some unopened boxes stashed in the living room and declared that they have been there since the movers placed them there thirteen years ago. "One of these days I'll get to them," he assured us.

I had not seen Jamal in a long time. Our friendship goes back about 45 years — when he was a student at UCLA. Jamal possesses a brilliant mind. It took him a total of only five years to earn a PhD in engineering (the allotted time for a BS in this field). He worked in research for a while and then became a consultant for various think tanks — overseeing contracts between the Department of Defense and aerospace contractors.

At the start of the oil boom, in the early seventies, he moved to Beirut, Lebanon, and helped found a consulting firm — a Middle East think tank, actually. With his help, I opened an architectural office there. When the civil war broke out and bombs started flying, I headed back to Seattle. About the same time Jamal accepted an invitation to work in Saudi Arabia. It came from his old friend of UCLA times, Hisham Nazer (then the Minister of Planning and later the Minister of Petroleum). For the next several years Jamal helped modernize the oil rich kingdom and became not so poor in the process. During the same period, I established an office in Saudi Arabia with the help of a member of the royal family. Jamal and I saw each other frequently. When the oil boom ended, Jamal retired comfortably to his properties in Southern California, an area that reminded him of his beloved Palestine.

As brilliant as Jamal may be, he has his faults and eccentricities. A compulsive smoker most of his life, he dropped the nicotine habit 15 years ago — "cold turkey." Three years later, during by-pass surgery, the doctor was astounded that his lungs were perfectly clean. "...As if I had never smoked. You see, Alex," he explained, "I also ate lots of fresh fruit and healthy food. That saved me." True. Jamal was an original health freak.

He was married twice. The first time the marriage lasted about a month. Another time the marriage lasted a whole year. Both women are still in touch with him and relate to him with affection.

"I guess, I'm not meant to be married," he conceded. "In fact, I cannot even have any room mates anymore. Even if my brother comes to visit me, I put him up in a hotel." Jamal was not always this way. For brief periods, he and I were roommates in Seattle, Beirut and Riyadh.

A passionate man who tends to do everything in extremes, Jamal seems to have mellowed somewhat, but his wit and humor is as infectious as ever. I was happy to hear that his compulsive gambling declined from five sessions a week to about two. The stakes (at poker) also have decreased from thousands of dollars to just a few hundred. "I calculated that last year I earned and average of $1.89 per hour playing poker," he said with self-effacing amusement.

Once a gourmet cook, he now spends little time in the kitchen. "I always go out to eat, especially during mid-day when it's hot. I prefer the local casino, which is air-conditioned. I play poker and eat their food — it's the finest cuisine. That way, I eat well, if only once a day, and I stay healthy." I had to agree. Jamal looked healthier and in finer shape then when I last saw him.

He was always a prolific reader (of non-fiction), but his main passion now is his garden. The latter is densely planted with dozens of exotic fruit trees and fruit bearing bushes. He introduced us to each and every specimen as if they were his children. He owns an avocado orchard in nearby Ramona. "Unfortunately, the avocado business costs me $20,000 a year to maintain," he laments. "The cost of water is killing me. But, I don't have the heart to let the trees die."

The farm, his home, and various properties are tended by a Mexican family — whom he supports almost exclusively. "The parents have nine children and I found them living in one small trailer — all of them! I could not bear to see that. I almost cried." So, he moved them into one of his rental houses in town, rent-free. "I love these Mexicans," he confided, "they are so warm and down to earth. And they have culture — they uphold old Mexican traditions. I have practically adopted them," he stated with considerable pride.

Today, their oldest daughter was having her 26th birthday party and we were invited. Their little compound consisted of an old house and the trailer. The space in between was covered with a large tarp which provided shade for the living / dining area. Several Mexican men, in cowboy hats and boots, were standing around, with a can of Budweiser in hand; a couple of them attended to the preparation of meat. This consisted of a giant pot with chunks of pork boiling in it. The other was an "earth oven" — a deep pit in the ground with a pig, wrapped in banana leaves, roasting on hot coals and covered by earth. The latter was a tradition that Jamal picked up in Palestine when he was a small boy. A couple of BBQ grilles were loaded with marinated beefsteaks. Kids were gleefully running around and helping their older sisters decorate the place with ribbons and balloons. The women were busy preparing traditional Mexican dishes inside the house. Drinks of wine, beer and rum cocktails were offered. I stuck to soda pop — due to overindulging the night before. Giedre was fluent in Spanish and the women enjoyed being able to talk with her. I was surprised to hear Jamal speak Spanish. Apparently, he took some lessons in order to communicate better with his hired help. His zest for life was evident as he helped orchestrate the preparations.

Jamal also invited a couple of his countrymen (a man and wife) to this fiesta and they contributed with homemade "Hummus." Giedre and I sat down with them and started into the various table snacks. Turmoil in Israel was in the headlines and our discussion gravitated to that topic. When Jamal overheard us he became visibly upset and asked us not to discuss politics today. "This is a birthday party so, let's keep it happy," he said. "The goings on back home are too upsetting." We switched to telling jokes.

The chunks of meat from the pot and from the pit were tender and flavorful. It was also a treat to eat real Mexican fare —

which was being disbursed in great quantities. Alas, Giedre and I had a standing commitment to visit other friends and we were running late. Reluctantly, we excused ourselves just as the party was gaining momentum.


## VIKTOR AND ILONA

Of course, we had no trouble finding the Peteris house on the mountaintop in nearby Vista. Viktor was a successful architect who recently retired. He was fortunate in having had a son who followed in his footsteps and who was able to take over his practice. As a final project, Viktor designed and built his "dream house" here. The panoramic views were spectacular. The sun was setting and the urban lights of San Diego were beginning to glow in the distance. Below the expansive crimson sky, the Pacific Ocean appeared as a sharp, dark line as if painted by the stroke of a broad brush.

Our hosts greeted us warmly even before we had a chance to ring the doorbell. To my surprise, two other old friends were visiting them, Kestas and his wife, Milda. We were all friends from the days before my exodus from California, many years ago.

Viktor gave me the grand tour of his masterpiece. Every room had floor to ceiling picture windows strategically located to capture the best views. The walls were adorned with remarkable paintings, mostly Ilona's semi-abstract oils. Various works of art proliferated in every room, including Viktor's photographs of their trips to exotic parts of the world. Ilona had her studio in an upstairs loft and, by all appearances, she was still very much in a production mode. Seeing this home, which reflected the life styles and interests of both occupants, made me wistful of the day when I would also design and build my "dream house."

Viktor was my childhood friend in Lithuania and, later, our families reunited again in Los Angeles. He was always like an older brother to me and influenced my interest in painting and the love for mountains. During those youthful days in LA, Ilona was my folk dancing partner before she even met "my older brother." When they did meet, it was love at first sight, I'm sure, for I was soon invited to their wedding.

The fireplace was roaring with dancing flames. We sat down in the living room to enjoy this reunion between old friends. Kestas was also a retired architect. I asked him what he was doing with his free time. He pointed to the collection of ceramics adorning various nooks and crannies of the house. I took a closer look and found that they were truly works of art and not just functional pottery.

Ilona, who was a culinary artist, as well as a painter, served dinner. This guy, Viktor, really lucked out when he married Ilona, I thought, but refrained from saying. After all, a good marriage is always a two way street. Viktor proudly served fine red wine selected from his ample collection in his "cellar." He was disappointed when I declined to imbibe and stuck to my fruit juice. I could not help but notice that Kestas was also drinking a non-alcoholic beverage. This was surprising. I remember him being a prolific drinker in the best Lithuanian tradition (only the Irish are better, I'm told). Apparently, his drinking got the better of him and Milda drew the line. He had no choice but to get "on the wagon." Milda was always one of my favorite people, a woman of substance and a dedicated wife. Kestas could not afford to lose her and I don't blame him. Yet, I was sorry to see Kestas drinking "near-beer" tonight. In the old days he was always the party humorist — with a mischievous smile on his face and an ever-present drink in his hand. His sense of humor and joking were legendary.    Tonight, twinges of his wit came through on occasion and I silently wished for more of it.

Giedre and I departed at a civilized hour, this time, and I did not need any prompting.   We still had a long drive back to LA. Tonight, I was the designated driver.  It was invigorating to see old friends again, especially, after a long lapse of time.  We recounted experiences in our lives that were good and we knew that, at times, they were not so good.  No one gets smooth sailing – I'm convinced of that.  Giedre seemed to have enjoyed the diversion of the last few days and I hoped it helped her cope with her mourning.  I must admit, I also miss my old friend, Rimas.  I intended to share many more adventures with him and it hurts when these expectations are denied with such finality.  He was one of the most colorful and inspiring friends I ever had.

# Chapter IX: A NEW LIFE IN THE NORTHWEST

*NORTHBOUND*
During the first week of January 1961, I packed everything I owned into my Citroën 2CV and headed north. I was full of optimism and confident that this move was a positive step in my life. When I crossed the California border into Oregon, I was elated—a new and exciting life awaited me in the Northwest; I could sense it. There were about ten days before the start of school, and I was keen on getting a taste of what the Northwest had to offer. A lot of snow had fallen in the mountains, and I decided to take a side trip to Crater Lake—an ancient volcanic cauldron filled with dark-blue water. The snowbank at the lodge was fifteen feet high; I had not seen so much snow since my days in the Alps. There was not enough room to sleep in the car, but I was prepared to bivouac in the snow—wherever I stopped. I continued north along Highway 99 and turned off toward

Mount Hood, the 11,240-foot volcano that I had seen only in pictures.

A few months earlier, I had read a *Time* magazine article about Timberline Lodge, located high on the southern slope of Mount Hood. It was built by the Civilian Conservation Corps. This organization, created by President Roosevelt during the Great Depression, hired unemployed youth, including many artists and artisans who were put to work building unique lodges throughout the West. Timberline was built during the thirties but lay dormant during most of the fifties. The article described how a wealthy businessman from New England had purchased the rights to the lodge and spent a lot of money refurbishing it. It was now open to the public again and the chairlifts were running.

I decided to stop at the lodge for a few days. There were expensive luxury bedrooms available for the well heeled, but there were also cheap bunk-rooms available for poor student types such as me. The lodge is an architectural masterpiece: huge timbers support three levels of public lounges dominated by a stone masonry column containing no fewer than six big fireplaces. All the wood detailing is beautifully handcrafted in wildlife themes. Big oil paintings adorn the walls. The view to the south looks across the broad Cascade Range with sharp-spired Mount Jefferson looming in the distance. The view to the north frames the summit of Mount Hood, always snow encrusted with intricately sculptured ice formations.

The weather was marginal when I arrived. The forecast predicted that a storm would move in. I desperately wanted to climb Mount Hood. I started asking ski instructors and ski patrol people if anyone was interested in accompanying me on a summit attempt. A young ski instructor agreed to join me; he was also an experienced climber. We set out at daybreak the next morning with overcast skies. We were turned back by bad weather not far from the summit. Some days later, I tried again with a new partner. By the time we reached the summit slopes, clouds had moved in and we continued in whiteout conditions. Fortunately, my companion had climbed the mountain before and knew the way. We reached the summit in poor visibility. The view I was hoping for was denied us, but I was not complaining. I was very happy to have climbed my first Northwest volcano.

By the time we reached the lodge, it had started snowing. It stormed for the next three days, and the snow accumulation was enough to shut down the highway. We were snowbound! No one could arrive at or depart from the lodge. The manager opened up the bar and everybody enjoyed free drinks for the next few days. There were several students from WSU and we all became friends. We even mingled with the blue bloods from New England, who were not enjoying the involuntary confinement nearly as much as the students.

Around the seventh day of our stay, it stopped snowing and snowplows finally broke through to the lodge. It was a challenge to find the right car, since they were completely buried in deep snowdrifts. I shoveled my little 2CV out of its cold tomb and headed down the mountain and east along the Columbia River. The Gorge was blanketed in snow and it was a spectacular sight. I crossed into Washington near the Tri-Cities and arrived in Pullman two days before the start of school.

## LIFE ON CAMPUS

I was housed in a dormitory called Kruger Hall—a sterile concrete structure containing about a hundred little dorm rooms. I was paired with a roommate who had been accepted onto the varsity football team (a prestigious accomplishment). I had joined the varsity gymnastics team and that must have been the reason for our being paired: we were considered "jocks," though we had nothing else in common. My roommate was a typical football player: big, bulky, and not very bright. Interestingly, several fraternities came to our room in order to entice him to join the brotherhood. I kept my nose in the books I was reading and pretended not to hear the dubious enticements that they were offering. Once in a while, one of the Greeks would nervously glance my way, but not one of them ever came over to me to ask if I was interested in joining their fraternity. On the outside, I must have had all the attributes of a good candidate. Did they sense that I would have refused them outright?

I took a heavy load of courses, perhaps too many, since I was also committed to participate on the gymnastics team. Fortunately, it was off-season and there were no meets scheduled. One of my teammates was a German exchange student named Rolf Vordervülbecke. He was president of the Cosmopolitan Club—an organization where local students could mingle with foreigners. Rolf informed me that there would be a dance on Friday night and that I should come. I accepted his invitation.

The room was full of students speaking a variety of foreign languages. WSU was proud of its tradition of hosting many foreign students.[43] Rolf pointed out a lovely young lady on the other side of the room and said, "She is from Munich, like you. You should meet her, so go ask her to dance." I walked across the floor and introduced myself to the young beauty. She said her name was Gisela. As we danced, the conversation continued (in German):

---

[43]Many foreign students signed up to attend Washington State University thinking it was a college in Washington, DC One classmate told me that he was confused when his plane did not land on the East Coast—instead continuing westward. He was surprised to end up on a campus surrounded by rural wheat farms instead of the monuments of our capital.

"Where did you learn to speak German so well?" she inquired."I used to live in Germany," I told her."Oh, where in Germany?" "In Munich," I responded with a smile.

Her face lit up and she said, "That's where I'm from! Where in Munich did you live?"

"In a neighborhood called Bogenhausen."

Now her expression changed to one of puzzled curiosity. "That's funny, I also lived in Bogenhausen. Do you remember by chance what street you lived on?"

"Yes, on Mühlbauerstrasse," I responded.

At that moment I had to hold her up, for her knees had suddenly gone weak.

"You're joking, aren't you?" she said. "That's so strange. You see, I also lived on Mühlbauerstrasse."

We stopped dancing and walked to a quiet corner. There we established that indeed, both of us had lived on the same little street in Munich during the same five-year time period! However, there was a good reason why we had never met, although we were the same age. I lived in a large apartment building and played in the street like all the other kids on the block. Gisela lived across the street (one block away) in a private boarding school for girls. The school grounds were surrounded by a ten-foot masonry wall. I do remember climbing to the top of the wall on some occasions to get a glimpse of the uniformed girls playing volleyball. Very likely, I may have seen little Gisela, who one day would become my wife.

Gisela and I became a couple and we really enjoyed each other's company. We had many friends in common. Unfortunately, I was having too much fun and my grades were suffering. Halfway through the semester, I decided to forgo the temptations of social life and try to concentrate on academics. I developed a rather unconventional schedule. After dinner, when campus social life went into high gear and the noise (and music) in the dormitories started cranking up, I went to bed and slept. Around midnight, when all was quiet, I hit the books and studied all night. Gisela felt abandoned, but our friendship survived.

The one activity that I continued was soccer. I signed up with the varsity team and became the team's top scorer. We played against several schools throughout the Northwest, including the University of British Columbia (Canada). Unlike major college teams that traveled in style, we had to provide our own transportation and pay for all expenses when going to games at other schools. This inequity was most unfair, I thought.

Upon my arrival on campus, I joined the climbing club. When its members found out my (modest) record in climbing, they immediately voted me the president of the club. This carried the obligation of taking novices on field trips and teaching them how to do roped climbs safely and how to rappel down a cliff. I remember one aspiring young mountaineer who was being coaxed to step over a precipice for her first rappel. She was rotund and weighed a good 250 pounds. We belayed her with a second rope so nothing could go wrong. Nonetheless, getting her to commit to the rappel became a problem. It took two strong men to pry her fingers from the top edge of the cliff. I don't think she came back for lesson number two.

The campus was surrounded by farmland—primarily wheat fields. There was ample opportunity to go hunting for small game. One time I stayed behind when some of my friends went on a hunt. My friend Armin Wüsten asked if he could borrow one of my guns—a 22-caliber pistol with hammer action. I agreed to loan it to him but warned him never to keep the hammer cocked while the gun was in the holster. "Cock it only when you are ready to shoot," I warned. "It's a safety feature." He nodded.

That evening, he came by to return the pistol and I noticed that his lower leg was in a cast. "What happened?" I asked. "Well," he responded with an embarrassed smile, "I forgot to uncock the hammer, and when a rabbit ran by, I went to pull the gun out of the holster and shot myself through the foot." A lesson learned the hard way.

Architectural design classes were demanding, but the instructors were good. I enjoyed drawing and designing and received good grades for my efforts. Unfortunately, I realized that I was running low on cash and that I would need to get a part-time job to support myself. Architectural firms were few and far between in this remote corner of the state. Reluctantly, I made plans to transfer to the University of Washington (Seattle) in the fall.

During this one semester at WSU, I was truly fulfilled with the academic as well as social life. I made more lifelong friendships here than at the other four colleges I attended—combined. Adli Qudsi was my architecture classmate and became my partner in the office we started in Beirut. Riad Kayyali, who graduated in engineering, would become my office manager in Riyadh, Saudi Arabia. Half Zantop became one of my best climbing partners. Edith Miles (of Auburn, Washington) remained a lifelong family friend. Gisela became the love of my life. Dave Rahm commissioned me to design his house but left on an assignment to Jordan before I could start. His hobby was stunt flying, and he was giving King Hussein a demonstration when he failed to pull out of a dive. His little plane crashed into the ground. He died in the arms of the king.

As the end of the semester approached, I made plans for the summer and the next year. I intended to join some friends (in Los Angeles) on a gold mining trip to British Columbia. I needed to return to LA to provision the expedition. Gisela was graduating with a bachelor's degree in psychology and had a job lined up at Shriners Hospital in LA for the summer. I agreed to take her along in my car. Her friend Anna joined us for part of the trip (her destination was San Francisco).

## THE LONG SUMMER

First we drove to Vancouver, British Columbia, where Gisela had some friends. Then we took the scenic route down the Pacific Coast. We camped on various beaches each night. One morning the tide came in sooner than we expected and the sea started lapping at the ends of our sleeping bags. Gisela was not used to camping like this, but she was a good sport and developed a liking for nature and the wild Pacific West.

While in Los Angeles, Gisela met my mother and they seemed to hit it off. My mother invited her to stay at our house for the summer while I was off in Canada. But first, Gisela and I took one more trip—down to Mexico.

I packed my two-man kayak into the back of the 2CV, and we drove south to the little island I frequented near the town of Ensenada (Estero Beach). We paddled across the small bay and set up camp on the desolate isle. There was not a human being in sight; we had the place all to ourselves. I set up a tarp for protection against rain and sun between the sand dunes. It stormed for the next two days, but we stayed warm and cozy in our makeshift shelter. When the stormy weather abated, we took a long stroll along the beach. The surf was still pounding hard, so we did not go into the water. In the distance, we saw many seagulls hovering over something they had found on the beach. As we approached, we realized that a school of manta rays had stranded themselves during the night. They were lying in formation (more or less) and were dead. The seagulls were after fresh brain food and started pecking at the heads. Blood was already trickling from some craniums. The mantas were black and their heads were beautifully sculpted. Gisela was wearing a pink dress and the contrast was macabre. I took a few photos but did not ever enjoy looking at them.

After a wonderful week of cavorting and swimming in our little paradise, we returned to Los Angeles. Gisela went to work at the hospital and I got busy rounding up equipment and a truck for our trip to the gold fields of British Columbia.[44] Before I departed, Gisela asked me if I would object should she choose to stay in America. Her question caught me off guard. Back home, she had parents, a brother, and a sister, not to mention many friends. *Why would she want to stay in America?* I wondered. I was certainly not ready to make any permanent commitments. I urged her to return to Germany.

Upon my return to LA (from Canada) at the end of the summer, Gisela had already departed. My mother informed me that she was still in New York. I contacted her by phone and offered to visit her one more time. Having parents working for UAL allowed me to fly to New York for free. Gisela was staying in a youth hostel just off Central Park, the rough side. It was September and the East Coast was enjoying an Indian summer. The weather was sweltering hot and humid. Getting a good night's sleep was a challenge. For a few days, we enjoyed visiting many museums and art galleries. The Guggenheim was our favorite, of course. One evening we were taking a romantic stroll through

[44]See story, *"Caribou Mountain Gold."*

Central Park when two police officers intercepted us.

"What do you two think you are doing—walking here after dark?" one of them asked. "Don't you know you are risking your life?"

"What's the problem, sir?" I replied. "Are we doing something illegal?"

"No, you're not. You're doing something stupid. You're obviously from out of town. Consider yourselves lucky that we found you first."

Then they proceeded to explain that Central Park after dark was a haven for drug dealers, muggers, and rapists. We got the point and took the shortest route back to the city street, Central Park West.

Gisela cried when I dropped her off at the airport for her flight back to Germany. I promised to visit her, someday.


*RELOCATING TO SEATTLE*
During our trip down the coast earlier that summer, I stopped in at the University of Washington and spoke to Dean Herman about transferring to his school for the coming fall. He read my transcript and seemed impressed with my record in architectural courses, as well as academic ones. I had so many credits he offered to enroll me in the fourth-year program. I was keen on taking many more electives and felt two years was not enough time for the education I was seeking. I replied that I would prefer to start with the third-year courses. He agreed.

I arrived in Seattle a few days before school started and rented a small apartment squeezed into the attic of an old Victorian house (near Group Health Hospital). I had a view of Mount Rainier from one of the little windows and that appealed to me.

My trusty old 2CV was on its last legs and running on one cylinder. I decided to donate it to a local Boy Scout troop. They were delighted with the gift and used it for mechanic training. It was perfect for that purpose.

I bought a ten-speed bicycle and it sufficed for my student lifestyle. The ride to campus was only three miles—mostly downhill in the morning and uphill on the way back. The first time that I made the trip home from school, I got soaking wet with sweat and fell into bed exhausted. Within a few weeks, I was breezing up the hill and seeking out the steepest streets for extra exercise. During some winters, it would snow and the streets would freeze over. On those rare occasions, I would sleep on the floor of our studio at school.

During the early sixties, bicyclists were a rare sight on Seattle streets, and drivers where not used to them. I would speed down Capitol Hill on my way to school. Once, I came down Interlaken and made a hard left turn onto the sidewalk of 24th Avenue East (without crossing the street). There used to be a gas station on the southwest corner of 24th and Boyer (now a vacant lot), and I was used to rushing past it (northbound). This time a car was pulling out of the driveway (southbound), and the driver was looking over his left shoulder to see if the coast was clear. He was beginning to move forward as I crashed into him—head on. I flew over his hood and landed, spread eagle, on his windshield. The look of surprise on the driver's face was astounding as we eyed each other a few inches apart; he had no idea where I had come from. I slid off the hood and he stepped out of the car. My bike was mangled into a pretzel. The elderly man started apologizing profusely, and I did the same. He offered to give me his insurance card so that all the damages could be paid for. I declined to accept it and assured him that I was not hurt and that the collision was really my fault, not his. Today a similar accident would probably have resulted in lawsuits.

I joined the varsity gymnastics team. My credentials as a California gymnast impressed the coach at the UW. The standard of competition was not nearly as high in Washington as it was in California. Unfortunately, my name got into the campus newspaper and Dean Herman found out about it. He called me into his office and looked at me angrily.

"Mr. Bertulis, you never told me that you intended to participate in varsity athletics. Do you think you can do justice to our architecture program while spending your afternoons working out with the gymnastics team?"

"Of course, sir," I replied. "I was successful in doing so for the previous two years, and my grade point average is quite good."

His response was "Our program is very demanding, more than any of those other schools you went to. So, you can choose between gymnastics and architecture. You're not going to do both while I'm dean of this school."

I was deeply disappointed with this ultimatum. I resigned from the gymnastics team but continued to train with them unofficially for the rest of the school year. I was later honored with an invitation to appear as a judge for the Washington State high school championships. I enjoyed the experience of sitting on the other side of the performances for a change.

Dean Herman was a stuffy old gentleman. He had been the dean of this school for most of his adult life. He was not much of a designer and did not teach any design courses. He did teach a basic course in architectural history. He had this course down pat, and it was popular with the students. The reason for the popularity was that he presented this course with flair and humor. However, he was wrong on one historic point: he considered Frank Lloyd Wright a fraud and thought his type of architecture was to be disdained. The reason for this prejudice was rooted in a personal encounter with Wright that Dean Herman had had many years earlier.

During the 1930s, Mr. Wright had very few architectural commissions, and he supplemented his income by lecturing as a visiting architect at various universities. As the story goes, Mr. Wright was critiquing the designs of the senior class at the University of Washington. Dean Herman was doing a private project on the side and decided to sneak his plans in with the student presentations (under a pseudonym). When Mr. Wright came to critique Dean Herman's design, the dean was listening and most of the students knew whose plans these were. Mr. Wright did not mince words in lambasting such an inferior design. The students were doing their best not to laugh out loud. Dean Herman returned to his office humiliated. Ever since, he had been getting even in his history lectures.

Overall, I was delighted with the academic life at the University of Washington. Our architecture class had many talented students who would later become successful architects. I always had an easy time with design courses, since I appeared to have a talent in this area of endeavor. I loved academia; there was so much to learn. I often overloaded my course load with more than my share of elective courses, such as creative writing, public speaking, foreign languages, art classes, even math courses.

A requirement for architecture was a basic course in watercolor, taught by the Art Department. I enjoyed this class so much that I continued to take extra courses in painting with this medium. A few of my paintings got B grades and most of them got As. The trouble with the A-grade paintings was that the Art Department would keep them. At the end of the school year, the department would hold an auction, and these painting were sold to the highest bidders. I could not afford to buy my paintings back. However, I would be rewarded at times upon seeing my paintings in various conference rooms of local architects and lawyers.

There was one classmate in architecture who also took his painting seriously. His name was Tom Rickard. Having already received a degree in landscape architecture from the University of Oregon, he was an experienced painter. He invited me to join him on weekend painting trips. These excursions were a lot of fun—not just because we always had a fruitful exchange of ideas about painting issues as well as world affairs, but also because Tom had the wherewithal to include good wine and cheese in our picnic basket. Tom remained a lifelong friend.

Despite the prejudice toward the architecture of Frank Lloyd Wright, my interest in his projects never waned. I acquired a Volkswagen bug, and during some school breaks, I would travel across the width and breadth of the lower forty-eight states in order to view and photograph completed Wright projects firsthand. Mr. Wright is said to have completed several hundred commercial and residential projects; most of them are still standing. I would seek permission to visit these masterpieces in advance of my arrival and photograph them from the inside (in most cases) as well as from the outside. I was also able to interview many of the original owners, who have since passed away. Unfortunately, I did not keep written records of these informal discussions. However, my slide collection became extensive. I gave lectures on Mr. Wright's works throughout North America and Europe.

Toward the end of the communist era in Lithuania, I was invited to be a guest lecturer at the University of Vilnius. I selected two architectural subjects I was expert in: one lecture was on the comparative differences of construction in Europe and the USA, the other on executed commercial projects by Frank Lloyd Wright. The latter presentation was quite popular.

## WORKING AGAIN

I needed money to pay for tuition, rent, food, and other expenses. I had no trouble finding good paying jobs in architectural offices in Seattle. Of course, I never told Dean Herman or my architecture instructors that I was working on the side. Some of them frowned upon the idea of getting on-the-job training before they were through indoctrinating you in the proper concepts of the profession.

There is a beautiful little office building that literally overhangs the corner of Eastlake Avenue and East Galer Street, near the south end of Lake Union. I was intrigued by its simple yet excellent design and figured the office occupants must be good architects. I was right. One day I walked into the office and introduced myself to the receptionist. I informed her that I was looking for part-time work as a draftsman. She responded that there were no openings, but she would inform one of the partners that I was there. Mr. Arthur Andersen came out to see me. He reiterated that there were no openings, but he was willing to take a few minutes to look at samples of my work. I rolled out the set of plans I had brought along, and Mr. Andersen began to peruse the sheets of construction drawings. He mumbled something that I did not understand and walked back into the drafting room. A minute later, he reappeared with his two partners, Messrs. Arden Steinhart and Robert Theriault. All three of them began looking through my drawings with serious interest. "This is your work?" one of them asked. "Yes," I replied. "When can you start working for us?" was the response.

This firm specialized in various commercial projects and some incidental residential work. Though modest in ambition (this firm deliberately tried to remain small), their work reflected conscientious design. The office had a congenial atmosphere, and the three principals of the firm remained my friends for many years after I left.


*CLIMBING TO HIGHER LEVELS*

The Pacific Northwest is full of raging rivers that attract the adventurous kayaker. Having had some flat-water experience in California, I was eager to test my mettle with whitewater kayaking. To get proper experience, I enrolled in a class given by Wolf Bauer. He taught his students all about hydrology and kayaking. I became proficient but not expert in this sport. I also tried my hand at scuba diving. The Pacific Ocean at Westport provided ample supply of lingcod, but Puget Sound waters were too murky for good diving. One summer a diving partner and I made some good money retrieving sunken junk in a salvaging operation in Elliott Bay; they were planning to expand a pier. It was hard work and that suited me just fine.

Once I arrived at the University of Washington, however, it did not take me long to find climbing partners for trips into the Cascades and the Olympic Mountains. Helmut Geldsetzer was a geology student, and we made a pact that we would climb a mountain every weekend during the summer of 1962. With our growing experience, our climbs became bolder and the trips longer. Sometimes, we would have to run back down the mountain in order to make it back to Seattle in time for Monday morning classes or work. Frequently, I would show up at work wearing sandals because my feet were too sore for street shoes after an arduous weekend trek.

Our final objective of the summer was an ambitious climb of

one of the remote peaks of the Picket Range: Mount Challenger. It was Labor Day weekend, and we had three days for a trip that normally requires four or more. It was a long way in, about twenty-five miles, and we hiked most of the distance without resting. On Sunday, we got our first glimpse of this magnificent mountain range. The nearest peak was Mount Challenger—with Mount Fury and then Mount Terror behind it. It became obvious that even Mount Challenger was too far for the time left in our schedule. Helmut and I figured that if we moved fast, we could climb one of Challenger's three satellite peaks.

We scurried over Perfect Pass and climbed alongside the glacier and over a ridge to the summit of a small spire. It was a first ascent, so we built a big cairn on top. The view of the Pickets was enchanting. At that moment, I decided to come back the next year, traverse the range, and climb all three major summits.

The following year, I was able to enlist my old friend Half Zantop for the traverse I dreamed about all winter long. Half was earning his master's degree in geology at the UW. We allowed ten days for the trip and arranged to have a friend to pick us up at the trailhead on the other end.

First we climbed the imposing Mount Terror. While taking turns sitting on the tiny summit, we looked down the other side into the McMillan Creek Valley—six thousand feet below us. Descending the first two thousand feet required continuous rappelling, which we accomplished in two days. A few days later, we climbed Mount Fury, making the first ascent of the South Peak in the process. Finally, we managed to climb Mount Challenger while the weather was deteriorating. On our tenth day, we ran most of the way out to the trailhead in order to meet our prearranged ride on time.[45]

---

[45]See story, *Our "Alps:" A Match for Europe.*

This traverse was historic and caught the attention of the leading local climbers. At the time, there was an Eigerwand Kaffeehaus in the U District where climbers and various eccentrics would hang out, drink exotic teas, and play chess. The proprietor was a well-known climber by the name of Eric Bjornstad. His passion in life was climbing mountains, especially by unclimbed and difficult routes. He was obsessed with the idea of climbing the notorious north face of the Eiger in the Swiss Alps. His Kaffeehaus, which mostly served tea, was decorated imaginatively in alpine motifs: old climbing ropes crisscrossed the ceiling; axes and crampons decorated the walls. These walls were planked with weathered cedar boards that he found on old (abandoned) barns in the foothills of the Cascades. When the city health department cited him for "unsanitary" tabletops—because they had too many cracks and nicks in them—he replaced them with marble slabs. When the city inspectors approved the new slabs, they did not know that these pieces of marble once served as urinal partitions in an old (abandoned) office building on Pioneer Square.

Eric was impressed with our traverse of the Picket Range and invited us to present our slides at Fred Beckey's party that Friday night. *Wow*, I thought; I would finally meet "The Legend" himself! Fred was in his mid-forties at the time and had probably made more first ascents than anyone else in the world. Some people were wondering why he was still climbing. After all, his reputation in history books had been secured and he was getting "old." Almost fifty years later, Fred Beckey is still climbing, and these same people are still wondering when he will retire.

Fred was also impressed with our traverse of the Picket Range and invited me on his next adventure—the first ascent of Spider Peak in the remote Wind River Range of Wyoming. I continued climbing with my own friends, including Eric Bjornstad, Hans

Baer, and Half Zantop, among others, but more and more frequently I would receive invitations to join Fred on some epic climb. During the coming winter, I teamed up with Leif Patterson (who taught mathematics at UBC) and invited Fred to join us on the first winter ascent of Mount Robson—the highest peak in the Canadian Rockies and one of the most challenging. Fred reciprocated by inviting me on the first winter ascent of Mount Sir Donald—an impressive peak dominating Rogers Pass in the Canadian Selkirks. A year later, Pete Williamson, Bill Sumner, and I made the first winter ascent of Forbidden Peak—a popular mountain near Cascade Pass.

During the winter and spring of 1965, Fred invited me to participate in the second ascent of the "Grand Wall" on the Squamish Chief—a 1,600-foot granite cliff an hour's drive north of Vancouver, British Columbia. One of the most impressive granite walls in Washington State can be found on the east face of Liberty Bell Mountain. Today it can be viewed from the observation terrace located at Washington Pass on the North Cascades Highway. In the early sixties, Steve Marts and I made a number of attempts to climb this face. I had made plans to leave for Africa,[46] so Steve finished the climb with Don McPherson and Fred Stanley. We named the route Liberty Crack. Today it is considered one of the classic climbs of North America. The crux of the climb is a twelve-foot overhanging ceiling—which Steve named the "Lithuanian Lip." I was first to climb over it.

A year later, I teamed up with Don McPherson and established a second route on the east face of Liberty Bell Mountain, which was even more challenging than our first route. It took us four days to overcome the 1,300-foot precipice. We named it the "Independence Route."

---

[46]See story, *Into The Mountains Of Africa.*

During the sixties, the Chinese government made most of the mountains of the Himalayas off-limits to climbers from the West. Aspiring climbers focused on the next best thing—the mountains of Alaska. Fred Beckey was a veteran of Alaskan climbing and invited me and two other friends to join him in an attempt to climb the highest unclimbed peak in Alaska: The Twaharpies (14,621 feet). The year was 1964. Four of us left Seattle in a 1957 Ford station wagon. During those days, the Alcan Highway was still unpaved. Seven flat tires and three thousand miles later, we arrived in the little town of Glennallen. From here, a bush pilot flew us into the Wrangell Mountain Range. Soon after we were dropped off on the glacier and established base camp, we were hit by a ten-day storm. We stayed in two little tents day and night. The conditions tested our nerves and friendships. When the weather cleared, we started up the mountain. Halfway up the route, a slab avalanche let loose. We survived without injury, but some of us were buried in snow up to our hips. It could have been worse. Fred decided to call off the trip and "live to climb the mountain another day."

During the presidential election year of 1964, when Barry Goldwater was running against LBJ, I was coming back from an attempt to climb Shiprock—a two-thousand-foot basalt spire in the New Mexico desert. Fred Beckey dropped me off at the airport in Las Vegas, and I got on a plane headed for Seattle. The plane was full, and I noticed that there were an inordinate number of tall young men on board. I sat down in the last empty seat next to one of the young men and asked if they were some sort of team. He replied with a heavy accent, "Yes, we are Soviet basketball team." I was impressed. I spoke a little Russian and informed my seat-mate, "I am Lithuanian." At that, his eyes lit up and he declared that there was a Lithuanian on their team. "Really?" I said. "Could you point him out to me? He stood up and shouted down the aisle: "Modestai!" With that, a tall young man stood up and looked back at us. My companion waved to him to come over and relinquished his seat.

I introduced myself in Lithuanian, and I could tell the young man was delighted to meet an expatriate countryman. His name was Modestas Paulauskas, one of the greatest basketball players to ever play on the Soviet national team. During the 1968 Olympic games in Mexico, he was instrumental in the first-ever defeat of a USA basketball team. Now we were sitting together in a plane, flying at thirty-thousand feet with lots of time to talk —and talk we did!

He was nineteen years old and eager to hear as much as possible about life in the West. This was during the time when the Iron Curtain was still solidly in place. I told him all I could about life in America, how much things cost, how much we earned, our laws, our politics, etc. He was most interested in our politics, and I tried as best as I could to explain to him our system of democracy. At one point, he leaned over to me and in a low voice informed me that, "the folks back home are all hoping that Goldwater will win." They figured Goldwater would be tougher on the communists.

We talked intensely and freely because no one else on the plane could understand Lithuanian. This did not make some people happy. One Russian fellow kept walking by us and giving Modestas angry looks. He was not particularly tall, and I figured he was one of the KGB agents assigned to "protect" the team. Modestas ignored him and we continued talking. The plane was bound for San Francisco, where the team had a game scheduled before coming to Seattle. Modestas asked me if I would be able to do him a favor and buy some small items for him to take home. I said I would be more than happy to. The list included prescription glasses for one of his parents, needles for an old Singer sewing machine (for his uncle, who was a cobbler), fishing gear (he was an avid fisherman), and a copy of *Playboy* (request made with a red face). He said that they would be staying at the Olympic Hotel while in Seattle, and I agreed to deliver the items there.

In San Francisco, I had to change planes. The Soviet team was ushered into a VIP waiting lounge where newspaper reporters and camera crews were waiting. Inadvertently, I kept talking to Modestas as we disembarked, and I was ushered into the lounge along with the Soviets. I was also handed a glass of orange juice with the rest of them. Very few of the players could speak more than a few words of English, and the interviewers were having a tough time. Suddenly, a reporter shoved a microphone in front of me and started asking me questions while a TV camera focused in. The reporter was delighted to have found someone who spoke English well, and he ran through a litany of questions. With a straight face, I answered all of them. I could only imagine how impressed the TV audience must have been with a "Soviet" player so fluent in English. We parted when I heard the boarding call for my flight to Seattle.

A few days later, I read in the local paper that the Soviet team had landed in Seattle and was scheduled to play in Key Arena. I phoned the Olympic Hotel and got Modestas on the line. He informed me that we should meet in the men's toilet located in the basement of the hotel. It was now a clandestine operation—no one was in the basement and the men's room was not in use. Modestas was not the same happy fellow I last saw on the flight from Las Vegas. His demeanor was serious and he acted nervously. I gave him my collection of purchases; he thanked me and left quickly. I could tell that the KGB must have had a frank talk with him about fraternizing with the "enemy."

That evening, I watched the game on TV and saw Modestas sitting on the bench (he had always been a starter). This time, he sat out the whole game. I am sure he was being punished. We never met again. Of course, during those days, corresponding with foreigners was all but impossible for Soviet citizens. I followed his brilliant basketball career through various news venues.

One of the most popular mountains in the Northwest is Mount Rainier. I first climbed it with Steve Marts, Fred Stanley, and Don McPherson via the challenging Ptarmigan Ridge route. A few years later, I climbed the route again with Rich Pellerin. When Fred Beckey heard my plans to climb that route with Rich, his response was "Why are you doing it? You already climbed it once!" Well, I like climbing classic routes not just to say that I have done them, but because the climbs are so enjoyable. I've climbed Liberty Ridge (on the north side of the mountain) nine times—once with my daughter Eugenia when she was eleven years old and once with my son Nik when he was twenty-five.

Over the years, I climbed mountains all over the world, including fifteen expeditions to the Himalayas. Mountain climbing has remained an activity close to my heart. Only my family and my profession (as an architect) have received more dedication.

One of my favorite climbing companions during those early years was Half Zantop. He was of German ancestry but grew up in Barcelona. He was a frequent guest at my mother's house in LA and spent one Christmas with us. I had the pleasure of spending the Christmas of 1966 with his family in Spain. While in Seattle, we often double dated. One winter we toured the major ski areas of the West—often spending the night sleeping under a tree with snow as our mattress. We made numerous exciting climbs in the Cascade Range of Washington, the Bugaboos of Canada, the Grand Tetons of Wyoming, and the Sierras of California, to mention but a few. Our last climb together involved a mishap. While leading a vertical face in the Tuolumne

Meadows area of Yosemite, Half took a fall and broke his ankle.
It could have been worse if I had not held him on a belay. He retired from climbing. In one of his letters to me, he reminisced:

> Last night it struck me that some of my fondest
> memories and most challenging feats of my life have
> been fully your doing. The traverse of the Picket
> Range and the wild-goose chase to climbing areas in
> the Canadian Rockies, the Tetons, and the Wind
> Rivers, and finally the Sierra Nevada, after we were
> snowed out of other possibilities. You saved my head
> when I fell on Echo Peak, and I suppose the broken
> ankle and meeting Susanne finally forced me to fin-
> ish my long-overdue PhD and embark on my profes-
> sional career.

Half became a professor of geology at Dartmouth College. He
and his wife raised two bright and beautiful daughters. Tragedy
struck one cold evening in January 2001. Half and his wife were
brutally murdered in their home by two teenage thrill seekers.[47]

## FEMALE RELATIONSHIPS

I was socially active during these first years in Seattle and got
involved with some wonderful women. I dated a beauty by the
name of Marti Hagan (of Tacoma). She was an aspiring ballet
dancer and certainly had the talent and figure for it. One year she
became the Seafair Queen here in Seattle. The following year,
she was elected Miss Washington State. I think she eventually
married a naval officer and moved to Texas. The city of Vancouver, three hours' drive north of Seattle, has a cosmopolitan reputation; it used to have a popular restaurant called Johann Strauss.

---

[47]A book about the Zantops, *Judgment Ridge*, was written by Dick Lehr and
Mitchell Zuckoff, and published by Harper Collins.

The reason for its popularity was not the good food but the opportunity to meet single women. The orchestra played continental and Latin music (waltzes, tangos, sambas, etc), and many people, mostly Europeans, would attend the evening dance sessions.

That's how I met an attractive young lady from Munich by the name of Rita Riedl. We would rendezvous at the Johann Strauss on weekends. One time we took a trip up the Sunshine Coast of British Columbia and drove to the northern terminus of Highway 101 (which starts on the Mexican border). It ended on a cozy little warm-water cove at the edge of Desolation Sound. Here we went swimming, built a campfire, and camped for the night under a star-studded sky. Lonnie Vaughn was an architectural sales rep in Seattle, and I met her when she came into the office I was working in. She was a few years older than I and became the proverbial "older woman" in my romantic relationships. I tried to introduce her to mountain climbing and took her up The Tooth, near Snoqualmie Pass. The peak was small but steep. I had her safely roped in, but she was too terrified of falling to enjoy the climb. We took too much time and spent an unexpected night sleeping on the trail on the way out. After that experience, I was not keen on teaching girlfriends how to climb.

Having been an avid hunter, I used to read countless hunting stories. The author of many of these was Jack O'Connor. He was a legendary hunter of game big and small. I had the pleasure of meeting him at his house in Lewiston, Idaho. It was a thrill to make the acquaintance of my long-time idol. He was congenial and showed me his remarkable collection of guns and rifles— stacked in long rows along different walls of his house. There were trophies of big game animals hanging on numerous walls and a special trophy room. When Jack learned that I was living in Seattle, he informed me that he had two daughters, more or less my age, who were "unattached." I became friends with Car-

oline and Cathy O'Connor, and we had some great times together before drifting apart. Forty years later, Caroline and I recognized each other at a social function in Seattle and renewed our
old friendship (we were both single again).

After finishing up my studies at the UW, I had no more obliga-
tions and the world was at my feet. My plan now was to save
enough money for the proverbial trip around the world. I continued working for various architectural firms and climbed mountains like there was no tomorrow. At Eric's Eigerwand Kaffeehaus, I met a girl from Ellensburg, Peggy Bull, who was an English major at the UW. We decided it would be more economical
if we moved in together. We opted to share a houseboat next to
the University Bridge. Our other roommate was her best friend,
Toni Pellegrini. Toni's fiancé was away at medical school. The
deal was I would pay for the food and the women would do the
cooking. I ate well for a change. Toni's father (Angelo Pellegrini) was an English professor and renowned for his gourmet
cooking as well as his numerous books on the subject. I still
have many fond memories of dining at the Pellegrini household.

During the spring of 1965, I made frequent trips to advance our
route on the Squamish Chief (north of Vancouver). Peggy would
often accompany us to the base of the cliff. One day she decided
to drive back to Vancouver (in my VW bug) while Leif and I
continued climbing overnight. When Peggy failed to return the
next day, we were forced to hitchhike back to Vancouver. We
found her in a hospital: she had collided with a parked car and
suffered some broken ribs. My car was badly damaged, as was
the car she hit. To make matters worse, I was informed that my
car insurance was not valid in Canada! That was not a pleasant
way to find out about the small print in my insurance coverage
(again).

I had plans to join Leif on a major climb that summer: Norway's unclimbed monolith called Trollveggen. Leif found some Nor-wegians to do the historic climb with. I remained in Seattle and worked for one more year to pay off the debt incurred by the claim for damaging the Canadian car. The repair bill amounted to several thousand dollars, more than my entire budget for the world tour I was planning. After I submitted the final installment payment, the Canadian insurance company sent me a formal let-ter acknowledging that the debt had been paid off and thanking me for my "splendid cooperation."

Peggy would also join us on many climbing trips. She had no in-terest in mountaineering, but she enjoyed camping at the base of the cliffs and taking telephoto shots of us climbers with my camera. With my friend Tom Rickard, we would go on weekend painting excursions—usually to one of the Puget Sound islands. Peggy would entertain us with her guitar, singing, and good hu-mor. When I finally departed for my world trip, she fully expect-ed to reunite with me a year later. She met me in New York when I returned, and I had the unpleasant task of informing her that I was now a married man. She took it very hard and, unbe-knownst to any of her family and friends, joined a mysterious religious cult. She would phone me every few years and even made a couple of visits to my house, where she met my wife. She would not reveal how and where she was living, and she would answer inquiries with a cryptic, "Oh, I'm living the dull life of a nun." Eventually, her cult members moved to San Diego, where they all committed suicide—with intentions of hitching a ride on Comet Hale-Bopp—which was passing by planet Earth at the time.

*LITHUANIANS IN EXILE*
When my family came to the USA, we assumed that our stay in this country would be temporary. We hoped that the illegal oc-cupation of our country would end and we could all go back

home. This hope diminished with time when it became apparent that the Kremlin continued to tighten its grip on the Baltic states. Washington refused to take a strong stance against the Soviets, lest it provoke World War III—though, to its credit, America never officially recognized the illegal integration of Lithuania into the USSR.

When I arrived in Seattle, I became friends with other Lithuanians in "exile"; among them were Viktor Lapatinskas and Anatanas Minelga.[48] We would get together and celebrate Lithuania's day of independence (February 16). We worked behind the scenes to help Lithuanians back home as well as the effort to regain Lithuania's independence. Because of my political contacts, I was often asked to help Lithuanians who were imprisoned in Siberia. Sometimes, I was successful in helping these people, but I was not always successful in keeping my efforts out of the news.[49]

Some American-Lithuanians criticized me for being too patriotic! Their sentiment was that Lithuania's freedom was a lost cause; it would never happen, they argued, and such a small country was not worth saving anyway. I disagreed strongly and never gave up hope. Some of these people even went so far as to forbid relatives to speak to their children in Lithuanian lest they be contaminated by this old culture. When my father saw that I spoke Lithuanian to my young daughters and they could reply in this language, he was moved to tears. In response, he composed

---

[48] Antanas Minelga remained in Lithuania after the war and became a guerrilla fighter in a futile attempt to resist the Red Army and the KGB. This little-known resistance effort is well described in the book *Guerilla Warfare On The Amber Coast* by K. V. Tauras (Voyages Press, NY).

[49] I tried to avoid publicity since I knew that the KGB was watching my activities, and I had hopes of going to the USSR to visit my relatives someday. See essay, *A Patriot In Exile.*

a sonata dedicated to Eugenia and Ruta.

I always enjoyed Viktor Lapatinskas's story of how he evaded capture by the Russians after WWII, thus avoiding being sent to Siberia. He and some other Lithuanians were trapped in the Soviet zone of Europe when the war ended. They were incarcerated at a "relocation" camp under Russian control. The border of the American zone was a few miles away, but Russian soldiers guarded that area. Viktor and a partner decided to escape and sneak into the American zone one night. When they reached the frontier (on their bellies), a Russian guard spotted them and shouted out, "Halt! Raise your hands and identify yourselves." Then the soldier asked them where they were coming from. They responded by identifying the camp in the Soviet zone. The guard escorted them back with his Kalashnikov at the ready.

A few days later, Viktor and his partner tried again to escape to the West. They were caught (by a different guard) the same way and were returned to their camp. At that point, they realized that the questioning had been almost identical—indicating that the Russian soldiers really did not know who belonged where during this phase of postwar confusion. The two young Lithuanians made another attempt to escape. This time when they were caught by a Russian soldier and asked where they were coming from, Viktor pointed to the west. The soldier dutifully took them over to the American zone and handed the two over to an American soldier. They were free at last!

*RELATIVES*
I never met any of my grandparents. They all died before I was born. In America, my mother was able to renew a correspondence with her two siblings in Moscow. After Stalin died, her brother Kasimir resurfaced—having lived in the shadows of Russian society for many years. He was a professional engineer but survived by playing in chess tournaments during these times.

He was a chess master. My mother often told me that I had much in common with him; he was also unconventional and adventurous. I was eager to meet him.

During the height of the Cold War, it was all but impossible for expatriate Lithuanians to visit their native country. However, a visit to Russia was a little easier. It was assumed that Lithuanians had no relatives in Russia. I made plans. First I took a year of intensive Russian classes at the UW so that I would be able to speak the same language as my uncle. Then I got a visa and booked a flight to Moscow. This was 1966, and Czechoslovakia was experiencing a little too much democracy under Premier Dubček. Three weeks before my scheduled departure, Khrushchev ordered the invasion of that poor country and the Iron Curtain came down even tighter. My mother received a clandestine letter advising me that now would be a bad time to come to the USSR. Sensitive information between my relatives was exchanged in prearranged code during the Cold War. Alas, by the time the political situation quieted down enough for me to travel, my uncle had passed away.

My mother's sister Sofia married a nuclear scientist and bore him two children. During the summer of 1976, I was participating in a mountaineering expedition to the USSR, under the umbrella of a "cultural exchange." This was a great opportunity to meet with my aunt, though by then she was close to ninety. I had an address for her in Moscow. It was a ten-story tenement building without an operating elevator. I knocked on the door, and a Russian woman answered. She recognized my aunt's name and said that she had moved to Rostov, near the Black Sea. The next day, my climbing team and I departed for the Pamir Mountains, but some Russian friends who stayed behind promised to search for my aunt in Rostov.

Six weeks later, during the last climb of the expedition, one of our American team members fell while climbing and sustained severe injuries. Rather than returning to my Moscow hotel, with a few days to spare for celebrations, I brought the injured climber to a Moscow hospital. I stayed at his side until I had to catch my plane back to America. I rushed to my hotel to pick up my belongings. The concierge handed me a note *written in my aunt's handwriting!* It said that she had waited for me at the hotel until the day before and had to return to Rostov. She passed away within a year. I was heartbroken.


*FAMILY MATTERS*
By 1960, our family finances allowed my father to quit his job as a janitor in LA and move to Chicago. This city had the largest concentration of Lithuanians outside of Lithuania (about two hundred thousand). He became an active member of that community and hardly ever spoke English again. He had no problems finding work—in his field of music this time. He was the organist at the local church. He became the choirmaster of a large group of singers. He gave piano lessons to various students, some of whom I still keep running into forty years later. He produced an opera that was staged by the local opera company. And he continued composing all kinds of classical music. Free passes with United Airlines allowed my parents to see each other frequently.

During his youth, a gypsy seer forecast my father's future. Nearly seventy years later, he came across the piece of paper that recorded the highlights of that encounter. Some of her predictions did not come to pass and some of them did. He was impressed that she predicted that he would spend his final years in America. This prediction was made before WWI! She also said he would die peacefully in bed at the age of seventy-four. This made an impression on him. He really believed that he would die at that age; he was about seventy-two at the time.

The first thing he did was to have me design his tombstone. It had to show an oak tree that was broken in half—symbolizing that his life had been cut short while he was still bearing fruit, so to speak. I executed the design as best I could, and he had it carved from a piece of red granite. He placed it on a plot in a huge (ethnic) cemetery in the middle of Chicago. He would visit me frequently in Seattle and I would visit him in Chicago. He was organizing his belongings in expectation of his imminent death. When he reached the age of seventy-four, he bade me farewell—never expecting to see me again. He was solemn. He did the same with his wife, my mother (who was still living in Los Angeles). Both my mother and I chuckled behind his back. The auspicious age of seventy-four came and went, and my father did not die. Then my mother and I chuckled real hard (still behind his back). Each time he came to visit me, he parted with a hug and kiss on both cheeks, informing me how sad he was to see me for the last time. Two more years passed and, totally out of the blue, my mother died!

Never in my life was I so devastated by any tragedy as this one. She had had a heart attack. We knew she had some heart problems, but we thought they were minor. She was only fifty-eight. We buried her ashes under the tombstone designed for my father.

A silver lining came with her death. My father and I became close for the first time in our lives. He came to visit me more frequently, and we would have a great time together. At one point, he admitted that he had always been jealous of my close relationship with my mother. It was clear that she always put me first. That must have been hard on him. My father was over eighty years old when he died. I was sad about his death, but happy that I had finally bonded with my father. It took thirty years.

My mother was undoubtedly the biggest influence in my life. When I returned from my world tour, I was a married man, but not yet a father (Gisela was pregnant with our first child, Eugenia). I came to Los Angeles and went to my mother's house. When she opened the door, she greeted me warmly and said, "Pupa, do you forgive me?" I did not expect that question, but my immediate answer was "Yes, of course." Perhaps, my answer should have been "Forgive you for what?" There had been lingering misunderstandings between us, and then, with those few words, they were behind us.

I had finally grown up and was on the brink of raising children of my own. The tables had turned. Lithuania survived fifty years of brutal occupation and rejoined the community of free nations. Totalitarian empires are all but a distant memory now. A new generation of my family has taken root in America.

# CARIBOU MOUNTAIN GOLD

*Beyond the shark-tooth ranges sawing savage*
*at the sky*
*There's a lowering land no white man ever*
*struck;*
*There's gold, there's gold in millions, and I'll*
*find it if*
*I die,*
*And I'm going there once more to try my luck.*
*Maybe I'll fail-what matter? It's a mandate,*
*it's a vow;*
*And when in lands of dreariness and dread*
*You seek the last lone frontier, far beyond your*
*frontier now,*
*You will find the old prospector, silent, dead.*

From "The Prospector"
By Robert Service

Gold fever can strike anyone at any time, even dumb students working their way through college. In fact, the dumber one is the harder the fever strikes, I found. We were pretty dumb.

There was a time when the US government would subsidize gold prospectors. It was called a "grub stake." Until recently, the Canadian government still had such a program. It encouraged the unemployed and unemployable to dig for gold. In their quest, prospectors would penetrate the impenetrable. They would suffer environments so harsh not even sport fishermen would venture into them. By law, if they were fortunate enough to find any gold, they were required to sell it to the government at the fixed price of $32 per ounce. On the black market an ounce would fetch a hefty $70 (in 1961). Visions of finding gold, a little or a lot, became an obsession called "gold fever."

Paul and I were college students tired of earning money the hard way, i.e., with desk jobs. So we headed north to Canada. At the border we had to stop for inspection. The station wagon in front of us belonged to a couple of burly men with intentions similar to ours. The Canadian customs officer was looking through their undergarments that were neatly stacked in one of their suitcases, when, lo and behold, he came across two 44 magnum revolvers. Canada has strict laws against handguns, and everyone knew it. These two guys looked at each other feigning total bewilderment and shrugged their shoulders. "Did you know they were there?" they asked each other in utter amazement. "Nope, I sure didn't put them there." The inspector was unimpressed and confiscated the guns. The only weapon we carried with us was a small shotgun, which we duly registered ahead of time.

Our research of gold lore told us that before the turn of the century huge amounts of the precious metal were extracted from the Caribou Mountain region of British Columbia. "Thar's gold in them thar hills!" was the refrain, and we could still hear it, loud and clear.

Driving north along the Frazer River we noticed major forest fires raging east of us. It was an unusually dry summer. Tumultuous mushroom clouds, laced with red and orange ash reached ten thousand feet into the sky. We were forewarned not to get caught at a roadblock, where the Canadian Mounted Royal Police had the authority to draft anyone into service to fight those fires. We were careful to keep our distance.

Our first evening in the wilderness was spent by a river called "Lightning Creek." We noticed that what we called "rivers" in the States, Canadians called "creeks." This "creek" was full of fish and we could almost smell fresh trout roasting over our campfire. We hauled out the fishing equipment and found that the smallest hook we had was large enough to snag a marlin. We put about ten salmon eggs on one rusty hook attached to a 100 pound line and threw it into the water. The fish were dumber than we were and attacked the bait; the water seemed to boil in the frenzy that ensued. The first fish grabbed the big hook and rushed off with dozens of his friends in hot pursuit. The hook was too big to swallow and, when it dropped free, the next fish would grab it and rush off in the opposite direction. This circus went on for some time. While Paul continued to play with the fish, I got my wetsuit on, pulled out my trusty old spear gun, and waded into the river. Instead of running away, the curious fish surrounded me. The big ones hovered at a distance but not out of range of my gun. We had fish for dinner that night.

Soon we were dredging and panning the sandy shores of the historically rich creeks identified in our mining journals. It was fun at first but, without any rewarding "color" in our pans, it got to be tedious work. We drove deeper and deeper into the remote wilderness. Occasionally, we would come across a grizzled old "sourdough" sitting lazily in front of his rustic log cabin. These old timers enjoyed visitors such as us and would spin long yarns about surviving harsh winters and close encounters with the legendary Sasquatch. Not a word, though, about the subject we wanted to hear: "where's the gold?" It was obvious to us that these old geezers had found their gold and were living off of it, albeit modestly; they might have been millionaires. Apparently, they had lived the lives of lonely, poor prospectors for too long and they could no longer go back to a conventional life style.

Ever deeper into the uncharted wilderness we pressed. Yet, everywhere we looked, signs of previous gold seekers were evident. Once we came upon a rather big operation. A bunch of cowboys from Montana had sold their ranches and invested that money in mining equipment — like "D6" caterpillar tractors and big dredges. They were in the process of digging up an area where the old creek bed used to be before it shifted to its present location. There they were sure to find undiscovered gold, they figured. A couple of years later I got a letter from Fuller, one of the Montanans, describing how they eventually reached the bottom of the old creek bed but found no gold. They went broke. Now they were trapping beaver, marten, and other rodents whose furs were highly prized. He went on to tell me how he had befriended Jimmy Angel (of Angel Falls fame) a few years earlier. The legendary pilot told him the story of how he had crashed on a remote plateau in Venezuela, near the falls bearing his name, and found emeralds on the shores of a river! Fuller felt he knew exactly where to find those emeralds and how to avoid the unfriendly headhunter tribes. "We'll use helicopters," he assured me and then added, "I got room for you to join us! Are you able to come?" I was still chasing a degree in architecture and not willing to risk my head over fabled emeralds. It's a good thing I declined the invitation. Fuller went into the jungle with a well-equipped team. Neither he nor the team was ever heard from again.

In our effort to penetrate the remotest area of this gold producing region, we followed a creek deep into the Caribou Mountains. This area was so remote, we were sure no one had prospected it in years. Just as we arrived at a spot that looked promising enough for a test (by panning the shore of the creek), we smelled campfire smoke. As luck would have it, this spot was already staked out! Two big, burly prospectors made their presence known and they were not giving us a friendly reception. On the contrary, their tone was threatening and the big six-shooters on their hips did not go unnoticed by us. We made it clear that we were on our way up the valley and over the next mountain (and into Alberta, if necessary). We got out of there, fast. Somehow, these two guys looked familiar. In fact, they were the same two Americans we had met at the border and watched as their revolvers were confiscated. Now they were sporting new ones.

Relieved to have gotten away from the intimidating prospectors unharmed, we continued up the narrowing canyon. The sides were getting so steep we could proceed only by hopping along the river's edge, from boulder to boulder. We came upon a little beach and were shocked to find the body of a man lying there, face down. He was still wearing a backpack, but he was dead. We turned him over and were aghast at the maggots that had begun to infest his eyes, nose and mouth. Otherwise, he did not seem harmed and we assumed he might have been dead for a day or two, at the most. Having just encountered two mean looking "hombres," we became suspicious that there may have been foul play.

Dumb as we were, we got really scared. We decided to go back to town and report this death, but we also had to avoid the two well-armed prospectors. The canyon walls were too steep to climb. We were able to avoid their camp by climbing directly over a headwall alongside a hundred-foot waterfall.

Eventually, we arrived at the town of Quesnel and reported our grisly find to the R.C.M.P. The weather was not conducive to helicopter flying. So the "Mountie" simply recruited Paul and me and two other hapless bystanders to go back into the mountains to carry the body out. I suggested that they bury it where we found it. Unfortunately, under suspicious circumstances, an autopsy would have to be performed, here in Quesnel. We spent another long day carrying him out on a stretcher. It was unpleasant and backbreaking work. I never imagined that a hundred-and-sixty-pound body could be so heavy.

We later learned that the poor fellow died of a heart attack. Evidently, upon finding some "color" in his pan he staked out his new claim. The excitement must have been too much for his heart.

As fate would have it, our little expedition did not have the good fortune of finding the elusive gold in quantities to pay for our expenses and we went broke. A sympathetic resident of the area told us there was an old gold mine still operating in a place called Wells, between the town of Quesnel and the ghost town of Barkerville. We might get hired there, he suggested. When we arrived in Wells we encountered a place time had forgotten. Most of the houses were boarded up and the dilapidated old mine was barely operational. Obviously, no Canadian in his right mind would work there. We Americans were hired with enthusiasm that should have aroused our suspicions. The pay was minimal and the conditions were hazardous, but we were happy to be earning money.

The "Caribou Gold Quartz Company" was once a thriving operation when, years earlier, it employed hundreds of miners and produced countless millions of dollars in gold. Now it was a derelict mine employing less than a 100 miners. The company town was nearly abandoned. It did have a public gathering place encompassing a grocery store, restaurant, post office and tavern, all under one roof. During time off we all got to know each other pretty well.

It was a rather interesting assortment of men who worked the mine and called this place home. There were several veterans of the German Wehrmacht. One of them claimed to have been Goering's staff sergeant — responsible primarily for organizing the field marshal's elaborate hunts. He told stories of how daring Goering was when facing dangerous game and the big drinking parties that followed. Other ex-Nazis were less willing to speak about their exploits during the Third Reich. There were also several young Italians from the province of Sicily. They came from poor families and were saving their hard-earned money so that they could go back to Italy and become "gentlemen." These Italians were always jovial and fun to be around. There was also an assortment of internationals whose backgrounds were mysterious, if not shady. Some were deserters from the French Foreign Legion, we suspected. One was a   scholarly American reputed to be a former Harvard University professor. There was only one Canadian among the miners, toothless old Jack, our supervisor. Actually, he had a few teeth, but they were few and far between. Jack had worked in this mine for over twenty years and had a lot of stories to tell about the days when there was so much gold here, "you could pry it out of the rock with your bare hands, like thick wire."

Paul was given a job shoveling ore into the conveyers above ground. I was given the title of "mucker" and sent deep into the bowels of the mine, 1,300 feet below. The "mountain," as the mine was called, was pocked with tunnels, most of them abandoned by now. It was the miners' job to carve out new tunnels by drilling deep holes into the rock and packing them with dynamite sticks. At the end of each shift, the fuses were lit, the mine was evacuated, and the subsequent explosions released the gold ore. The rubble would then be pushed into vertical shafts where it would flow down to a lower tunnel and be gathered in carts pushed by an electric trolley. Filling the carts and driving them to a central conveyor shaft was the mucker's job.

This mine was dangerous! Most of the tunnels were about six feet wide and six feet high. The timbers supporting the ceilings were old and in various stages of decomposition. The rusted old rail-carts and electric trolley cleared the timbers by mere inches in some places. Invariably, an occasional timber would slough downward and, if the mucker failed to duck in time, his head would be crushed. Occasionally, a trolley pushing fully loaded carts would collide with a protruding piece of broken timber and the whole ceiling would collapse. Hours of delicate work would be required to extricate the train without causing a major cave-in. Understandably, the turnover in muckers was high.

A thousand or so feet below ground oxygen becomes rarefied. It would take three or four wooden matchsticks, struck at once, to light a cigarette. We all smoked. Ventilation was poor and the humid air was stale. Most timbers were decorated with abstract formations of white fungi. Along the iron tracks, large puddles of mineral laden-water would accumulate. The only light emanated from the "torch" on the miner's helmet. The illuminated puddles would reflect deep ruby red, sometimes reminiscent of blood. Discarded old rubber gloves or boots appeared as so many body parts. The job of mucker was lonely, claustrophobic, and at times spooky.

Once I got stuck behind a collapsed crossbeam and did not get out to the elevator in time, by the end of the shift. I knew that the dynamite fuses were being lit in the tunnels above and that the explosions would soon start. The possibility of a cave-in was real. Muffled "booms" went off at various intervals while I hid in a dark corner of a cave, the safest spot I could find. The mountain shook. My hard hat fell off and my light went out. The "booms" kept getting nearer. With effort I suppressed the urge to panic, and thus avoided going stark, raving mad. As a child during WWII, I would tremble in dark basements when Allied planes dropped their deadly load of bombs on us. This suppressed angst arose in me as the explosions shook the earth again. After what seemed like an eternity, the "bombing" stopped. I lit a cigarette and eventually found my way back to the elevator. I was a nervous wreck. I began counting the days when this job would end. Going back to school was a prospect I abhorred just a few months earlier; suddenly, I found the thought rather appealing.

My final day of employment in this god-forsaken mine was memorable. The only other time that I yearned for a termination of tenure with such eager anticipation was while awaiting my discharge papers from the US Army. My spirits were up, for I knew I would never have to face this awful hell-hole again.

At work that night I was assigned a new employee and had to teach him my job. The day before had been his first day at work, but he had become sick and had to quit early. Today Jim was working with me and I noticed that he was a little nervous (his hands were shaking). I assured him that there was nothing to fear here and that he would soon get used to it all. We were on the 875-foot level and at first everything went well. In one spot deep in the tunnel a beam hung a little low and the situation became dangerous.

When I allowed Jim to drive the train for the first time, he had barely begun to move when he failed to duck and struck his head on the low beam. The ceiling, which had only six inches of clearance above the wagons, suddenly settled on top of the load. The rock walls started shaking all around us and pieces began falling down. I yelled at Jim to run for it since the rest of the ceiling could cave in at any moment. Jim jumped from the train but could not move any further because his helmet was stuck under the train — he was tied to the helmet by the electrical cord connecting his light. I told him not to move. I crawled over to him, extricated his helmet, and we retreated to a safe spot.

Since I did not dare move the train, I called the shift boss. When he arrived he looked the situation over and instructed me to pull the train forward. I warned him: "Jack, if I move that train the whole ceiling is going to come down!" "Move it out!" the boss ordered. I had just started to move the train when everything around me exploded. I glimpsed the ceiling and walls collapsing around me. Like a bullet I dove over the train and landed on my stomach in the acidic water between the tracks. I did not dare run since rocks were falling all around. My helmet had fallen off somewhere. With my face in the dirt I covered my head with my hands as if in a bomb attack. I was certain I would be buried under tons of rock. I waited for the first onslaught of muck for what seemed an eternity, but the rock did not bury me. I jumped to my feet and ran as fast as I could. When I was a safe distance away from the cave-in, I stopped and realized that my legs were shaking so hard they could barely hold me up; I sat down to recover from the shock.

The loud noise had not abated as I tried to approach the train. I did not know if Jack and Jim were alive on the other end. I could see nothing; there was so much dust, as if in an inferno. The stench was terrible and I could barely breathe. Once again I returned to my safe spot and sat down. I tried to calm my nerves, then approached the train again. The same thing happened and I could not breathe or see. I did not dare go any further. Concerned about the two men I decided to return to the elevator station and phoned the safety officer. It was a long walk through the tunnel and I was painfully aware of how close to being killed I had come. When I talked to the safety officer he came down quickly and we went back down the tunnel. At that moment we met Jack and Jim who were looking for me. Jack asked me if I was hurt. I informed him that I was alive and healthy and that I managed to escape the cave-in, but just barely. He looked at my wet clothes and added cheekily: "Why, you just got a little wet!"

That was my last run. I took the rickety elevator to the top, breathed the clean, fresh air outside, and joined the ranks of the unemployed. I was finally cured of any lingering signs of gold fever.

# OUR "ALPS:" A MATCH FOR EUROPE[50]

Some of the most impressive mountain country in the world lies almost unnoticed in our back yard.

I'm speaking of the North Cascades, often referred to as the Alps of America. Until recently, only a few mountain climbers and fishermen (a hardy bunch) have ventured into the rugged wilderness of our "Alps." I have climbed mountains in Europe, throughout the West, Canada, and Alaska, and nowhere have I seen a mountain range that could match the rugged beauty of the Cascades.

With keen interest I have been following the construction of the new trans-Cascade highway. Now mountain climbers can drive to the foot of one of the most popular and imposing mountains of the range. The Liberty Bell Mountain massif consists of Liberty Bell Mountain, Lexington, Concord, and the Early Winter Spires. The east face of Liberty Bell is a smooth wall of granite over 1000 feet high and nearly vertical.

---

[50] First published in the *WEEKENDER MAGAZINE,* Seattle Post-Intelligencer, August 5, 1967.

It was on this face that Don McPherson and I found ourselves inching our way toward the summit. How long it would take us to climb this route we did not know since no one had preceded us. We prepared ourselves well. Unable to find good footholds we resorted to artificial means of staying on the rock. This way, we were supported by slings and stirrups that were suspended from pitons that we had driven into small cracks. One man would climb while the second man would sit in a sling and belay the first man. That is, he would hold the rope tied to the leader in case he should fall.

We hauled our equipment, food, and water behind us with a separate rope. In this manner we progressed about 300 the first day. Dusk found us impeded by an overhang. We spent the night sleeping in hammocks, a little discouraged at the slow progress we were making. The next morning Don continued "nailing" up cracks that were so small that he could only use knife blade thin pitons that barely held his weight. When he reached the end of his lead I followed, extracting his pitons along the way.

The next lead took me over a small overhang and then over three ceilings where the pitons had to be placed upside down. Don got another half a lead done before darkness overtook us and again we slept in our hammocks; we were not uncomfortable. The weather was good and the scenery spectacular.

The third morning, while Don was climbing and I was sitting in my sling, I had time to scan the vast Cascades around us. I tried to identify some of the mountains that looked familiar. It was like picking out a few waves in a restless sea of rock and snow.

A thin yellow line demarked a dirt road snaking through the heavily timbered valley far below us. Ant-like was the heavy equipment used for construction and the men operating them were too small for the naked eye to see. I thought of the many people who would soon come to enjoy this area. To the east of the pass a parking lot was being graded. Then I visualized gas stations and tourist stands and I shuddered.[51]

My thoughts were interrupted by Don's voice from above. He had reached another overhang and it was my turn to climb. That afternoon we came upon some ledges large enough to stand on and the climbing became less difficult. For the first time we were able to sleep on a tiny ledge huddling close together. The sun was painting the mountains around us crimson while we spoke of the pleasures of the climb.

The following day we reached the summit, tired, dirty, hands bruised, yet filled with elation. We signed the registry that we found under a cairn and christened our route "Independence."

We rappelled down the south side of the mountain that is the normal route of ascent. Inspired by our accomplishment, I returned two weeks later with three other Northwest climbers and repeated the Liberty Crack route, a similar climb on the left side of the East Face.

---

[51] Fortunately, the area became a National Park and was permanently preserved from commercial development.

# ART NOURISHES THE SOUL

I was born into a family that deeply appreciated the arts. There was always music to be heard somewhere: either live performances, by recordings playing on gramophones (78 rpm), or on the radio. When I was still a small child my mother often took me into the big city (Memel) to hear performances in music halls where my father played the bass or the piano in the orchestra. She also took me to plays that were appropriate for small children. One such performance was a musical called: *Peterlein's Mondfahrt (Little Peter's Trip to the Moon)*. My mother also enjoyed hosting parties and would invite guests from far and wide. Since we lived in the country, our house was designed to accommodate many people for overnight stays. Some of these soirées were black tie affairs with a live musical ensemble. At other times they were smaller gatherings with couples dancing to the music playing on the gramophone. It was my job to keep the record player cranked up, a chore which I performed with great pride.

Each summer, my mother would get together with various neighbors and organize children's plays. On one such occasion the play was *Snow White and the Seven Dwarfs*. Of course, I was one of the dwarfs. As I remember, it was a hot day and my white beard, which was made of fluffy cotton, irritated my skin to no end. I got overheated and threw up all over my robe and "beard." The play turned into a tragic-comedy.

The walls of our house were adorned with paintings. Various works of art sitting on shelves, tables and desks could be admired throughout the many rooms of the house. One of my favorite pieces was an 18th century desk set depicting a bull elk with a large rack, reaching high in order to nibble on the acorns of an oak tree. It was designed to hold (quill) pens on the tray space and contained a crystal well on each side — one for ink and one for ink drying powder. It was intricately sculpted from Russian silver and commissioned by an ancestor on my mother's side of the family who was fond of hunting in the forests of Russia. This item still graces a shelf in my study in Seattle.

Our idyllic life came to a sudden end when the invading Soviet Army threatened to overrun our corner of the world. The year was 1944. My mother and I had to leave almost everything behind and run for our lives. My father was caught behind the advancing lines of the Soviet Army. He was desperately trying to evade the Soviet Secret Police (NKVD) who had an arrest warrant out for him. He and other intellectuals of Lithuania were considered "public enemies" during Stalin's reign of terror.

In addition to what we could carry, my mother also took along the silver desk set, which could be disassembled. It came in handy during our flight south when she bartered parts of the ornately carved silver branches for food. The times were chaotic, but we had to eat. Paper money was worthless.

After we finally arrived at the relative safety of southern Austria (part of the *German Reich)* I would go out and shop for food with money that my mother gave me. On one occasion, as I was passing a flea market, I saw a postcard sized watercolor depicting Hänschen Klein - the fictional little boy of German nursery rhymes. I bought it with my food allowance and gave it to my mother, who was bed ridden at the time. She kept that little painting near her bed for the rest of her life (see *Hänschen* story*)*. It was my first purchase of a work of art.

Before the war ended we moved to Ismaning, a sleepy little farming community on the outskirts of Munich. The rent was cheap here and we were relatively safe from Allied bombing raids. German war veterans on crutches and with missing limbs often came to our door begging for food. One such soldier was a dilettante painter who offered us a little watercolor — it was a landscape scene that he had done. We gave him a small sack of potatoes in exchange. This little painting now hangs in a corner of my bedroom. It is not a great work of art, but the memory it evokes is. Another veteran did a pencil sketch of me when I was six. He seems to have caught the spirit of a youngster who may have been traumatized by war.

After the War ended, we moved into an old neighborhood of Munich, called *Bogenhausen*. Officially, we were "Displaced Persons" (DP). Stateless (Lithuanian) refugees like us, were all planning to emigrate to countries willing to take DPs: Argentina, Venezuela, Australia, Canada, the USA, et al. At the University of Munich my mother befriended a young student in the art department whom she recognized as an up and coming artist. His name was Kurt Moser. When she had money to spare, she bought a couple of oil paintings from him as an investment. "Starving" students were known to sell their works cheaply. We knew that our future lay in the "new world," but we did not know what to expect there. So, buying art was a hedge on that uncertain future. Besides, my mother just loved art.

As an adolescent, I was already showing signs of entrepreneurship. One source of my income was in the sale of cigarettes. Cigarette addiction was high in post-war Germany and name brand cigarettes were available only on the black market at prohibitive prices. In those days, as well as today, smoking was not allowed on public transit lines. Smokers catching a streetcar would drop their cigarettes on the ground when the trolley pulled up. There was a streetcar stop near our apartment building and, on a good day, I would find as many as a dozen cigarette butts on the ground with some usable tobacco still left in them. I would take these remnants home, cut them open, and salvage the good tobacco. Once I had gathered enough tobacco I would roll them into "new" cigarettes using neatly cut pieces of toilet paper held together by my saliva. When a cigarette addict came knocking at our door for free handouts, I offered him my special brand for the cut-rate price of a few Pfennig. Soon I was making good money.

On one occasion, my mother brought some fresh herring home for dinner. I was allowed to "gut" them. I found that their lungs were neat little bladders that held air. I collected all I could and sold them to neighborhood kids eager for any kind of novelty. Regular toys were non-existent. I made some good money that way, as long as my mother brought home fresh fish.

By the time our emigration appointment neared (May 1950), I had accumulated over 50 Deutsche Marks ($12.50) from all my enterprises. My mother suggested that I invest my savings in one of Kurt Moser's paintings for the trip to the "new world." I ended up buying a large (2'x3') oil painting: a still-life depicting a farmer's table setting of bread and vegetables. Years later, while browsing through the art department of a large department store in Los Angeles, I noticed some oil paintings (reproductions) depicting Bavarian scenes. I took a closer look and saw that they were signed by "Kurt Moser," now a painter of some renown. My mother knew how to judge talent.

Despite our economic plight, my mother kept her interest in the arts alive. Within walking distance of our home on Mühlbauerstrasse was a premier concert hall called *Prinzregenten Teater*. It had musical events as well as theatrical performances. Tickets were heavily subsidized by the government and school children my age could attend free of charge on certain weekends. Once, my mother took me to a small theater that completely mystified me: it showed a film! I had never seen this theatrical medium before. I was still assuming that this performance was a staged play. Unlike the play called *Peterlein's Mondfahrt,* where I was savvy enough to figure out how the special effects were done (e.g., flying to the moon, sailing over the ocean), I was totally befuddled as to how a team of horses could run at high speed on a small stage without ever running out of space. I soon learned that films were a new high-tech kind of art form.

Eventually, we were reunited with my father who was able to get a job with UNRRA (United Nations Relief & Rehabilitation Administration). He had managed to outsmart Soviet agents and escape to West Germany. During the summer of 1950 we sailed to America and ended up in Los Angeles. We found the housing market most affordable in the low rent district of Watts. By and large, Americans were friendly and helpful to newly arrived war refugees. I made fast friends with neighborhood boys and girls, though I could not get into the American teenage culture of dating, hot-rods, and rock and roll. Ironically, I loved Country & Western music, which I was exposed to in Germany when the GIs arrived. My favorite musical venue was the *Hollywood Bowl*. It had outdoor seating; the cheapest seats were on the lawn. Carmen Dragon was a regular conductor at the *Bowl*. Many years later I had the good fortune of meeting him at a dinner party in Seattle. He was delighted that I recognized him form his *Hollywood Bowl* days. Opera had not yet made its way to Los Angeles, but my father would take me to operas shown on film. *Shriner's Auditorium* was one such venue. I was luke-warm to this medium, until I saw a performance of Verdi's *Rigoletto*. Thereafter, I was hooked on opera for life.

We were living in the city famous for being home to Hollywood and movies carried the day. On Saturdays local movie houses allowed school children to see Saturday matinee performances for 9 cents! I went often. By the time I reached high school age I took greater interest in staged plays again. Ironically, for a city that was famous for having an abundance of famous actors, it had very few live theaters. I found one little theater tucked underground just off of Hollywood Boulevard. I don't remember its name, but it had excellent performances. I was too young to drive and I would spend a good hour or so, hitchhiking to see these plays. Two performances remain in my memory: *The Mouse That Roared* with Peter Ustinov, and *Mark Twain Tonight,* starring a very young Hal Holbrook. Over the years I saw numerous performances of *"Mark Twain"* by Holbrook, by which time he no longer needed to wear gray wigs.

After living for eleven years in "the city of angels," I packed up and moved to the Pacific Northwest. As architecture students at the University of Washington, we were all required to take at least one course in watercolor painting given by the school's art professors. Architects in those days had to present their designs beautifully rendered in watercolor — the favorite medium. I found that I not only enjoyed painting, but I was good at it. Instead of the required one course minimum, I signed up for a year's worth of painting instruction.

During my world travels, I continued my mother's example of "investing" in art. I acquired works from the European continent, from the Middle-East, from China, and Latin America. I have also collected small sculptures cast in bronze, silver, ceramic and some carved out of wood. The storage area in the basement of my house is stacked with paintings (framed and unframed), rare posters and lithographs, some dating back to the 18th century. The practice of architecture was a fickle business (and still is). During hard times, when commissions were far and few between, I would reach into my "treasure trove" of rare art and sell whatever I could at cut-rate prices. After all, I had a family to support. Money from my art collection would save the day, but it was painful to part with works that I had collected out of admiration and not just as an investments.

Today, the artwork on my walls is in seasonal rotation — a custom I learned from the Japanese. Seeing these works of art when I wake up in the morning gives me pleasure — not just from the joy of being greeted by something that is beautiful, but also from the memories these creations evoke. Every work of art has a story behind its creation. The enjoyment it brings is the same whether they are my own creations, the creations of my children, those of my old painting partners, or of artists whose works I have admired and collected. Art nourishes the soul.

# VOYAGE INTO YESTERYEAR

During the 1960s East Africa experienced more change than during the preceding 100, or even 1,000 years. While colonialism took root over decades, independence ("uhuru," in Swahili) came suddenly. Africans were on the threshold of the twentieth century — ready to join nations which had governed themselves for centuries. The principal cities of Kampala, Nairobi, and Dar Es Salaam were full of many trappings of any cosmopolitan metropolis. Yet, a few miles beyond these bustling cities, life continued as if the twentieth century had never arrived.

I was in this area mainly to climb the region's principal mountains: Kilimanjaro - an exotic hike, Mt. Kenya - a challenging spire of rock and ice, and the Ruwenzori - the fabled "Mountains of the Moon." In between expeditions and safaris I needed some "R & R." Three English engineers working in Nairobi suggested: "Alex, if you really want to get off the beaten track, go to the island of Lamu in the Indian Ocean." Then they added, "While you're there you can also inspect the status of the construction of our boat (a forty foot ketch) which we plan to sail around the world. They have no phones on the island and,

God knows what they've been doing." To me, it sounded like a perfect excuse for a trip to a remote island. Anyway, I was tired of high mountains and the dry savannah. A trip on the ocean sounded refreshing.

These were the days when I was traveling on a shoestring. I hitchhiked southwest from Nairobi to the port city of Mombasa. Hitchhiking in East Africa during those days was a cinch — if you were white. There were enough former colonialists still living there who felt that it was improper for a white man to stand on the side of the road with his thumb out. They would pick him up immediately! Thus, I found myself in the back seat of a car owned by a middle-aged couple who had not seen Mother England in decades. We got along quite well, until I mentioned where I was planning to stay that night. When they heard me say, Rainbow Hotel, gasps of dismay emanated from the front seats. This hotel was recommended by fellow shoestring travelers from Los Angeles, who assured me it was "the best deal in town."

My British hosts declared that they could not allow me to stay at the Rainbow. "It just would not be proper," the woman said with an air of English propriety. "Hey, I am a vagabond with a beard trying to get by with very little money," I protested. None-the-less, when we arrived in Mombasa they pulled up at the Empress Hotel and escorted me right up to the reception desk, to make sure I registered. Then we sat down in the lounge where they bought a round of cold beer as a gesture of their good will. While sitting at the table with these well-intentioned folks, I saw (through the big store-front window) my friends from LA walking by. And, they saw me! I quickly rushed out into the lobby to intercept them and assured them that I would soon meet them at our prearranged destination.

As soon as my British friends departed, I cancelled my

reservation at the Empress and left. The Rainbow did not have a reception desk. Instead, I was directed to the bar where the bartender was doubling as the receptionist. This bar was primarily occupied by the most beautiful assortment of voluptuous black maidens this side of the Playboy mansion in Hollywood. The room rate was $1.50 per night and that included breakfast! Now, that really suited my budget. However, this was not a private room, I was advised, and I would have to share it with another American (all single rooms were booked). "Who might that be?" I inquired. The bartender pointed to a young Peace Corps volunteer from South Dakota, who was flanked by two scantily clad maidens. Smiling, he nodded my way, indicating it was OK with him that we share the room. I paid up and went upstairs.

I had dinner with my friends from LA, who were on an extended tour of Africa, now into their third year. They were a fun couple full of stories and good advice. I got back to my room at the hotel around midnight and fell asleep quickly. Early in the morning, as I was getting out of bed, my room-mate staggered in. He was either very drunk or completely exhausted (or both). I could not help but notice that his lips were visibly swollen as he crashed (face down) onto his bed.

I packed my backpack and proceeded to hitchhike northward, up the Kenyan coast, to the town of Melindi. There were fewer "Anglos" around these parts and the trip took a little longer. I was dropped off at the edge of town at dusk. Melindi was a coastal village. The architecture was Afro-Arabic with a couple of mosque spires piercing the sky. There were practically no lights because the region lacked electricity. What really made it eerie was the sound of mullahs wailing their prayers from high up in the minarets. I walked past the adobe buildings in the diminishing daylight until I reached the beach. I found some palm trees for shelter and settled in for the night.

I needed transport to the Island of Lamu. My friends in Nairobi informed me that it would be in this town that I would be able to find a boat to take me there. Eventually, I found the only English speaking person in this quaint little place. He was the postmaster, customs officer, head of communications, and general expediter of miscellaneous affairs. He understood my needs and was most helpful. He assured me that when a captain with Lamu on his manifest came across his schedule, he would let him know about my request.

Two days later I was introduced to a captain of an Arab dhow whose next port of call was Lamu. I was struck by the resemblance of this man to the then president of Egypt, Gamal Nasser. He could have been the president's younger brother, I thought. The fee for this voyage would be $10. I paid it gladly. The "postmaster" interpreted while I received instructions about when and where to meet for the voyage. It was to be one hour after sundown at the beach in front of the Customs House.

Arab dhows are sailing ships of ancient design, single masted with a lateen sail, meaning, the boom is fixed at the top of the (forward sloping) mast rather than at the bottom. They are broad beamed and have no keel. This allows them to beach and, when the tide goes out, they simply lean over on one side at about a 45 degree angle — allowing for easy loading or unloading of cargo. When the tide moves in, the boat rights itself — no need for modern piers or docks. I watched these boats being loaded with tons of grain in hundred pound sacks.

I showed up after sunset at the prescribed location and was soon met by the captain and three of his shipmates. We sat on the beach for almost an hour watching the tide come in. They smoked an occasional cigarette, but there was no discussion. Then, from the darkness in front of us a distant light swung in a repetitive arc. In response, the captain raised his kerosene lantern and swung it in a similar fashion. About ten minutes later a rowboat appeared and beached directly in front of us. They motioned for me to climb in with the rest of them. In total darkness (no moon) we rowed back out to sea. Upon reaching the dhow, we climbed aboard and the skiff was hoisted topside. Every square inch of the deck was covered with sacks of grain. I was offered a seat in the comfort of the skiff. I understood that this was now the "luxury suite" on this primitive vessel.

Since there was nothing to do, I lay down and tried to nap. We were in a waiting mode. The moon was soon peeking through passing clouds. There were a few specks of light visible in the town. Once in a while, the captain, who was sitting not far away, would ask me in Swahili what the time was. I was the only person on board with a watch. In my limited grasp of this language I proudly responded with the exact hour. To my dismay, the captain (and his shipmates) would shake their heads at the information I provided. This happened several times and I was really befuddled. Many days later I learned that the people of this region were not only on the lunar calendar but they were also on solar time: the first hour came with daylight! My modern contribution on this ship proved useless.

I soon realized that the captain was waiting for the moment when the tide began to ebb, to give his ship a boost away from the beach and toward the open sea. I was dozing off in my skiff when I heard a command being barked by the captain. Out of nowhere men sprang into action — twenty or thirty of them. The anchor was weighed while the sail was being hoisted. The sudden commotion broke the night's silence like a call to battle. With an enormous bang, the sail filled with air when the boom reached the top of the mast. I could feel this lumbering ship accelerating as the bow crashed against the waves. We were under way and the excitement on deck was contagious.

345

I remained asleep in the skiff well into daylight. The undulating movement of the ship was definitely sleep inducing. We were experiencing high rolling waves — remnants of a monsoon storm off the west coast of India. Most of the crew seemed to have vanished, again. The sky was clear, the wind was brisk and the waves were large and consistent. I was getting nauseated and had to keep my head below the gunwales of the skiff to avoid throwing up. Some of the waves seemed dangerously large and would break against the ship causing it to shudder. I tried to hide my apprehension and remained in my "luxury suite" with my eyes mostly closed. If the ship sank, I was in the best compartment, I figured. I felt a shadow come over us and just got a glimpse of a giant wave cresting over the boat. It crashed clear across to the other side of the dhow — engulfing the entire deck. I was protected by the skiff, otherwise, I would have been swept overboard, I'm sure. The anxious looks of the captain and his crew indicated that this was a serious close call. The rest of the voyage went by without any more unpleasant incidents.

Except for the old car tires that were used as fenders, I saw no equipment on board that could be associated with the 20th century. We arrived at the ancient port of Lamu the following morning. It was an impressive sight. A battery of ancient Portuguese cannons pointed out to sea. Above the old Moorish town there was an imposing fortress — which caught my attention. It looked abandoned, but I could imagine that the dungeons of this old "Bastille" were filled with rotting prisoners chained to dank granite walls. If I got arrested there would be no American consular mission around to bail me out. I determined to be on my best behavior while on this remote speck of land in the Indian Ocean.

Deposited into a foreign environment without a clue as to what to expect, I proceeded to scout out the harbor before venturing into town. The people here were dressed in native garb dating back to previous centuries. The men wore a variation of Arab dress while the women were covered in black from head to toe, only their feet, hands and eyes were visible. Obviously, this was a strict Muslim culture.

I was still strolling around the port area when a local native in "western" clothes addressed me in broken English. He was definitely fashionable in his Khaki shorts and Hawaiian shirt. With a polite demeanor he offered me seashells to buy. Well, I was certainly not in the market for such tourist trinkets and I declined his offer. None-the-less, he continued to follow me around and, at every opportunity, he persisted in offering to show me his collections of very special seashells. By now, I had seen all there was of the port area and was ready to go into town. In a moment of weakness, I consented to see his collection. What harm could there be in this, I thought.

With renewed vigor, he motioned me to follow him. The streets were really narrow: at times I could touch buildings on both sides with my outstretched arms. This type of architecture was designed to keep the rays of the equatorial sun out of the streets. The whitewashed structures were two or three stories high. I admired the exquisitely carved entrance doors to each building. Eventually, my guide opened such a door and we entered a passageway leading to a cool courtyard. We took the first side door into a small foyer adjoining a larger room. The room was sparsely furnished with a chair and a bed. Everything was tidy and clean. With a smile he politely asked me to wait until he returned with his collection of seashells.

I had waited no more than fifteen minutes when the curtain to the doorway opened and my guide presented his collection of "sea shells" with undisguised pride. What followed through the door were not nautical specimens but several young women clad in their black "chadors." They lined up in front of me and proceeded to disrobe, right down to their undies. The smiles on their faces were of unrestrained anticipation. To make matters more difficult, these dark skinned girls were incredibly beautiful — with distinct Arabic features. Unlike their sisters in the Rainbow Hotel in Mombasa, these prostitutes had no make up on and their underwear was home made (of white cotton like our great grandmothers must have worn).

Thoughts of the fortress and its dungeon flashed through my mind. I was concerned: I heard that Muslims behead adulterers. Was this my ticket to oblivion? I did not even negotiate for these "seashells." With utmost politeness and diplomacy, I declined his generous offer and made a fast exit from whence I came. In subsequent days, I passed this pimp in the streets but we ignored each other.

My English friends in Nairobi had given me the name of a contact on this island. He was the local Indian merchant and overseer of the nautical construction project. I had no trouble finding him and he put me up in the top floor of his three-story house. The place was spotless. Even the primitive toilet was sanitary. There was no running water, electricity nor any glass in the windows. But, everything seemed to work. Through the window I could see the ocean — framed by swaying palm trees. The sunset was worthy of a painting.

The next few days were spent exploring this little island. Most of the surrounding land was occupied by coconut groves. I decided to hike to the unoccupied side of the island where there were endless long beaches. As I crossed through a large coconut grove I came upon a man who seemed to be a caretaker. He asked me if I was thirsty. He then picked a nice specimen off the ground, and with an expert slash of his panga, he sliced the top off just enough to reveal a slight opening to the core. The coconut water inside was cold and refreshing.

The sand dunes guarding the shore were huge. I struggled up the final mountain of sand and glissaded down to the beach below. Here, I took off my clothes and dove into the surf. The water was clear and bathtub warm. If ever I would choose a place to spend my honeymoon, this would be the spot, I thought.

As I had promised my friends in Nairobi, I made an inspection trip to the boat yard where their boat was being built. This island is probably one of the last places on earth where the ancient way of sailboat construction was still practiced. These extremely sea worthy ships (dhows) have not changed in design for over a millennium and they seem to last for centuries. One of the reasons: they are put together without a single piece of metal. Every piece of plank is dowelled together. I watched the shipwrights drilling away with primitive string bows with long wooden drills held between their teeth! Labor was cheap, but the skill level was high.

This was definitely a place modern progress had forgotten. I figured a cup of "Turkish coffee" cost me less than a penny. A good meal varied between ten and a twenty-five cents (paid in Kenyan shillings, of course). I could have retired here and lived comfortably for the rest of my life.

In fact, I did find two "retirees" on this island. Past the far end of the harbor, there was a small hotel with a bar that served alcoholic drinks! It so happened that two life long colonial administrators could not readapt to Mother England when "Uhuru" came around; they decided to retire here. They opened this little beachfront hotel and bar despite the lack of clientele. What the heck, Africa was their real home and this was as close to being in paradise as you could get.

I was sad leaving this lovely little island, seemingly displaced in a different century. Ten years later, while on a visit to Munich, Germany, my attention was caught by a flashy ad in a travel agent's window. It beckoned German tourists to visit the "exotic island of Lamu" in the Indian Ocean. Non-stop flights would take you directly to the "Lamu International Airport."

# Into The Mountains of Africa

I came to Africa on the "Emin Pasha Memorial Expedition," though my interests lie closer to mountain climbing than historical research. The year was 1966. After touring historical locations of the 19th century explorer in Kenya, I relocated to Uganda in hopes of connecting with local climbers. As luck would have it, President Obote had just staged a coup against the hereditary king of the Buganda tribe, centered on the capital of Kampala. His chief military commander, Idi Amin, was seen driving around in his open jeep gleefully shooting at fleeing Bugandans with his mounted 50 cal machine gun. White people were not threatened, but it was a good time to seek safer terrain, like the mountains to the north.

I was fortunate to connect with two British climbers working as teachers in the town of Fort Portal, not far from the southern border of Sudan. They invited me to join them on an ambitious expedition into the Ruwenzori Mountains, located on the Uganda/Congo border. Ptolemy of Egypt called this range, "The Mountains of the Moon" and identified them as the source of the Nile, though, no European had ever set eyes on these legendary peaks until the latter part of the 19th Century, and then only from a great distance.

The plan proposed by Ron Hockey and Chris Robson was to approach the Ruwenzori from the southeast via the Lamya Valley, which had never been penetrated by any Europeans. Climbing objectives included the unfamiliar Portal Peaks (14,400'), and Mt. Stanley (16,763'). The latter would require a new traverse of the Mt. Stanley massif from the Congo to Uganda. We would exit the range to the south via the normal approach route back to Fort Portal. On August 5 we drove to the road-head located by a small hillside village. Along the way we picked up Joseph Matte, a college student and an avid mountaineer. Matte was invited as our fourth climbing companion and proved to be invaluable as an interpreter during the many conflicts with our porters. At the town of Bundibugyo, we found ourselves surrounded by curious villagers, but our porters were nowhere to be seen — they were hiding in the hills! Rebel mountain tribesmen were threatening to kill any porters working for us Europeans, not because they had any issue with white men, but because of old enmities between tribes. To counter the threat, we spread (false) rumors that we were armed with military rifles.

Around noon, just as our patience began to run out, our eight porters and one headman showed up sporting embarrassed smiles. Late that afternoon we reached a small promontory and camped inside the forest line. Cultivation, scattered huts and villages, and the vast expanse of the Congo were visible far below us. Ahead was the Lamya Valley. Our food supply included the usual assortment of climber's grub. We supplied our porters with native food: cassava flour, ground nuts, smoked fish, curry powder, salt and tea and cigarettes.

On August 6 we hiked up a steep ridge and entered the giant bamboo zone, which we never left for two days. The bamboo forest was thick, cool and dry. The hunters' trail we tried to follow was cluttered with dead bamboo and vines — at times too dense for our pangas (machettes) to hack through. At times we had to resort to crawling along on hands and knees. Besides soldier ants, there were thorn trees, thorn grass, and thorn brush, all of which we tried hard to avoid. We could not avoid the solid wall of nettles that accompanied the bamboo. It was a long continuous sting that did help us forget the strain from our heavy rucksacks. Fortunately, we did not encounter any elephants or buffalo. (On Mt. Kenya we were charged by a screaming bull elephant, which came within 15 feet of catching up to our Landrover as we ambled along uphill on a muddy road.)

Late the third day, after gaining considerable height, the terrain changed into a strange and velvety "giant heather" forest. On the fourth day the porters decided that the going was too arduous and refused to continue. After an exchange of arguments and threats a mutiny was averted. We sent back only three men, two of whom had sustained minor injuries, the third a troublemaker. The terrain became increasingly difficult and we were forced to abandon the steep sides of the valley for the soggy bog in the middle. By late afternoon Ron and I reached Bukurungu Pass and established camp on the knob in the middle of the bog. Toward dusk the last of the straggling porters arrived. So far we had been lucky with the weather. If it had rained, as it frequently does in these parts, I am sure that not just the porters would have been eager to turn back.

August 9 we spent climbing the Portal Peaks by a new route from the west. The porters spent the day resting and hunting. On our climb up we had a dramatic view of the mountains around us as the clouds drifted about. By the time we reached the summit, for a third ascent, we were enveloped in mist. Back at camp we celebrated over a meal of stewed rock hyrax, which our porters had managed to catch. The hyrax is a rodent-like animal about the size of a marmot. It is distinguished by its throaty screaming, which we heard continuously throughout the night; it was a hideous, eerie noise perfectly suited for horror movies. The following morning Matte, who had fallen ill, and two other sick or injured porters turned back to Bundibugyo while the rest of the party continued over Bukurungu Pass.

It was a perfectly clear day. The valley was thick with exotic Lobelia and Giant Groundsel plants, providing the panorama of the Ruwenzori a science fiction like setting. Mts. Baker, Stanley and Speke, all over 16,000 feet in elevation, stood before us covered in flowing glaciers. Very few people preceded us in experiencing this remarkable view. Far below, at the foot of Mt. Baker, we could see Bigo Bog where our route would meet the regular trail. It was all down hill, but also the most treacherous day so far. For hours on end we fought through the dense Helichrysum brush. This plant, with attractive blossoms that stay in permanent bloom when picked, has dry and wiry branches that refuse to bend, but break when you least want them to. Then they gouge your skin or rip your clothes when you snag the broken ends. We finally reached the valley bottom where we were in for some knee-deep bog hopping. We were intent on reaching Bujuko Hut that same day — just two and a half hours march from Bigo, but our porters refused to take another step. Debating the situation was a problem in itself since the men hated the Lutoro language of the plains people, which Ron could speak. Reluctantly, they agreed to continue for double pay.

The following morning Chris, Ron and I headed over Stuhlmann Pass and into the Congo. It was the seventh day of our trip and the weather held miraculously. We crossed over Mt. Stanley's northwest shoulder and began to traverse the Alexandra Glacier in order to reach the Belgian Huts for the night. The steepening ice slope and the diagonal direction we took made for awkward footing. Behind me I heard Chris slip and fall. We were still unroped. Instantly, he began speeding down the glacier studded with loose sharp rocks, but managed to arrest himself within a hundred feet. In his fall he crumpled a crampon, ripped his parka, and injured his right hand. We decided it was time to rope up. That night we camped lower down in the Congo on the shores of Lac Du Vert. Our spirits improved with the warmth of a large fire built from the peculiar Giant Groundsel. Chris was in no condition to continue with our intended traverse, but insisted that Ron and I make the climb without him.

The following day we hiked back up Alexandra Glacier and escorted Chris to a notch in the northwest ridge of the mountain. From this point he could return to Bujuku Hut in a matter of a few hours without difficulty. As we parted, Chris pulled out his 8 mm movie camera and started filming as Ron and I disappeared into the mountain mist.

Ron and I continued to traverse across to the formidable west face. Due to the geological tilt, the Stanley massif is much more dramatic from the Congo than from the east. The big faces drop off abruptly and are encrusted with hanging glaciers of spectacular proportions. We left the main glacier and started up a rock buttress that pierced the glaciers hanging from above. We now faced four pitches of steep ice climbing. The uppermost part was overhanging and the icicles were huge — more than a foot in diameter and ten feet long in some cases. With the crux of the route behind us only a three hundred foot rock face remained between us and the top of the mountain. Unfortunately, it started to snow. Since it was late in the day we did not savor bivouacking on the summit. Instead, we settled for a semi-protected ledge on the northwest ridge.

The morning was crisp and clear. The sun illuminated the sharp slopes of Mt. Emin (Pasha). I shook out the ice rime that lined the inside of my bivouac sack. After some hot coffee and porridge we continued with the rock climbing. At a strenuous section of rock the high altitude and the rigors of the last nine days began to take their toll.

Yet, for the most part we were well acclimatized and still feeling strong (I had recently hiked to the top of Mt. Kilimanjaro). We rested on the summit of Point Albert still early in the morning. Margherita, Mt. Stanley's highest point, seemed to float on a sea of clouds in front of us. Point Alexandra was another hundred yards, or so, further on. On Uganda's highest point we took some pictures and congratulated ourselves for the new route we had just established.

We marveled at the good luck we were having with the weather. The notoriously stormy "Mountains of the Moon" must not have seen such a long spell of good weather since the first ascents by the Duke of Abruzzi, sixty years earlier.

We wasted no time rappelling, scrambling and cramponing down the complicated East Face of the mountain. Unfortunately, our expedition was not coming to the happy conclusion that we were anticipating. Exhausted, after strenuous three days of climbing, we reached Bujuku Hut and were stunned to find out that Chris had not returned! He should have been back no more than three hours after we parted. This meant that he had lost his way or met with tragedy.

With just four hours of daylight left I set out to retrace the route Chris should have taken back. Ron remained in camp to organize a bigger search party for the next day, including aerial searches with the help of the British embassy. It was after nightfall when I reached the notch in the ridge where we had left Chris. Along the way I searched for clues of his whereabouts, but found nothing. Calling out his name once in a while made me feel even worse. I bivouacked under a boulder that night to mitigate the storm that was closing in. In the morning I woke to see the terrain around me under a blanket of fresh snow. For five depressing days I searched all possible areas of exit and found only leopard lairs and an abundance of fresh kills. Chris had two lightweight sleeping bags with him, but lacked any other equipment vital for survival, such as matches or a compass. My conclusion was that he must have lost all sense of direction and either walked off into the Congo, where a battle with Simba rebels was raging, or he simply walked off a cliff, in which case he was dead.

Deeply distraught, we called off the increasing, but futile ground and air search and decided to hike out. Back at Fort Portal informing Chris' young wife (they had two children) that there was little hope of her husband ever being found alive was one of the most painful experiences I've had to endure. The next day a runner arrived from the mountains with a message that Chris had walked into camp at Bujuku!

After we reunited with our scraggly partner, Chris related the details his misadventure. Within fifteen minutes after we had left him on the ridge of Mt Stanley, he put the camera back into his pack and found himself enveloped in mist. He got disoriented and proceeded to hike down into the Congo. Once he reached lower elevations and the mist was behind him, he noticed that the sun was setting in front of him — which had to be west. He should have been heading east! It was too much for him to climb all the way back up to the pass, so he reasoned that it would be no big deal to circumnavigate the "little hill" that he was facing. He was wrong: it took him six days to accomplish this feat!

During his seven day ordeal he ate a total of twenty berries. Chris learned from the mistakes that he made. Ron and I seriously underestimated the perseverance of a young man, who is determined to survive.

357

Clockwise: Alex panning for placer gold. Guiseppe setting fuses at the end of his shift. Bruno driving a trolley down a tunnel. Alex with fish for dinner (note the dredge on the truck). Bottom: the mining town of Wells, BC, as it appeared in the summer of 1961.

Top: Shiprock - the 2,000 foot spire that dominates the surrounding desert in the northwest corner of New Mexico.

Left: Sunset over the Pacific Ocean, which won a showing at the Annual NW Watercolor Show of the Seattle Art Museum. Right: Liberty Bell Mountain, East Face. All watercolors painted on location of the subject by the author.

Right: A painting of
an Arab Dhow, simi-
lar in design to one
that Alex sailed on to
the island of Lamu,
in the Indian Ocean.

Ron Hockey on the
summit of Peak
Margherita, Ruwen-
zori Mountains of
East Africa.

360

Left: Alex inspecting a school of manta rays that beached themselves during a storm on the (Baja) Mexican coast. Photo: Gisela von der Borch

Gisela looking through the top of Alex's Citroen 2CV on Estero Beach, Baja California. Picture taken during the trip down the Pacific coast in 1961.

Right: Gisela enjoying a beach on the Pacific coast in Oregon.

Alex and Half on the summit of Mt. Fury after making the 8th ascent of this remote peak in the North Cascades of Washington.

Half Zantop during the first traverse of the Picket Range in the North Cascades. Mt. Terror is the middle peak on the horizon.

362

# EPILOGUE

## A SON'S WORDS OF ENCOURAGEMENT

For my 63rd birthday my youngest son Nikolas gave me a spiral
notebook with these words of encouragement written inside:

*July 17, 2002*

*[Dear] Papa,*

*I know a journal is probably not something you need right
now but consider it a symbol of how much I want you to
write your memoirs. These stories of your life, especially
the ones I was a part of, have become an indelible part of
me, not always an easy part but one I cherish nonetheless.
To leave the retelling of your stories to the whims of your
children would not do them justice. Write them for your
grandchildren and their children and their children and
write them for the world. Do whatever it takes to get the
words pulsing in the
stream of your blood and into your imagination and onto
paper or a computer screen or wherever. Write about your
climbing, your childhood, your parents, your wife, your
travels, your architecture, your friends, your dreams and
your reflections. I hope you can capture both the intensity
and the subtlety of how you live. Write on. Right on.*

*Happy birthday.*
*[Your],*
*Nikolukas*
*P.S.  I look forward to creating many more stories with*
*you.*


## My response:

*February 23, 2005*

*[Thank you] Nikolukas,*
*You have given me the push I needed.  And, though this*
*book does not include you (nor Tomi, Eugenia or Ruta),*
*the next book will.*
*[Your],*
*Papa*
*P.S.  Happy birthday!*

# MAP OF EUROPE
## (During WWII)

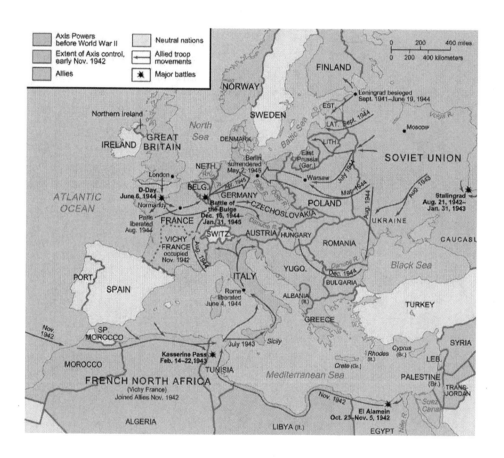